GOOD TO GREAT TO GONE

Diversion Books
A Division of Diversion Publishing Corp.
80 Fifth Avenue, Suite 1101
New York, New York 10011

www.diversionbooks.com

For more information, email info@diversionbooks.com.

First Diversion Books edition September, 2012

ISBN: 978-1-938120-11-4

1 3 5 7 9 10 8 6 4 2

This book is dedicated to the thousands of Circuit City Employees at all levels and their families. For over sixty years these dedicated men and women gave their best to provide customers with a great shopping experience. This book is especially dedicated to those, who, through no fault of their own, lost their livelihood and their dreams when the company faltered and then collapsed.

GOOD TO GREAT TO GONE

THE 60 YEAR RISE AND FALL OF CIRCUIT CITY

Alan Wurtzel

DIVERSIONBOOKS

2012

CONTENTS

CHARTS

ACKNOWLEDGMENTS

It takes a village to write a book.

While I am solely responsible for the errors and omissions, I relied on multitudes to write the story of Circuit City's sixty-year passage from Good to Great to Gone.

First and foremost I want to thank my father, Samuel Wurtzel, for having the trust and confidence to bring me into his business and the patience and love to teach me most of what I needed to know to build and run a large company. Ditto for his partner, A. L. Hecht, and the original board of outstanding individuals, including Hyman Meyers, Sam Winokur, and Fredrick Deane. I hope they would be proud of the company Wards became and will forgive my candid assessments of interim challenges.

I also owe a great debt to the "five horsemen" who were my fellow riders on this journey: Bill Rivas, Dan Rexinger, Walter Bruckart, Ed Villanueva, and Bill Zierden. Their abilities, dedication, and common sense helped keep me straight and the company on a sound track. I also owe my successor, Rick Sharp, a great deal for successfully building on the base that my team laid and taking the company to new heights. While Rivas, Rexinger, and Bruckart are no longer with us, all the others, including Rexinger prior to his death, helped me tell the story.

For the arduous job of collecting sixty years of data and the research and critiquing of the manuscript, I am much indebted to Ann Collier and Steve Richman, both former Circuit City executives, and to Rachel Miller, a talented recent graduate of the University of Virginia. Ann challenged many of my interpretations, and those disagreements sharpened my understanding.

In the course of writing this I interviewed many members of the Circuit City village, including two of my successors, Rick Sharp and Alan McCollough, and a few directors. They were uniformly generous with their time and their thoughts. A few requested anonymity, which I have respected. My sincere thanks to: Bob Appleby, Sooho Bae, Bruce Besanko, Richard Birnbaum, Dennis Bowman, Ed Brett, Bob Burrus, Steve Cannon, David Cecil, Richard Cooper, Joanne Cronin, Ben Cummings, Pete Douglas, Phil Dunn, Jack Fitzsimmons, Doug Foley, Mike Foss, John Froman, Gertrude Gibson, Mike Jones, Jerry Lawson, Brian Levy, Carl Liebert, Austin Ligon, Bruce Lucas, Jim Marcum, Doug Moore, Jonathan Reckford, Dan Rexinger, Steve Richman, Mikael Salovaara, Shelly Shapiro, Ralph Smith, Ann Marie Stephens, David Strasser, Jeff Wells, Jim Wimmer, Tom Wulf, and Bill Zierden.

In telling the story, I have tried to be as objective and factual as I know how. I hope that any unflattering assessments of Circuit City leadership are perceived as they are intended— an honest attempt to explain what happened to a public company as it tried to navigate the waves of change.

Several good friends read the manuscript and provided useful input. They include my two daughters, Judy and Sharon Wurtzel, plus Linda Cashdan, Tracy Fitzsimmons, Rod Heller, William Klepper, Ed Kopf, Frank Loy, Beth Stewart, Michael Salovaara, Walter Salmon, Clara Silverstein Schnee, Leo Zickler, and my agent, Ron Goldfarb. All provided valuable insights and identified errors of fact, grammar, and judgment. Judy Kern and Andrew Rosenberg were invaluable editors.

In addition to helping with the story, Tom Wulf added great value to this project with his amazing stock of Circuit City photographs from over the decades and his imaginative and dedicated insight of what photos to use and where to place them.

Closer to home, I am deeply indebted to my assistant, Kris Megna, for her amazing computer skills, patience, and cheerful willingness to take on any task. Finally, I am eternally grateful that Irene Wurtzel agreed to be my partner for life and that she was willing to read and comment intelligently on more versions of this manuscript than either of us can remember. To the extent that this book is more than a boring business history, it is attributable to her amazing literary skills as a successful playwright.

GOOD TO GREAT TO GONE

Prologue

BANKRUPT

In business, the competition will bite you if you keep running;
if you stand still, they will swallow you.

— William Knudsen

Dateline: January 16, 2009. U.S. Courthouse, Richmond, Virginia. The courtroom is crowded with reporters as well as lawyers for Circuit City, its numerous suppliers, and the creditors committee. Tensions are running high. There have been ten days of round-the-clock negotiations. The parties and their counsels are tired and frustrated at not having reached agreement.

Over the previous two years, the company has shed over $5 billion in stock market value. It posted just one profitable quarter since mid-2006.[1] It owes its creditors more than $1.5 billion, including $650 million to its suppliers and $900 million to its banks.[2] Circuit City's net worth has shrunk to little or nothing. It is bleeding cash, having run through more than $200 million between March and August 2008 and untold sums since.

U.S. Bankruptcy Judge Kevin R. Huennekens, in what he says is one of the hardest decisions he has made during his two years on the bench, orders Circuit City Stores Inc. to liquidate its assets to meet the claims of creditors. Circuit City is ordered to close all 567 store locations by March 31, putting 34,000 employees out of work.[3] Going-out-of-business sales at Circuit City stores all over the country are to begin immediately. The desperate last-ditch efforts to find a buyer have ended in failure.[4]

It has been a long fall from the top. Since the late 1980s Circuit City had been recognized by Wall Street and business insiders as the best-run, best-managed, and most profitable specialty retailer of electronics and appliances in the country.

From 1982 to 1997, Circuit City's stock price had outperformed that of the general stock market by an incredible 18.5 times, far better than any other Fortune 500 company for any fifteen-year period since 1965. Yet just twelve years later, Circuit City was no more.

In the process of growing from a single store located in the front of a tire recapping shop to a nationwide colossus, Circuit City transformed consumer electronics retailing; launched Car-Max, a revolutionary new way to sell used cars; and provided employment to hundreds of thousands as well as excellent savings and service to millions of consumers.

This is the sixty-year saga of a company that grew from a Richmond, Virginia, mom-and-pop TV store to become an industry leader before it ultimately stumbled and subsequently died.

I know the story well. My father, Sam Wurtzel, founded Circuit City (then known as Wards) in 1949. I joined the company in 1966, became CEO in 1973, and held that position until 1986, when I retired to pursue other interests. I remained on the board until 2001.

I recognize that my direct involvement as the son of the founder, as the second CEO, and as a longtime board member is both an asset and a liability. On the plus side, I was an interested observer for the full sixty years of Circuit City's existence and an active participant for more than thirty years; in the course of writing this book, I was able to interview more than forty people who could add color and context to the years that I was not directly involved.

On the liability side, I am, admittedly, not a totally objective observer. It is impossible to escape the human tendency to admire one's own successes and "explain away" one's mistakes. In writing this account, I have tried to be as objective and self-critical as I know how to be. Only the reader can judge if I have been successful.

Some of the decisions I criticize were mine; some were made by friends and colleagues, including my father. I have tried to be impartial in my examination of both the good and the not-so-good decisions that were made. All of the judgments are mine, but I am reassured by the fact that every one of them is shared by other key individuals who played significant roles in the business.

My purpose in telling the story, however, is not primarily to record the company's history but to shed light on the strategic decisions, good and bad, that successive management teams made, especially at key times in the life of the company—and to see if there are any lessons to be learned from these decisions.

In a sense, this book can be viewed as a case study, illustrating some of the principles developed by Jim Collins in his two books, *Good to Great* and its sequel, *How the Mighty Fall*, neither of which was published until well after I left Circuit City. When Jim called to interview me for *Good to Great* in 1998 I didn't know that Circuit City was one of only eleven companies to outperform the Fortune 500 by at least three times for fifteen years. Nor did I have any idea that I had, during my tenure, unconsciously followed many of the management principles shared by his eleven "good to great "companies. I had simply been doing my best to make commonsense, long-range strategic and operational decisions in collaboration with the board and my senior colleagues. I knew, for instance, that people were the key to success, but I did not talk about "who gets on the bus." I did try to be analytical and honest, without calling it "confront[ing] the brutal facts." With a strong push from my board, I simplified our business and became a "hedgehog," knowing one thing well, instead of a fox that knows many things superficially. I also built the company patiently and step-by-step, or, to use Collins's term, "tended the flywheel." When I read *Good to Great*, however, I realized that these were brilliant metaphors for many of the policies my associates and I had followed in the course of building Circuit City.

More recently, as Circuit City was dying, I had another conversation with Collins about *How the Mighty Fall*. Although I was not an officer, director, or even a shareholder during Circuit City's last eight years in business, when I read that book I was struck, once again, by how perfect his metaphors were:

- Hubris, Born of Success
- Undisciplined Pursuit of More
- Denial of Risk and Peril
- Grasping for Salvation
- Capitulation to Irrelevance or Death

They all described the last days of Circuit City. I am grateful to Jim for creating an intellectual framework for thinking about the fall as well as the rise of Circuit City.

Turning Points

In the multi-decade life of any company, indeed any industry, there are turning points at which the company needs to be "reinvented"—moments when the business model needs to be revised to accommodate changes in the competitive landscape, including the economy, technology, customer preferences, and so forth.[5] The retail scene is littered with examples of companies that made, or failed to make, these necessary transitions.

In looking at the sixty-year life of the business that ultimately became Circuit City, I have identified five turning points at which the company's very existence was in question and it needed to be invented or reinvented.

- The first was the initial decision to open a TV store in Richmond, Virginia, shortly after the South's first TV station went on the air.
- The second occurred in the early 1960s when the discount store revolution caused conventional mom-and-pop TV and appliance stores to struggle.
- The third took place in the early '70s, when most of the many acquisitions my father and I had made were losing money and all the company's discount store landlords filed for bankruptcy.
- The fourth was in the mid-'90s when the Circuit City Superstores

began losing market share to Best Buy and the mass merchandisers.

- The fifth occasion was in 2000, when the company understood the need to reinvent itself but proved unable to do so.

In the course of this book, I will pay special attention to these critical turning points, the ways in which Circuit City's management responded to them, and what we can learn from these decisions.

Habits of Mind

While this book is organized around Circuit City's history, the focus is on the business strategy. Circuit City's sixty-year run in the most dynamic segment of American retailing provides an excellent window onto the ways business strategies interact, both negatively and positively, with the ever-changing economic and competitive landscape. My premise is that there can be no "rules" or "formulas" for business strategy. Strategies are situational; they are specific to time and place. What works today will generally not work tomorrow, in another place or in a different economic environment.

Behind every strategy, however, lie the Habits of Mind of those who developed the strategy. Pessimists see the world differently from optimists. Curious people see problems and opportunities differently from know-it-alls, and gamblers differently from paranoids. Habits of Mind are not situation-specific, but ways of thinking about one's organization in relation to the world in which it exists. It is these Habits of Mind that drive strategic decision-making and lead either to success or to failure. This book attempts to identify the successful and unsuccessful Habits of Mind that guided Circuit City's strategy over its lifetime.

Following are the Habits of Mind that I consider essential to organizational success. I will refer to them again at the end of each chapter as they are relevant and as I share my perspective on key moments in the company's history and the lessons learned from the results of the strategic decisions made.

Be Humble, Run Scared: *Continuously doubt your understanding of things. Business success contains the seeds of its own destruction. Worry about what the competition knows that you do not. Andy Grove, the legendary co-founder of Intel, got it largely right in his book* **Only the Paranoid Survive.**

Curiosity Sustains the Cat: *The world is constantly changing. Be open and curious and strive to learn from others. Continuously try to understand the market and the changing economic, demographic, and other relevant forces at work that impact your business. Study your competitors. They may have insights and practices worth emulating or refining.*

Evidence Trumps Ideology: *In business, as in politics, decisions are too often based on unproven assumptions about what works and what doesn't. We all need operating assumptions about human nature, the economy, and the like, but when things do not work out as planned, we need to determine whether our assumptions were based on evidence or ideology. Evidence about the real world trumps ideological assumptions every time.*

Confront the Brutal Facts:: *The worst person you can fool is yourself. Ignoring or denying reality does not help it go away. Once you understand the issues, be bold enough to take decisive action.*

Chase the Impossible Dream: *Do not be limited by what Collins and Porras, the authors of* Built to Last, *call the "Tyranny of the OR." Be willing to embrace the "Genius of the AND." Two worthwhile goals that seem mutually exclusive can inspire an organization of "ordinary" employees to achieve extraordinary results.*[6]

Maintain a Current Road Map: *If you don't know where you are going, any road will take you there. Regular strategic planning based on how the company relates to its external environment, including the economy, competition, and the customer, is essential to success.*

Boldly Follow Through: *Big ideas require bold leadership and attract loyal followers. The effort comes to naught if the execution is tentative or not well disciplined.*

Mind the Culture: *Create a caring and ethical culture where employees can make mistakes without fear of adverse consequences. Beware of employees who are more concerned about their own success than the success of the business. Understand, exemplify, and reinforce the company's positive history and culture.*

Pass the Torch with Care: *Succession is critical. Most companies cannot withstand successive top management failures. CEOs need to select and groom their successor with care. Boards need to be bold enough to replace the CEO when necessary and to take the time to be sure the right successor is in place.*

Encourage Debate: *Learn from dissent. Involve senior staff and the board of directors in an open process to find the best answer. Create a board that will raise thought-provoking questions and challenge management to justify its* plans.

Keep It Simple and Accountable: *Develop a clear and well-articulated set of policies for dealing with customers, suppliers, and employees. For any organization to succeed it is essential that each and every employee internalize the company's goals and values. Employees should also be held accountable and incentivized to pursue those goals and values every day.*

Focus on the Future: *Manage for the long term and not the short. Don't let short-term earnings swings divert a long-term strategy. Ignore the skeptics and short-term market gyrations. If things go well, the value of your company, whether public or private, will respond over time.*

So, to begin at the beginning...

GOOD (1949-1970)

PART I

Chapter One

DISCOVERING THE OPPORTUNITY

*The secret of success in life is for a man to be ready for
his opportunity when it comes.*

— Benjamin Disraeli

Sam Wurtzel, a 41-year-old New York businessman, was having his hair cut in Richmond, Virginia. The barber at the next chair was telling his customer that in April 1948, not quite a year earlier, the South's first television station had opened in Richmond.[7]

Living in New York, Sam had occasionally seen television programs in public spaces such as bars or at the homes of wealthy friends who were proud to show off this hottest of postwar products. For most Americans, however, television was still a miracle they had heard about but never actually seen.

News and entertainment over the airwaves was not new. From the earliest days of his presidency, Franklin Roosevelt had galvanized the nation with his "fireside chats" on the radio. Americans had followed the war by listening to famed broadcaster Lowell Thomas. Most kids were addicted to the serialized adventures of Superman, the Lone Ranger, and Uncle Don. And adults were hooked on weekly radio shows such as *Amos 'n' Andy* and *The Jack Benny Show,* as well as soap operas like *The Romance of Helen Trent* and *Our Gal Sunday*.

But *pictures* of the news were captured only in newspapers, in *Life* and other news magazines, or on movie theater screens. Mass entertainment occurred on the stage, in movie houses, or in other public arenas, not at home. Only a relative handful of Americans, mostly in New York and Los Angeles, had ever watched a television, and even fewer had done so at home.[8]

As the barber continued to cut, Sam began to think about what a new TV station in Richmond could mean. He knew something about retailing from working in his mother's grocery store. His mother, Flora, had emigrated from Russia in her early twenties. When her arranged marriage did not work out she was left to raise two boys and two girls, all under ten years old, on her own. With help from her parents, Flora opened a neighborhood grocery store behind their home in Perth Amboy, New Jersey. Life was hard, but Sam's mother was a tough and disciplined woman. She demanded that her four children graduate from high school and make something of themselves, and, in fact, all four became very successful in their chosen fields.

Like many boys without a father in their lives, Sam was often a discipline problem, He was bright enough to graduate from Perth Amboy High School in 1924 despite his less-than-studious habits, but he did not have either the inclination or the opportunity to go on to college.

During the Depression years, finding and holding a job was difficult, but Sam was energetic, personable, and extremely bright. He also found that he had an aptitude for business. For a time, he and his older brother ran a wholesale butter and egg business financed by their estranged father, who also sold butter and eggs to retail grocery stores. After a falling out with his father, Sam moved to another wholesale food firm, June Dairy, in the greater metropolitan area. He was laid off but again landed on his feet

Sam made a favorable impression. Slightly over six feet tall, with a pencil moustache and good bearing, he was polite, charming, and had an excellent sense of humor. Recognizing his educational deficiencies, he took night courses in accounting and business. As he matured, he studied a few chosen fields, such as biblical archeology, and became a serious amateur. He excelled at bridge as well as double acrostics and other complex word games. In 1931 Sam met Ruth Mann, from Mount Vernon, New York, at a party in New Jersey and gallantly agreed to drive her and a friend home in his sporty roadster with a rumble seat. A year later they were married. Ruth came from the opposite side of the tracks—the good side. Her father, Leon, was born in this country and graduated from City College, actually a high school in Baltimore, Maryland. Leon moved to New York and became a successful manufacturer of men's clothing, a pillar of the Mount Vernon Jewish community, and a founder of both the local hospital and the leading Reform synagogue. The city dedicated a small park to his memory.

Samuel S. Wurtzel – circa 1940.

Through Ruth and her family Sam was exposed to a standard of living and a level of refinement he had never known. Her family had servants and she had made the grand tour of Europe with her parents and sisters while she was still in elementary school. Unlike most women of her generation, she had graduated from college.

Leon, an early venture capitalist, had a habit of supporting struggling inventors. One of them was a nearly illiterate Russian immigrant who had invented a two-story-high machine to make papier-mâché packing materials for eggs. The new material dramatically reduced breakage during shipping, thus reducing insurance costs. Unfortunately, however, a patent dispute arose between Leon's protégé and another inventor. To settle the case, Leon agreed to give up the U.S. market and sell the new packing materials only in Europe and South America. In 1938 he enlisted Sam to assist him in that effort. The business they created, Packing Products, was intended to market and sell egg-packing materials.

In Leon, Sam found a surrogate father, and Leon in turn found the son he never had. Leon not only taught Sam about business, but, more importantly, gave him the polish and skills that would benefit him for the rest of his life. Every morning Leon would come into Sam's office and write "HU" on his calendar. "HU" stood for the two precepts Leon believed we should live by: humor and humility.

When World War II broke out a year later, exporting to Europe was no longer possible. Leon was by then 73, and Sam, who was in charge of the day-to-day operations of the company, turned his attention to South America. But with few railroads and highways in place, eggs were rarely shipped long distances, so there was limited opportunity to sell egg-packing materials. To overcome this hurdle, Sam built an import-export business shipping a wide range of products to and from South America.

Packing Products was a broker, matching buyers and sellers, but not taking an inventory position without a confirmed sale in hand. Unfortunately, in 1948, while Sam was away, someone violated that rule and purchased steel that had not been pre-sold. The steel market collapsed and, as a result, the business failed. At that point, Sam's sole material asset was his home, and Leon, now in his eighties, was not in a position to help him start a new business.

Sam and Ruth decided to take a golfing vacation to gain some perspective and make plans for the future. Just before their departure for North Carolina, however, Ruth's mother, Nettie, took ill, and Ruth decided to stay behind in Mount Vernon for a few days until she recovered. Sam, who had a business appointment in Washington, D.C., went on ahead. He would keep his appointment, and then drive on to Richmond and wait for Ruth at the home of her sister before they proceeded together to North Carolina.

As it turned out, Ruth never got there, but while Sam was waiting, his restless mind kept returning to what he'd overheard in the barbershop. He believed that television was destined to bring about major changes in the way Americans were entertained and informed. It was only a matter of time, he thought, before almost every American home would have a television set. In fact, the number of TV stations on the air almost tripled in 1949 alone, growing from 27 to 76. And the number of homes with TV sets went from 1.2 million to 4.2 million.[9]

Sam began to think about how he could benefit from what he was certain would be the television revolution. At 42 years old he was still young enough to start over. While he had never been a retailer, he was aware that he lacked both the capital and the technical knowledge to manufacture TVs. However, through his friend and future partner, Abe Hecht, he knew someone at a TV manufacturing company, Olympic Television, located in Long Island City. And through his sister and brother-in-law, both well-connected, longtime Richmond residents, he had access to local bankers, real estate agents, and their network of business friends and acquaintances, whom he could trust to give him advice about how and where to get started. Leaving New York, where his business had failed, and moving to Richmond had appeal as well. But first, he had to think through the issues of going into the retail business and betting his future on a new and unproven technology.

In making the decision to start the company that would become Circuit City, Sam had to consider the larger economic context, how demographic and social factors might affect consumer preferences, and trends in the retail industry. The essence of any viable business strategy is to define a product or service that meets a real world need and that can be sold at a profit. Understanding the economy, demographics, customer buying preferences, and the competition are all essential to strategic decision-making.

The Real World in the '50s

The Second World War, which had ended scarcely three years earlier, left an indelible mark on American society and its economy. The ability to shift from Depression-level civilian production to extraordinary military production in a year or two had won the war and catapulted the country onto the world stage as the undisputed superpower.

Following the Japanese surrender, there were 12 million Americans in uniform, of whom seven million were overseas.[10] These veterans had returned home ready to begin families[11] and create a baby boom that would continue for the next two decades. The nation's population increased by one-third in the twenty years after the war.

This, in turn, created unprecedented opportunities for businesses that catered to the needs of young families. New mothers, despite their contributions to the workforce during the war, largely went back to their traditional roles as homemakers, though many returned to the workforce once their youngest child was off to school. All this Sam knew. It was the ideal economic environment in which to enter the TV and appliance business.

U.S. Population by Age Group 1949-1960

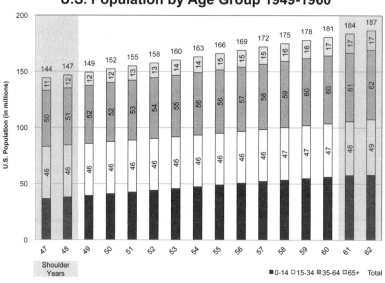

What he did not know was that the dramatic readjustment from prewar depression to postwar prosperity would also spawn remarkable social change. The G.I. Bill, designed to soften the impact of the sudden influx of veterans into the workforce, provided educational grants and low-cost housing loans to millions of Americans who had never even considered a college education or owned a home. Many families used the loans and their education-enhanced earning power to escape the overcrowded cities and move to the suburbs. By 1960, facilitated by the new Eisenhower-initiated interstate highway system, suburbia had grown by 35 percent, becoming home to nearly one-third of the American population as well as the center and the symbol of the American dream[12]. Immediately following World War II, many feared that the postwar economy would revert to depression levels of output and employment. Instead, the economy in the 1950s continued to boom. By the middle of the decade, productivity, spurred by high employment, technological advances, and the rise of higher education enabled by the G.I. Bill, was growing at the rate of 3 percent annually.[13] This tremendous growth increased real income per capita and introduced many Americans long ac-

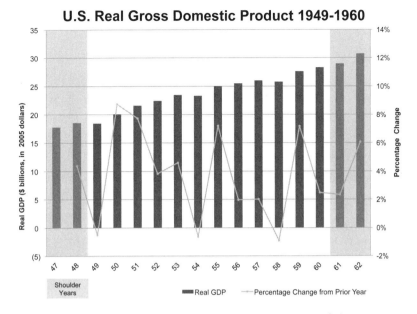

U.S. Real Gross Domestic Product 1949-1960

Shoulder Years

Real GDP — Percentage Change from Prior Year

customed to living hand to mouth to the concept of discretionary income. For the new postwar consumer, the American dream was not complete without a car, a refrigerator, and a television set.

At midcentury, American retailing was dominated by independently owned and operated downtown department stores, such as Miller and Rhodes and Thalhimers in Richmond or Macys in New York. The only significant department store chains at the time were the popularly priced Sears Roebuck and Montgomery Ward, neither of which carried many brand-name goods. Woolworth, and SS Kresge, both large variety store chains, were still important, although declining. Outside of the traditional department stores and these national chains, individual mom-and-pop stores and small regional chains were the important retail outlets both downtown and in most neighborhoods. There were no regional malls, no discount stores, and very few grocery or supermarket chains.

In the electronics industry, all eyes were on television. During World War II the government had limited the production of TV sets and discontinued licensing new stations in order to conserve scarce electronics materials.[14] As a result, there were only eigh-

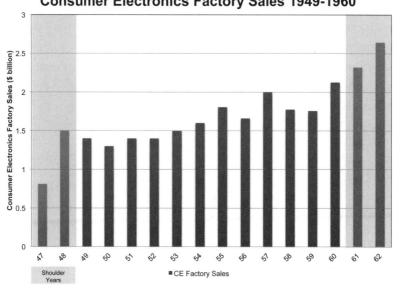

Consumer Electronics Factory Sales 1949-1960

teen TV stations operating in the United States when the war ended. Three years later, when Sam decided to take the plunge, there were but twenty-seven, centered in a few large cities.

The upside was that wartime restrictions had enabled manufacturers to focus on research and improve their technology while also creating pent-up consumer demand, which was further stimulated in 1955 by the opening of ultrahigh frequency (UHF) channels. Almost immediately, programming, the lifeblood of television, exploded across more than seventy channels, creating demand for TVs with new UHF tuners.[15]

In 1950, only 9 percent of U.S. homes had a television set. Ten years later, 85 percent of homes had at least one.[16] At this point, all broadcasting was still in black and white. The introduction of color television, long heralded but still in its infancy, held the promise that the industry would have another miraculous "rebirth" by replacing virtually all of the 50 million black-and-white sets still in operation.[17]

At the same time, the appliance business was experiencing a boom. With their newfound wealth, Americans purchased as necessities new products that had once been luxuries. And paying

for these appliances also became easier with the growing availability of "buying on time"—in monthly installments—thereby
giving even lower-income families access to refrigerators, washing machines, and electric stoves.

As all these work-saving appliances significantly reduced the
amount of time it took women to complete their household
chores, they also "helped her decide she had time for a bigger
family."[18] And then, as family size grew and more women were
employed outside the home, they began to rely even more on appliances, further stimulating sales. By 1954, 85 percent of American homes had refrigerators and 70 percent had washing machines, compared to 39 percent and 41 percent before the war.[19]

Saturation became a real industry concern. Continued growth
would depend on more people marrying and starting families,
replacement sales, and the introduction of new products. Dish-
washers and freezers, whose unreliability and high prices limited
their mass appeal, were two growth prospects in an otherwise
stodgy industry.

Inventing the Business Strategy

How much of the foregoing economic and retail context Sam
explicitly understood is not clear. But he was smart, alert to the
events around him, and an optimist by nature. Opportunity was
in the postwar air, and he was confident that television would
revolutionize the way Americans were entertained and informed.
Consequently, a month after having his hair cut in Richmond,
Sam decided to sell his Mount Vernon home and move his family
to Virginia's capital.

Sam decided to call his new business Wards TV. He thought
Wurtzel was too difficult a name for many Southerners to understand, especially on the phone, so he chose a family acronym, W
for Wurtzel, and the rest of the letters for his immediate family:
Alan (me), Ruth, David (my brother), and himself. He said, jok-

ingly, that the name was not "Ward's" because he did not "want to be separated from the rest of his family by an apostrophe."

Back in New York a few days after his Richmond barber shop visit, Sam arranged to purchase twelve Olympic TVs. In the process, he talked the manufacturer, which was small and looking to grow, into granting him an exclusive franchise for the entire state of Virginia. Olympic was to be the only brand Wards carried for more than a year.

In starting Wards TV, Sam was either lucky or smart—probably a bit of both—but he was not unique. All around the country entrepreneurs were eager to grab a piece of the exciting TV revolution. Some were appliance dealers, some had a background in selling furniture, and some, like Sam, were simply looking for an opportunity. Within the next five years, most major cities would have a leading TV and appliance chain: Silo in Philadelphia; VIM and Newmark and Lewis in New York; Lechmere in Boston; Luskin's in Baltimore; Polk in Chicago; and Highland in Detroit. Over the years, some of these early market leaders expanded out of town and quite a few went public, but only the company Sam founded went on to become a nationwide chain with sales in the billions and more than 500 stores.

When Sam returned to Richmond in March 1949, he rented the front half of a tire recapping shop on West Broad, the main shopping street in Richmond, twelve blocks west of the downtown department stores. TV sets were displayed on top of the cardboard boxes in which they were shipped, but there was no advertising or signage to tell people this was a place they could come to see and buy a TV. Instead, he bought a pickup truck and hired George Martin, a young man just back from the war, as a driver and helper.

When Wards opened for business, very few Richmonders had ever seen a TV. There was only one station, WTVR, an NBC affiliate, which had begun operation in April 1948 and broadcast programs only five hours a day, from 6 p.m. to 11 p.m. The rest of the day it aired a test pattern. The idea was so new that the Richmond newspapers did not publish a TV schedule, and WTVR, run by a thrifty curmudgeon, refused to advertise its own schedule. In an act of chutzpah, Sam took out his own newspaper ads and began publishing the schedule "as a public service."

While there was little independent competition, Wards did not have the market entirely to itself. Both downtown department stores carried big name brands including RCA, Motorola, Dumont, and Zenith. Sears carried its own private-label brand. And there were also many mom-and-pop shops, often run by young men who had learned electronics during the war, which sold and repaired both TVs and appliances.

To engage the Richmond buying public, Sam needed something unique to offer. He began by advertising, in the classified ad section of the paper, a "free home demonstration," meaning that he would deliver a TV set to a home one evening and return the next night to either pick it up or collect cash or an installment contract, which he could then discount at a local bank for cash. Credit cards had not yet been invented, so most transactions were based on 18- or 24-month installment contracts.

Most of Sam's early customers were from the lower socioeconomic strata. The middle and upper classes bought the more popular brands from the local department stores or private-label brands from Sears, which, in addition to brand recognition (no one in Richmond had ever heard of Olympic TV) and institutional credibility (no one had ever heard of Wards TV), offered charge accounts.

Initially, Sam personally handled all the telephone "leads" he received in response to his ads or through word of mouth. He depended on George Martin, the young man he had hired, to lift and carry the heavy wooden TV cabinets. Then, as the volume of calls grew, he hired "outside" salesmen who appeared in the office every morning to get their leads and make appointments for free home demonstrations.

From the beginning, Sam believed he was building a big business. He knew he couldn't do that as a one-man band, and within

Typical Wards TV ad – 1949

a few months he had persuaded his longtime friend Abraham L. Hecht to move to Richmond and join him. Hecht put in $13,000 (equivalent to $125,000 today), the same amount Sam had raised by selling his home.

A born entrepreneur, Hecht had made his living during and after the Depression by buying up bankrupt estates, generally at auction. These estates often included oddball assets, such as an apple orchard in Virginia, a privately owned sewer system on Long Island, stock in private companies, and lots of receivables. To monetize these receivables, Hecht became an expert "skip tracer," finding debtors who had disappeared or "skipped" to avoid paying their bills.

Sam was the somewhat impulsive visionary, Hecht the more conservative voice. They were both memorable personalities. Hecht wore a trademark beret, Sam a bow tie. They both had an infectious sense of humor, and despite their northern origins, both quickly adopted the apparently laid-back attitude that make Southerners so charming. Together they were a great team.

A few years later Martin Rosenzweig, a New York accountant with strong retail accounting experience, joined Sam and Hecht. Although Marty was not an investor, Sam and Hecht gave "Ross," as he was known, a stake in the business that the three of them would run together until the mid-1960s.

Selling Strategy

After a year of selling door-to-door from leads generated by classified ads, the partners were ready to open a "real" store. Believing that they could compete toe-to-toe with the nation's largest hard-goods retailer, they chose a location across the street from Sears Roebuck's largest Richmond store. By 1952 Wards had added major appliances from Frigidaire plus other TV brands, including RCA, Motorola and Philco.)

Central to Wards' success was the ability of its salespeople to convert a lead to a sale. The basic selling strategy was to promote low-priced, minimally featured products, known as ADVs (or "advertised specials"), that the company really didn't want to sell because the margins were too low or the stock was too hard to replenish, and then, whenever possible, to "step up" the customer to a more fully featured and more profitable model. This practice, known as "bait and switch," was endemic in the industry.

Sam studied various books on selling techniques and attended sales training sessions provided by manufacturers, especially Whirlpool, that had well-developed sales training programs. Based on what he had learned, along with his own highly developed instincts, Sam then devised a training program for his own employees that consisted mainly of a series of lectures, role-playing, and fun-filled contests. The sales process was broken down into a series of steps. While this may seem like fairly standard sales practice today, at that time the idea of breaking down a sales conversation into a series of steps was actually quite new. After the greeting (*"Welcome to Wards"*) came the warm-up (*"My name is Sam, what is yours"?*) and the qualification (*"What do you need today? When do you need it?"*), after which the salesman would begin to explain the product's features and benefits.

The features would be the basics—the product's characteristics, such as the cubic feet of storage in a refrigerator or the size of a TV screen. The benefits were whatever the salesman determined would be of greatest interest to each customer. For a TV the benefits could include watching sports, improving children's education, keeping families together in the evening, or saving money by not going to the movies.

Believing that customers preferred to make small decisions rather than commit to a major purchase, Sam taught the salesmen to ask for the order by assuming that the customer had already decided to buy: *"Shall I deliver it Tuesday or Wednesday?"* or, *"Would you prefer it in dark or light wood?"*

If the customer did not buy on the spot, the next step was to ferret out, and then try to overcome, his or her reservations or objections. If the issue was cost, the salesperson would ask a lot of questions

Wards TV sales floor – circa 1960

Sam Wurtzel Sales Training Session – 1950s

about the intended use. Based on the responses, he would select a product and put the monthly cost in a larger context (less than a dinner a month for the family at a local restaurant). If the objection was to the size or appearance of a tabletop TV, the salesperson was taught to suggest a console with doors that hid the screen. If there was still not a positive response, he would create urgency: *"If you buy today, I can throw in a free outdoor antenna or a tabletop lamp."*

To train salesmen to overcome objections and close the deal, Sam would have one of them role-play the family he could not close the night before. He or another salesman would play the salesman role. At the conclusion, he would ask the other salesmen watching this role-playing what they would have done, and together, they would come up with strategies for overcoming the objection and making the close. Often, the salesman who had presented the case would then call the customer for a second appointment to see if what he had learned would prove successful.

Each lead was precious, and Sam taught his staff how to formulate a strategy that would win the customer's heart, mind, and wallet. To keep competitive spirits high, he held monthly sales contests, sometimes with opposing teams of ten or more salespeople. The winners won steaks and the losers ate beans, or he would issue Monopoly dollars that could be bet in a game of roulette or blackjack, with the winnings redeemed for desirable prizes.

Unlike most of his peers, Sam made systematic sales training the cornerstone of his business strategy. He was a born teacher and was able to dramatize the training with personal stories or examples that made the lessons both enjoyable and memorable.

For example, he would hold up a worn leather coin purse and ask the sales class how much they would pay for it. Generally, the highest offer was a dollar or two. Then Sam explained that he had bought the purse in Rome and had it blessed by the Pope. Now he asked: "Given that you know the Pope blessed it, what would you pay for this purse?" Of course, the bids were higher. His point: You are not just selling a commodity, like a purse; you are selling a ticket to education or entertainment that can transform the lives of your family. You need to treat the product not as a TV or, subsequently, a refrigerator or washing machine, but as the gateway to a better life. Twenty years after he retired, Circuit City trainers were still telling many of Sam's stories.

Sam's sales force was a disparate lot, most of whom were schooled in the college of hard knocks. He didn't care how much education or what kind of manners a salesperson had, so long as he could sell. He also did not care about race. When the all-white sales force threatened to quit en masse because he had decided to give a smart, personable African American service technician a chance to prove himself on the sales floor, Sam faced down the revolt. And even though the man proved not to be good at sales and eventually returned to the service department, Sam had made his point and continued to hire African Americans.

Sam also took a personal interest in the lives of his employees. One rough-cut fellow had a prison record and a drinking problem, but he could sell. After a while, Sam insisted that this fellow come to his desk each morning to take an anti-alcohol pill that would make him terribly sick if he took a drink. That sobered him up, at least for a while. Others had financial problems or marital issues to which Sam would patiently listen, offer advice, and help to resolve. Often he would lend valued employees money to get past a financial crisis. Hecht once bought a worker a car so he could commute at odd hours and not be dependent on a bus schedule. Over time, the partners built a fiercely loyal and devoted following among the employees and their families.

Merchandising Strategy

Unlike most of their independent competitors, Sam and Hecht developed an elaborate program for buying and selling their products. Because they could buy and stock only a small fraction of the dozen or more brands and thousands of models available in any category of goods, they believed that very item on the sales floor had to be there for a reason. At the low end of the price range for each category of merchandise was the "ADV," or advertised price leader. From there, the Wards merchandising team created disciplined "steps," generally in increments of $10 or $20, designed to entice the customer to purchase a higher-priced item. For each step, there needed to be a logical reason for the customer to pay more, such as improved features, convenience, or appearance.

Done properly, the "steps" would practically sell themselves. Just as most auto buyers will pay extra for air-conditioning or tinted windows, most TV and appliance buyers opted to move up one or more "steps" for justifiable reasons. However, producing a compelling step-up program for each category of goods also required great expertise in picking the brands and models.

In order to make a profit, Wards had to offer a reasonable selection of the most popular brands, such as RCA or Zenith, to bring customers into the store, while also making available more profitable brands that provided the customer a better value and the company a higher margin—in those days Sylvania or Magnavox TVs and Magic Chef or Hotpoint appliances. Mixing and matching brands, price points, and gross-margin opportunities was a complex and ever-changing challenge.

Equally important as merchandise "programs" was building a sales force that could sell the products Wards wanted to emphasize. By doing both, Wards was able to deliver to its manufacturers an order flow with a reasonable proportion of their better goods, and since better goods carried higher margins for the manufacturer as well, Wards was, in turn, able to negotiate better pricing.

With a prominent store location and brand names to sell, Wards began advertising in the main pages of the paper instead of just in the classifieds. The store did very well—so well, in fact, that two years later, Sears bricked up its door on the side facing Wards to discourage its customers from cross-shopping. Sam was always proud of that brick wall.

Within a few years of its launch in 1949, Wards opened three more TV and appliance stores in various shopping areas of Richmond. They were moderately successful, but each drew the majority of its customers from a limited geographical area. The population of Richmond in 1950 was only 230,000, and most shopping in those days was concentrated downtown, so adding more volume by adding locations was problematic.

Out-of-Town Stores

Opening stores out of town was the obvious strategy to increase sales. Thus, in the mid-1950s, Wards opened stores in Roanoke, Virginia, and Greensboro, North Carolina; however, both were closed within a year of launching.

An out-of-town store, in a market with different competition and different suppliers, turned out to be much more difficult to manage from afar than Sam and Hecht had imagined. The challenge began with selecting the right manager. In Richmond, Sam could select a lead salesman with some limited management abilities. If something went wrong, he or Hecht was only a phone call or a fifteen-minute car ride away. In a remote market, however, the manager was on his own. He had to hire the store staff, prepare and place the weekly ads, and purchase a lot of the products from local factory branches or independent wholesalers. In those days, manufacturers did not allow retailers to buy goods in one market, such as Richmond, and sell them in another. Finding a manager who could do all of these tasks at the salary a small store could afford was a major challenge.

Equally important, the Richmond office did not know what was happening day-to-day in the remote markets. Relying on the mail involved delays, and long-distance phone calls were expensive. Once, Hecht went to visit the Roanoke store and found it closed in the middle of the day. The manager, an aspiring pilot, was out taking a flying lesson! Shortly thereafter, they closed the store. Sam realized that before expanding, he needed to develop systems to delegate decision making to the store level while maintaining the ability to monitor critical metrics centrally. The key was having better information both in the store and at headquarters.

Data Processing

Chain-store retailing attempts to provide the same customer experience over and over, across countless transactions in multiple stores. That requires knowing where each piece of merchandise is, what it costs, and how well the model is selling, as well as how much, and which items, each salesman has sold. Today we have automated technology to do this. But in the '50s, it was all done by hand.

As early as 1955, long before any of his peers or competitors, Sam brought in IBM punch card equipment to keep track of inventory. By 1966, he had a large data processing department. Shortly thereafter, he signed on for the new cardless IBM 360 computer system. Sam's decision to invest in computers, then still in their infancy, was both gutsy and visionary, especially for such a small company.

Within a few years, the system was tracking sales by merchandise category, brand, and model, as well as inventory, gross margins, sales commissions, and store-level expenses and profits. Cross-store analysis was used to compare expenses in dollars and percentages as well as the mix of merchandise sold. Exceptions were quickly spotted and action initiated to get the offending store back in line. Sam called it "management by exception."

In addition to helping control expenses, data processing was a great management-training tool. The store manager, his division manager, and the headquarters staff could all look at the same data and see the same patterns, exceptions, and trends. It was an important foundation for training future store managers and building a bigger business.

Habits of Mind

The events discussed in this chapter demonstrate the following Habits of Mind that lead to success or failure.

Curiosity Sustains the Cat: *The world is constantly changing. Be open and curious and strive to learn from others. Continuously try to understand the market and the changing economic, demographic, and other relevant forces at work that impact your business. Study your competitors. They may have insights and practices worth emulating or refining.*

When Sam heard that the South's first television station had recently opened in Richmond he was curious to learn more. Based on his instincts, he believed that the television business would thrive in the United States. Once he checked out the opportunity, he acted within weeks to become Richmond's first TV specialty retailer, and he quickly learned what it took to operate a successful mom-and-pop TV and appliance business.

Boldly Follow Through: *Big ideas require bold leadership and attract loyal followers. The effort comes to naught if the execution is tentative or not well disciplined.*

From the beginning Sam believed he was building a big business. Investing everything he had to move to Richmond and start a new life in an untried business was a bold move. His enthusiasm and optimism attracted longtime friend Abe Hecht and New York accountant Marty Ross to join him. Sam's audacious ideas, sometimes implemented against his partners' more conservative advice, continued to attract loyal followers for the rest of his career.

Chapter Two

SETTING THE VALUES

There are so many men who can figure costs,
and so few who can measure values.

– Author Unknown

Core values define an organization. Every organization has them, whether explicit and written down or implicit and transmitted by story and example. They define "who *we* are" and differentiate "*our* company" from our competitors.

A company's values are different from its mission. The mission focuses on *what* the organization is designed to do. A mission is usually defined as providing a better product or service. The mission may be altruistic (cure cancer, build affordable housing), or self-serving (maximize profits). Initially, Wards' mission was simply to make a profit by selling TVs and appliances at competitive prices and with superior service. As the company grew, however, it increasingly strove to be a good corporate and community citizen.[20]

Core values focus on *how* the company achieves its mission: How, for example, does it value and treat customers, employees, and suppliers? Some organizations emphasize respect, civility, and compassion. Others create a competitive environment in which success depends on getting ahead, regardless of process or whose ox is gored.

From the beginning, Wards' core value was the "One Face Policy." To Sam and Hecht, that meant fair and honest dealing with customers, employees, and suppliers. It meant telling the truth, even if it was not convenient. It meant telling suppliers, customers, and employees the same thing. Sam and Hecht believed that it was hard enough trying to keep your stories straight if they were true and impossible if there were different stories for different audiences.

The two partners put great emphasis on hiring people who shared those values, training them by example, and weeding out those who did not accept these goals.

Customer Values

Reconciling the company's core philosophy with its selling practices was an intellectual challenge. Although Wards advertised low-priced, low-featured products to bring customers in, the ultimate goal was to sell them higher-priced merchandise that would provide a higher profit margin. Critics call the process "bait and switch"; Sam called it "step-up selling."

Although it may sound like self-justification, Sam truly believed that a salesman owed it to his customers to point out the better features available so that they could determine if the more expensive product better fit their needs. He taught salesmen to ask questions about how the customer planned to use the product. If he had a large family, he probably needed a larger refrigerator or a bigger TV screen. If the customer was elderly, he might need a remote control. If, after an extended pitch, the customer was not ready to buy a step up model, he might be "TOed," that is, turned over to another salesman, generally introduced as the buyer or the manager, to see if the substitute could "close" the customer.

Sam believed that this was not a "bait and switch" because, in the end, if the customer was not persuaded to buy the "step-up" model, the company would sell him the ADV or provide a better model at the same price. One way or another, the customer was satisfied.

Harder to justify was the fact that the company did not have a fixed price for any product. The prices for most of the merchandise (with the exception of the ADVs) were well above what the company was ultimately willing to accept. In addition to the stated price, each price tag had a code that showed the lowest price the salesman could charge. At any price in between the asking price and the lowest acceptable price, the salesman got a percentage (also coded on the tag) of the difference. As a result, less sophisticated and less aggressive shoppers paid more. While not consumer friendly by today's standards, "caveat emptor" was a regular business practice in the days before the consumer movement. In this respect, Wards was no worse, but not a lot better, than most of its peers.

On the other hand, once a customer bought from Wards, the company stood behind the sale. A complaint, Sam believed, was

Abraham L. Hecht – circa 1960

"an opportunity to make a friend." He preached, "If you go to a store and buy a shirt that shrinks in the wash, and they give you a new shirt or your money back, they have avoided making an enemy. If, however, in addition to replacing the defective shirt, they give you a tie, they have made a friend."

Salesmen were required to call customers after the product arrived to see if they were fully satisfied. Sam recognized that besides the inevitable mistakes any business makes, the products Wards sold were often temperamental, and the customer would blame the retailer if he missed his favorite TV show or the food in the refrigerator spoiled. The company policy, therefore, was to do whatever was required to correct the mistake and, in addition, to send disgruntled customers a set of steak knives or kitchen towels or, in more egregious cases, a coupon entitling him to dinner for two at a good restaurant.

Sam believed in disproportional word of mouth. "If a customer was treated well," he proclaimed, "he would tell two or three people, but if he felt mistreated, he would tell ten." To avoid badmouthing was worth an extra effort and the expense of a gift.

Supplier Values

While Sam focused on sales, Hecht had the primary responsibility for buying and vendor relations. In addition to his gentlemanly manners, he had a perpetual twinkle in his eye, a wonderful sense of humor, and the gift of gab. His demeanor, paired with his trademark beret, made him a memorable and loveable character in the industry.

Hecht believed the world is small and that what comes around goes around. If you lie to a supplier today, he will remember it tomorrow. And if you brush off a salesperson today because you have no interest in his product, he may be working for your key supplier tomorrow and remember how rudely you treated him.

In addition, Sam and Hecht understood that suppliers, just like retailers, had a bottom line and that they, like Wards' salesmen, had families to feed.

Employee Values

From the first day he opened the doors, Sam understood that management means getting results through the efforts of other people and that if he wanted to get the best from others he had to treat them with respect and provide an opportunity for them to advance. He believed that most people are inherently honest, willing to work, and want to be successful. All he had to do was give them the training and the opportunity to move ahead.

George Martin, the first man he hired (to help him carry TVs into customers' homes), stayed and grew with the company for more than forty years. In his spare time George learned to be a "tube jockey." In the early days, before transistors, TV sets had lots of vacuum tubes, and many repairs were made by replacing defective tubes. George gradually learned to read schematics and to repair TVs by changing condensers and resistors in addition to tubes. Sam encouraged George by letting him observe experienced service technicians and by sending him to school. He then went on to train and supervise service technicians. George was his poster child for growing with the company.

Sam also believed that "the primary need a man has in his vocation is to be creative. Creativity in business can take several forms. You can be creative by being imaginative. You can be creative by being analytical, finding the things that need to be done, to be changed, to be improved."[21] You could also be creative by understanding what customers or suppliers really wanted and figuring out how to get them to a win-win solution.

In addition, Sam understood that employees, being human, would make mistakes, and that mistakes should be treated as learning opportunities. He once told an interviewer, "When an executive starts to build up his own ego by bawling out someone under him, he is not helping that person or himself because he is inhibiting future decisions by that subordinate, who will be afraid that he will make another mistake and get another bawling out."[22] So "one of the basic philosophies here is that if something goes wrong, the person who supervises must start off with the premise that the fault is his own. Something has gone wrong here. It's my fault because I either didn't provide adequate staff or enough income or adequate authority to do the job."[23]

Human Resource Policies

What began as instinctive principles gradually developed into a full-blown human resources philosophy. Many of Sam's principles predate the publication of Douglas McGregor's groundbreaking book, *The Human Side of Enterprise*,[24] which now serves as the basis for modern management theory.[25] Once he read that book, however, the disparate elements of his homegrown personnel philosophy fell into a coherent pattern.

Theory X and Theory Y

A professor at MIT's Sloan School of Management, McGregor identified two theories of human nature and of work. Theory X assumes employees are inherently lazy and seek to avoid work. As a result, workers need to be closely supervised and controlled to ensure that the work gets accomplished. McGregor's model for such organizations was the military.

Theory Y assumes that most people enjoy mental and physical activities and want to be creative and succeed at work. Theory Y managers believe that *given the right conditions*, most employees will seek out and accept responsibility and exercise self-control in accomplishing objectives to which they and the company are committed. The job of a Theory Y manager, therefore, is to create an environment in which subordinates understand the company's objectives, share in the decision making, and welcome the opportunity to do a good job.

When Sam first read *The Human Side of Enterprise*, he was so excited that he called McGregor's office and asked for an appointment. When it became apparent that he was not going to get one on the phone, he flew to Boston and called McGregor's secretary, again asking to see the professor. When he was once more told that McGregor was not available, Sam said, "I am staying at the XYZ hotel and will wait here as long as I need to get an appointment."

In a few minutes the secretary called back and arranged for him to meet McGregor the next day. At that meeting, Sam asked where he could hire a person with McGregor's Theory Y philosophy to be his vice president of personnel.[26] McGregor told him that there were no such people available, and added, "You need to build your own."

So Sam returned to Richmond and, shortly thereafter, hired a young man whom he knew socially. Larry Yoffy had inherited a small chain of failing Ben Franklin five-and-ten stores that he ultimately closed. He was smart, thoughtful, a good listener, and had the nonjudgmental temperament required to be a good vice president of personnel. Together, he and Sam began to develop, articulate, and implement the basic human resource policies that enabled Wards to grow.

There is no doubt in my mind that this was the key to the company's success. Like almost every retailer, Wards had no patents or trade secrets of any consequence. The TVs and refrigerators it sold were the same brands and models offered in a dozen or more stores in any city in which it operated. Therefore, Wards could succeed only if it bought the products better, advertised them better, sold them better, and delivered, serviced, and accounted for them better than the competition.

This meant that it needed highly motivated and better-trained people to carry out all these functions. Sam used to say, "To be successful, you need to do a hundred things right, but to fail you need only do one thing badly." He recognized early on that if

Wards were to become a big company it needed a set of personnel polices to ensure that it attracted and retained the right people with the right attitudes and the right training and experience in every position. To communicate these values, Sam developed a set of rubrics that he continually taught and followed.

Sam's Personnel Rubrics

Hiring: Who Gets on the Bus?

From the beginning, Sam was careful whom he hired or, to use today's jargon, "who gets on the bus."[27]

Initially, he was primarily hiring commissioned salesmen. As Wards grew, however, he needed to hire or promote people to management positions. From the beginning his approach to hiring was not to find someone with multiple years of experience in a nearly identical job, which was the traditional way of going about it. Instead, he often hired salesmen who had failed at something else, so long as he detected persistence and an appealing sales personality. His early hires included a suave Frenchman who had sold lingerie to dress stores, a former convict who had no significant work record, and an air-conditioning contractor whose business had failed.

Over the years, as the company grew and expanded out of Richmond, Sam developed the following commonsense rules for hiring, promoting, and firing.

Talent Trumps Experience

Sam fundamentally believed that a smart person with the right temperament and the right training could learn to be a successful manager. When evaluating applicants for a job or a promotion, he distinguished between the man with ten years' experience in another field and the man with "one year's experience ten times" in precisely the same job he was applying to fill. Initially, the former would need to learn the job and would be less productive. However, Sam believed that a smart and well-grounded person without direct experience would, in a short time, catch up with and surpass the more "experienced" but more limited individual.

"When I look for a man to bring into our management team, primarily I look for a man who I think is bright and capable of learning," he explained. "Those who grow on the job can create and define their job. If he has the capacity to accept responsibility, he can develop his job so that he can take on additional responsibility. What we do is provide the man with the opportunity to accept responsibility."[28]

Interpersonal Skills are Essential

Brains were necessary but not sufficient. A supervisor also needed "empathy"—what today we would call good "interpersonal skills." Sam warned, "If he is not...thoughtful enough or lacks empathy, and steps on somebody else's toes and creates dissension in an organization," that is a problem.[29]

He and Hecht also liked self-starters. Hecht talked about employees who went around with "their wheelbarrow turned up," ready to take on a new challenge or assignment. Employees whose "wheelbarrow" was always upside down did not progress or last very long.

Early on, Sam hired industrial psychologists to administer a battery of personality tests to applicants for important jobs in order to determine if they had both the skills and the right personality traits to succeed at Wards. Sam's willingness to spend significant sums prior to hiring an important executive is testimony both to his forward thinking and to the importance he placed on finding the right person for each job.

Make Hiring a Priority

Building a company is all about hiring the right people. Finding people with the right skills, energy levels, and values is not generally an easy or a quick task. Initially, at least two of the three principals—Sam, Hecht, and Ross—interviewed every applicant for every job. For important jobs, all of them were involved.

Never Hire a "Warm Body" Just to Fill a Slot

Although operating with vacant positions is a disservice to customers and unfair to other employees who are picking up the slack, it is better to be short-staffed for a while than to compromise on finding the right person. It may be tempting to hire someone and scratch the need to hire off your "to-do" list. The easy path is not the way to build a strong organization.

Have Multiple Interviews With Shared Feedback

No one could hire even a stock boy or a driver without having a supervisor or trusted subordinate also interview the candidate. To get exceptional results, Sam believed, you needed exceptional people at every level. The higher the position, the more people were involved in evaluating the applicant. For senior and often middle management jobs, the entire executive team interviewed the applicant one-on-one. Then they would gather in Sam's office or a conference room to compare notes at the end of the day. It was surprising how many applicants told different stories to different interviewers, thus demonstrating that they did not share the core value of honesty. Often a particular interviewer would make an important observation that had escaped the rest of the group, and, when combined with some general concerns, that might be enough to tip the balance. Altogether, it was a good process that minimized the inevitable hiring mistakes and created in the executive team a shared culture and a common view of where the company was going and how it might get there.

Promotion and Demotion: Where Do They Sit?

Just as important as who gets on the bus is where they will sit once they board. Human organizations are fragile things. Every decision to hire, fire, or promote has consequences both for the caliber of the personnel at all levels of the business and for the "message" it sends to other employees concerning the skills and temperaments the organization values.

Promote from Within

Building a loyal team was a priority for Sam. He believed that the best way to build loyalty was for employees to see that there were opportunities for advancement. Ambitious employees would leave if they perceived their job to be a dead end. Therefore, he felt, it was better to make some mistakes by promoting someone who subsequently failed than to hire only outsiders and never take a chance on an existing employee.

Provide Training

Sam believed that it was irresponsible and unfair to promote someone to a new level of responsibility without providing the tools that person needed to do the job successfully. Training was important, not only for salespeople but also for clerical personnel, service technicians, and managers. He encouraged and reimbursed employees who elected to go to school at night to improve their knowledge and skills. He knew from personal experience that ongoing education was critical to success. Today, widespread corporate training is commonplace, but in the 1950s and '60s it was pioneering.

Store or department managers were the linchpins of the system. In the early days they bought the merchandise from local distributors or factory branches, shopped the competition, planned promotions, and approved the advertising. They hired, trained, and supervised salespeople, cashiers, and stockroom personnel.

They were responsible for recordkeeping and reporting and for setting up merchandise displays on the floor. They were expected to do personal selling when the department was busy and, when necessary, to help unload the trucks. Having the right manager was especially important as the chain expanded out of town and the home office was "managing at a distance."

"You were an entrepreneur with financial backing," recalled David Blanset, a store manager in Oklahoma City in 1964. "You might see someone from the home office every three or six months. As long as your results were satisfactory on the P&L, you operated on your own."

As the company grew throughout the 1960s, Sam developed a formal store- management-training program. He seldom hired experienced store managers from the outside because he believed it would be difficult for them to "unlearn bad habits." Even those with extensive retail management experience were required to undergo at least six months of formal on-the-job training and take a rigorous promotion exam before they were awarded a store to manage.

At higher levels, a new executive's training would include working in a store over the busy Christmas season to better understand the pressures and problems the salespeople and store manager faced. In addition, Sam believed in moving managers to new areas of responsibility. The key operational executives, including Bill Rivas and Dan Rexinger, who would later help take Wards from "Good to Great," had each served a year or more in merchandising and store operations and had at various times line responsibility for warehousing, delivery, and product service. As a result, they understood all aspects of the business and how the parts fit together to support the whole.

Coffee Conferences: Organized Employee Feedback

By the mid-1960s, when sales were only about $20 million per year, Sam instituted a series of "Coffee Conferences," at which the VP for personnel sat with rank-and-file employees at the lowest levels (accounting clerks, warehouse workers, salesmen, and so forth) once or twice a year and asked what the company could do to improve their jobs. He was looking for working conditions or compensation issues that might adversely affect morale. Sometimes the feedback was as trivial as complaining about the quality of the paper towels in the bathrooms. Sometimes, however, the employees' complaints led to important policy changes, such as instituting flexible scheduling or a more tolerant sick leave policy. In every case, notes were made and the actions taken on the issues raised were reported back to the group at the next meeting.

The VP of personnel was also looking for productivity improvements that could reduce costs or increase job satisfaction. He would ask, "How can you work smarter, not harder?" This would generate discussions that often led to changes in the work flow, elimination of unnecessary steps, computerization of manual functions, and the like.

Make Hard Work Fun

Annual store managers meetings were held, sometimes in exotic locations like Puerto Rico, the French Riviera, or Hawaii. After three days of intensive training and feedback, the spouses (in those days they were all wives) arrived for a weekend of fun. Many of the managers had never traveled out of the country before, so these meetings made them feel special and rewarded for their long hours and hard work.

The meetings also provided a unique opportunity to listen to what was on the managers' minds and understand how the company could make their jobs less stressful and more rewarding for them and their families. Feedback sessions allowed store managers to feel that their voice counted and provided them with a top-management perspective on the company's goals.

Recognizing the importance of spouses to the managers' mental well-being, and understanding that long store hours and frequent relocations were hard on a marriage, Sam often held question-and-answer sessions with the wives. He also funded an informal spouses' network called Wards Wives. In cities with multiple stores, spouses would meet in casual groups to share their stories and help newly arrived families get settled. To this day, longtime Circuit City managers and their spouses remember with fondness Wards Wives and the fact that the company included spouses on the trips they took to faraway places for a weekend of fun.

Fair Compensation; No Negotiation

Sam wanted above-average employees and was willing to pay them above-average wages—generally somewhere around the 75th percentile of what his market research told him was the "going rate" for each position.

He believed in annual salary reviews but would not negotiate wage increases. He believed that if someone needed to ask for a raise, the company had failed because it was his responsibility as a manager to keep salaries competitive. If the research indicated a requested raise was justified by market conditions, an adjustment was made. If the demand was above market, he would not make an exception and would risk losing the employee.

Making Incentives Work

Sam also believed in incentive compensation. For sales personnel, he was constantly adjusting the commission system to maximize both sales and margins without motivating salespeople to be too aggressive. For service technicians, Sam paid a flat fee based on each job they did, not unlike a doctor or an auto mechanic. But he added a twist. If the customer brought the product back within thirty days and the new problem was not clearly different from the earlier one, the service tech had to repair it at no charge to the customer and no commission to the tech. That kept them from moving too fast and doing sloppy work.

Store managers and their supervisors were paid a significant monthly bonus based on achieving budgeted sales and margins.

Annual bonuses were based primarily on profits but also included rewards for such achievements as getting paperwork in on time, keeping expenses within budget, reducing shrinkage (missing merchandise), or other administrative matters. The relative emphasis on these factors changed annually to reflect current needs.

No Vacation Policy

Wards had the usual forty-hour workweek expectations for hourly paid employees. For management at all levels, however, there were no set hours and no vacation policy. Managers were expected "to get the job done" and to manage their schedules in order to have time for family and take vacations as needed to stay fresh and productive. If a prospective employee expressed surprise that there was no specific vacation or sick leave policy for executives, Sam would reply, "Would you rather work forty hours a week on my schedule or fifty on yours?" Most chose the latter. Few, if any, executives took unfair advantage of this self-monitoring system. Often, the biggest concern was to get an executive to take *more* time off to spend with his family or to clear his head.

Firing: Who Gets Off the Bus?

Here again, Sam developed a number of principles that served the company well for many years.

Freedom to Fail

Sam believed that it was wrong to fire someone for making a mistake, even a big one. People needed to learn from their mistakes and not make the same mistake again. However, he believed that too much pressure not to make any mistakes would cause employees to not make decisions. Creating an atmosphere in which employees are afraid to act is a worse disease than giving them the freedom to make mistakes.

Downgrades with No Pay Cut

Sam was reluctant to fire an honest, hardworking employee just because he was not successful in the job.

Often a failing store manager would be offered the opportunity to go back to the sales force, and many did. Likewise, a warehouse manager or a data processing manager might be offered the job of assistant manager or programmer as an alternative to being fired. In many cases demoted employees were relieved not to be fired. They generally knew in their hearts that they were in over their heads and the pressure was getting to them. If the person accepted the demotion, Sam would not cut their salary or downgrade their corporate title, if they had one. To do so, Sam believed, would belittle the employee and create resentment. Instead, he told the employee he would receive no further annual raises until the salary of his new position caught up with his current rate of pay. That might take years, but, whatever the cost, it bought respect and loyalty that was priceless.

Separate from People Gently

In the end, if he could not keep an employee, Sam would tell the person that the job at Wards just had not worked out. He would not blame them or say they had failed. Rather, he would blame himself by saying that he (or the company) had made a mistake in hiring or promoting the person in the first place. Sam believed that what goes around comes around, and someday this former employee might be in a position to help or harm the company. Having their goodwill was an asset.

Discharge as a Win-Win

He also believed that if someone was not appreciated at Wards, he was doing them a favor by letting them go. He would cite a particular example of a sweet, hardworking assistant who had been given multiple opportunities to prove his worth. The employee's bumbling performance, however, had kept him from progressing in both compensation and position. When he was finally let go, he went back to the auto dealer where he had previously worked as a salesman and was soon named vice president of truck sales. He came back to see his friends at Wards and was immensely proud of his new title and position. It proved, Sam thought, that someone who is not a success at one place could find a career at another company with different expectations. Letting this man go was a win for him and for Wards.

Habits of Mind

The events of Chapter Two demonstrate the following Habits of Mind that lead to success or failure.

Mind the Culture: *Create a caring and ethical culture where employees can make mistakes without fear of adverse consequences. Beware of employees who are more concerned about their own success than the success of the business. Understand, exemplify, and reinforce the company's positive history and culture.*

Sam and Hecht developed a coherent code for fair dealing with consumers and suppliers ("One Face") that was followed successfully for more than fifty years. For employees, the many personnel policies designed to allow employees to grow, to make mistakes, and to learn from their mistakes were critical to the success of the company for more than fifty of its sixty years. They motivated and informed the decisions of thousands of managers and hundreds of thousands of employees. The supplier, customer, and employee policies, taken together, were the "company culture" that took Wards, and later Circuit City, from Good to Great.

Keep It Simple and Accountable: *Develop a clear and well-articulated set of policies for dealing with customers, suppliers, and employees. For any organization to succeed it is essential that each and every employee in-*

ternalizes the company's goals and values. Employees should also be held accountable and incentivized to pursue those goals and values every day.

Sam and Hecht developed both the necessary IT tools and the practice of delegating P&L responsibility to the lowest possible level. They provided not only a road map but also a system for rewarding managers and holding them responsible for the financial results of the units under their control.

Chapter Three

PUTTING THEORY INTO PRACTICE

Great things are not done by impulse, but by
a series of small things brought together.

—Vincent Van Gogh

By the late 1950s, Wards had first-rate policies operating in a second-rate business. Sales in the four Richmond stores were not even $2 million. Out-of-town expansion attempts had failed and the Richmond market was never going to be big enough to satisfy Sam and Hecht's ambitions. Then they stumbled onto the greatest expansion of retail sales the country had ever experienced: the Discount Revolution.

The Real World in the '60s

During the 1960s the postwar economy moved briskly ahead. From 1962 to 1966 the United States enjoyed the longest uninterrupted expansion in its postwar history: real Gross Domestic Product increased at an average annual rate of 5.4 percent a year. Manufacturers and retailers alike clamored to ride the wave, taking advantage of easily accessible credit to fund new factories and stores.[30]

Consumers were also availing themselves of this free-flowing credit. In 1966 Bank of America introduced the first general purpose credit card, BankAmericard (which became Visa.) That same year the Interbank Card Association (later known as MasterCard) launched a competing service. Both cards quickly gained acceptance, reaching 16 percent of households by 1970.[31]

Employment in the '60s was high (over 95 percent),[32] inflation was low (around 2 percent),[33] and Americans were feeling optimistic. Consumer confidence, as measured by the University of Michigan Index Of Consumer Sentiment, peaked at 105.4 (on a base of 100) in May 1965, a level that had never been achieved before and would not be achieved again for more than thirty years.[34]

Despite, or perhaps partly because of, the good economy, baby boomers who were coming of age began to rebel. Many joined the counterculture and feminist movements, rejecting the traditional emphasis on settling down and starting a family. Facilitated by new and more readily available methods of birth control, population growth slowed, marriage was postponed, and couples had fewer children. In order to live the good life, many married women returned to the workforce while their husbands worked overtime or more than one job and took further training or graduate courses that would allow the family to move up the income ladder. Nonetheless, the population continued to grow. Between 1950 and 1970 the number of Americans grew from 150 million to 200 million—33 percent in twenty years.

At the same time, plagued by racial tension and social unrest, cities were becoming increasingly difficult places to raise a family. As the interstate highway system expanded and incomes rose, growing middle-class families fled to the suburbs in record numbers. An amazing 15 million new housing units were built between 1945 and 1955, mostly in the suburbs.[35] No available plot of land was safe from development, and entire communities sprang up around newly minted malls in the middle of nowhere. Compared with downtown, shopping in the suburbs was easy, parking was free, and greater ethnic homogeneity also brought a greater sense of "safety."

Before long, employment also began to move outside the beltways that now encircled most major cities, reinforcing the flight to suburbia. By the mid-1960s, suburbanites had become a majority of the nation's metropolitan population, and regional malls

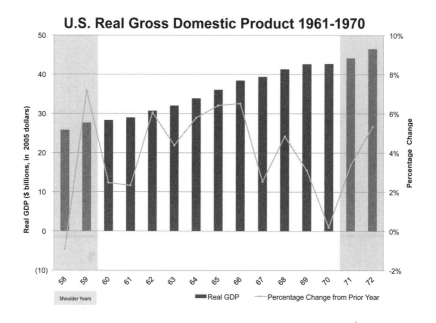

U.S. Real Gross Domestic Product 1961-1970

became the suburbs' "downtown."[36]

At the same time, retailing was undergoing a transformation of its own. As a result of increased competition from new stores, traditional retailers were experiencing declining profit margins. Savvy shoppers were suddenly in a position to bargain. High factory productivity led to periodic oversupply, and discounting—the practice of selling at prices below the manufacturer's list price—became commonplace even among traditional department stores.

In this highly competitive environment, a new business model emerged: the discount department store. In 1953, an entrepreneur opened a pioneering department store in an abandoned New England textile mill called Ann and Hope.[37] Virtually all the store's merchandise was offered at less than the manufacturer's suggested list price. Ann and Hope was conceived as a kind of Turkish bazaar, with a group of independent merchants gathered under one roof. But unlike a bazaar, all advertising was done under one name and the customers thought it was one store. All essential merchandise categories were represented, from men's, women's, and children's apparel to shoes, health and beauty aids,

U.S. Population by Age Group 1961-1970

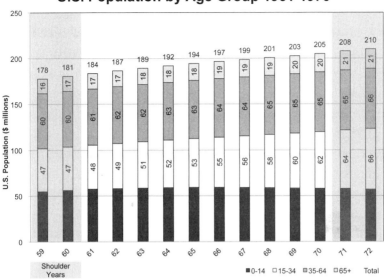

sporting goods, and so on. But a specialist, such as a traditional drug or sporting goods chain, merchandised each category.

Copycat discount stores blossomed like desert flowers after a rain. Real estate entrepreneurs often developed the early ones. They were soon joined by expansion-minded multi-store specialty retailers, which licensed out the departments they were not able to run themselves. Discount stores reached 15 percent of total retail sales by 1954.[38] The first Kmart,[39] Target,[40] and Walmart[41] stores opened in 1962, and by 1965, discount store sales surpassed department store sales, becoming the country's preeminent retail format.[42] Discounters appealed to both white-collar and the increasing number of blue-collar workers in the suburbs. Unlike downtown stores, they were open (when legally possible) on Sundays, offered free parking, were self–service, and were easier to get in and out of quickly.

Meanwhile, the retailing colossus Sears Roebuck was also increasing its already significant market share. Instead of relying primarily on what manufacturers offered, Sears began to determine what goods it wanted to carry and at what price point. It then worked backward, finding a manufacturer or, if there was not a satisfactory one available, organizing and sometimes owning the production chain at every step from raw materials to the sales floor. Sears created its own brands, like Kenmore and Craftsman. As a result, it became a formidable competitor, especially for durable goods. In 1972, about 10 cents out of every retail dollar was spent with Sears.[43]

For Wards, the emergence of discounting and the explosion of consumer electronics was the perfect storm. The total value of U.S. factory shipments consumer electronics more than doubled in the '60s, largely facilitated by sales of long-awaited color TVs. By 1968, dollar sales of color units exceeded those of black-and-white TVs.[44] In addition, the increasing popularity of television began to overcrowd the available airwaves, so in 1965 the FCC mandated that by 1971 all new sets include UHF tuners,27 expanding the number of channels they could receive from thirteen to more than seventy.[45]

At the same time, the enormous popularity of the Beatles and other music groups motivated manufacturers to produce, and millions of young people to purchase, high-quality, high-priced hi-fi components. New technical terms like wow and flutter, hertz, and amps entered the popular lexicon as hip young professionals and music buffs clamored for ever more high-performance equipment. Different brands and models of amplifiers, tuners, tape decks, and speakers could be mixed and matched to produce the sound and technical specs that most appealed to each customer. Audio buffs wanted the best, almost regardless of price.

Increasingly, the manufacture of electronics moved offshore, where low wages, high productivity, and engineering skills enabled foreign manufacturers initially to copy and then to design and produce high-quality products at highly competitive prices. Because they represented better values, imports of Japanese radios, TVs, phonographs, and tape recorders climbed from $96 million in 1960 to $368 million in 1967, accounting for fully 70 percent of the U.S. market.[46]

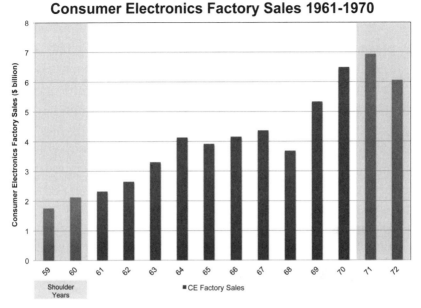

Consumer Electronics Factory Sales 1961-1970

Another fortunate development for retailers was the exploding capability and rapidly declining cost of information technology or, as it was then called, data processing. IBM's new 360 line of mini-mainframe computers debuted in 1965. Utilizing integrated circuits instead of individual transistors, they dramatically increased computational power at substantially lower cost. At that point, technical advancements were progressing so quickly that Intel co-founder Gordon Moore, in what would become known as Moore's Law, predicted that the number of transistors on a silicon chip would double every twelve (later revised to twenty-four) months with no appreciable cost increase.[47] Put another way, every two years the cost of computing power dropped by half or, for the same cost, computing power doubled.

For small- and medium-sized retailers, the IBM 360 could manage data for the entire business, without the full-time high-tech attention a mainframe required. The new technology dramatically sped up processing, reduced errors, and improved logistics without increasing costs.[48]

Wards Joins the Discount Revolution

As the first discount stores were popping up around the country in the late 1950s, Robert Wolfson, who was a friend of Hecht's from the Midwest, had invested in GEM International, a new chain of closed membership discount stores. Wolfson wanted Wards to run the TV and appliance department in one of GEM's early stores in St. Louis, but, not wanting to go so far afield geographically, Wards declined. Wolfson then introduced Hecht to National Bellas Hess, a discount chain based in Kansas City, Missouri, that was planning to open stores in Atlanta and Norfolk, Virginia. It also operated closed membership stores, called GEX (Government Employees Exchange). Membership discount stores were only open to government employees, union members, and other defined groups. Their "exclusiveness" gave them additional appeal. Sam and Hecht studied the opportunity and decided they were ready, so Wards opened its first licensed department in Atlanta in July 1960, another in Norfolk in September, and a third in Camden, New Jersey, in November 1961.

Both open and membership discount stores were a novelty and immediately drew large crowds. The stores were big, generally 100,000 square feet, and Wards was assigned a certain selling space (typically about 3,000 square feet), usually against the back wall opposite the entrance, and a separate stockroom off the selling floor. Wards added its own fixtures and paid for the required electrical and antenna installations. The department employed a manager, salesmen, cashiers, and one or two stock boys who unloaded the trucks and carried merchandise to the floor or to customers' cars. The store did the advertising for all its departments, for which Wards paid its pro-rata share.

The Wards licensed departments were an instant success. In December 1960, the TV and appliance department in the Norfolk store made an astonishing $100,000 in sales. For the first nine months of 1961, the combined sales of the two new licensed departments almost equaled the sales of the four conventional stores in Richmond. For the same nine months, the company, which had grown to 92 employees, had sales of $2.5 million and a net income of $48,000 (1.9 percent after taxes). Based on this unprecedented success, Sam, ever the optimist, believed that the world was his oyster and Wards was ready to go public.

GEX store – circa 1960

Going Public

In the early '60s, Wards was the only company in the country operating TV and appliance licensed departments away from its home base. As a result, it was frequently being offered expansion opportunities. Unfortunately, Sam and Hecht lacked the capital to expand. Wards was earning them a good living, but not a fortune.

Going public would be a way to raise new capital for opening new departments and also to expand by acquisition. For a small company like Wards, the price of new capital was steep, but for the go-go discount industry, going public was fashionable. In July 1961, *Discount Merchandiser* listed fifty-seven companies that were publically traded. With sales of only $2.5 million and profits of less than $50,000, Wards was not an obvious candidate. But Sam and Hecht found a willing underwriter: Stein Bros. & Boyce, a small but hungry Baltimore securities firm.

In December 1961 Wards sold 110,000 shares, equal to 40.4 percent of the company, for net proceeds of $536,250.[49] This valued the company at $1.8 million after the new money. Although the sum seems paltry by today's standards, Sam was thrilled. Instead of having the money wired to a Richmond bank, he chose to receive the check in person. His lawyer recalled that as they drove back to Richmond, Sam would touch his coat pocket every ten miles to assure himself that it was still there.

In retrospect, giving up 40 percent of the company for only half a million dollars seems like a high price to pay for the capital needed to open roughly ten more licensed departments. After Wards went public, the Wurtzels and Hechts together controlled 50 percent of the common stock, as compared to 84 percent before.[50] But they loved the idea of being public. It gave them more status in Richmond and in their industry. Every quarter, the newspapers carried a press release on Wards' sales and earnings, and Wards' executive salaries were reported annually alongside the salaries of the CEOs of Reynolds Metals, Phillip Morris, and the other big public companies in Richmond.

Down the road, it meant that the founders would never rival Sam Walton or even many of their counterparts in the consumer electronics business in terms of personal wealth. But Sam and Hecht were impatient to grow quickly and this seemed to be the best alternative.

Licensed Department Expansion

For the first three years after going public its sales and earnings grew consistently as it opened more licensed departments in discount department stores. By 1966 Wards had 27 licensed departments from Boston to Oklahoma City in addition to the four conventional stores in Richmond, and was doing $22.8 million in sales with earnings of $616,000, a respectable 2.7 percent after taxes.

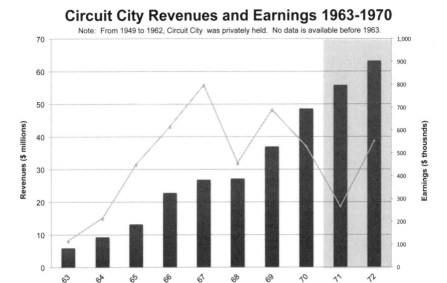

Circuit City Revenues and Earnings 1963-1970

Note: From 1949 to 1962, Circuit City was privately held. No data is available before 1963.

Starting in 1961, when it went public, Wards fiscal year ran from April 1 to March 31. In 1979, the company moved the fiscal year end to February 28 in order to have the best month, December, offset the worst two months (January and February), and thus smooth out quarterly sales and earnings. Hence, whenever the text refers to a fiscal year the year in question is composed of ten months in the prior calendar year and January and February, the two weakest months, of the named fiscal year.

This kind of erratic geographic expansion, dependent on where compatible chains of discount stores opened, also had its challenges. As Wards expanded into new markets, it encountered significant local vendor resistance. Under the traditional three-tier distribution system that existed at the time, manufacturers sold to factory branches or independent regional distributors, who in turn sold to retailers. While the products were the same, the prices that retailers paid for any given model might vary, sometimes significantly, from one market to another. Since retailers were prohibited by their franchise agreements from moving goods bought in one market to be sold in another ("transshipping"), when Wards entered new markets it generally tried to do business with local distributors.

As a participant in a discount store, however, it was especially resented by the existing TV and appliance dealers in town, which regarded Wards as an outsider, a dirty discounter, or "trouble-making Yankees from the North."[51] They complained to the distributor and to the manufacturer. When Wards could not make a satisfactory local deal, it transshipped and manufacturers were generally willing to look the other way, but they were also under pressure from their distributors and their local dealers. Sometimes, bowing to this pressure, a manufacturer would threaten to stop doing business with Wards.

When caught, Hecht and Sam would go hat in hand to the manufacturer to work out the problem. Transshipping was not simple for manufacturers to track, and they also liked the sales volumes that Wards and other transshippers were providing.

Over time Wards increasingly put pressure on manufacturers to loosen the rules for larger dealers, and by 1969 it had fifteen "national account" arrangements. As a national account, the company could buy directly from the manufacturer or from its distributors at uniform pricing. This brought significant economies and lower prices, and materially reduced that challenge of managing stores from a distance.

Why It Worked: Better Format

For the first ten years of its existence, Wards had focused on small stores (three thousand to five thousand square feet) in Richmond, and a few out of town. The Richmond stores made money, but not a lot. Small TV and appliance stores are a difficult business model. They generate little store traffic and require lots more advertising than the sales volumes can justify. They are open long hours, have a very small workforce, and are thus hard to staff, especially if someone is off or sick.

By contrast, the licensed departments in discount stores were far easier to manage. The manager of the licensed department did not have to worry about creating or placing the advertising (just picking the items to be advertised) or customer credit (the store did that) or physically maintaining the store. In addition, discount stores had a one-price policy that precluded negotiation. That made training salesmen a lot easier. And there was some backup supervision on the spot. If the Wards manager was absent or there was a problem in the department, the overall store manager would alert Wards' management in Richmond.

Most important, both the novelty and the joint advertising provided by a discount store created a far higher level of awareness in the community and generated a lot more foot traffic for all departments than a small freestanding store could attract on its own. As in a mall, some of the customers who came to buy toothpaste or shoes saw the electronics and appliances and ended up buying something more than they had intended.

Why It Worked: Better Systems

Despite these advantages, managing from afar was still an issue. Since the days that they determined the Roanoke store was too difficult to manage from Richmond, Sam and Hecht had put three other programs in place to facilitate management from a distance. As we have seen, the decision to build an IT infrastructure was the first step. Developing structured sales training and store management training programs was another. A third was creating chain-wide budget and merchandising programs.

For Sam, no recurring expense was too small to escape his attention. By tracking monthly store expenses down to the postage and telephone bills he could compare managers and send a message that every dollar counted. In addition, tracking monthly store sales, by brand, model, and category of goods, as compared to the merchandising program, became another essential tool for managing the business. Why, he could ask, did the Atlanta store sell so many more refrigerators than the Mobile store, or why did it sell so many fewer top-of-the-line refrigerators? Or fewer Whirlpool items than those of the more profitable Hotpoint?

To focus the store managers' minds on the bottom line, Wards paid them significant monthly bonuses, as much as one-third of their annual compensation, based primarily on sales and margins as compared to budget. It also paid annual bonuses to everyone involved in store operations, from the store manager to the vice president, based on annual profitability compared to budget. Thus, budget versus actual proved a powerful tool for delegating decision making and accountability to the lowest possible level.

After ten years of trial and error, Wards had found a viable business model. Licensed departments in discount stores carefully monitored from Richmond enabled the company to grow and prosper—at least for a time.

Building a Board

Once it went public, Wards needed an independent board of directors. Together with the underwriter, Stein Brothers, Sam and Hecht determined that there would be five members, and they were somewhat frustrated by the fact that one of those seats would go to the underwriter, who seemed to them more a watchdog than a contributor. From the beginning, they wanted the best board they could attract. Their criteria were:

- **Independence of mind.** They did not want "yes men," but independent-minded, successful businesspeople who would challenge their thinking and contribute ideas based on their own experiences.
- **Diversity of experience**. Retailing experience was, of course, highly valued, but they also wanted a lawyer, a financial expert, and, as the company grew, people with other relevant experience, such as in marketing, investment banking, or data management.
- **Debate and dissent.** From the beginning, they sought to get honest feedback and fresh perspectives from their directors on how and what they were doing. They did not always follow the

advice they got, but they always listened.

To implement this philosophy, their first choice was a lifelong friend of both: Sam Winokur. Sam was first in his class and editor in chief of the *Yale Law Journal*. After a short and highly successful career at Sullivan and Cromwell, he was recruited by Grand Union supermarkets to be in line for CEO. When he was passed over, he moved to become CEO of White Rose Tea, a large regional wholesale grocer, whose business he grew dramatically.

Next to be elected was Fredrick "Rick" Deane, the up-and-coming executive vice president, later to be chairman and CEO, of the Bank of Virginia. Rick was one of Richmond's leading bankers and citizens. He was able to open doors in both Richmond and New York financial circles. Always cheerful, upbeat, and generous with his time, Rick was a fierce ally and a wise counselor to Wards, a very small fish in his much bigger pond.

Morton Wallerstein, a Harvard-trained lawyer and company counsel, and a highly respected member of the Richmond bar, also joined the board right after the company went public. Finally, Sam and Hecht added Hyman Meyers, also a personal friend, who ran Heilig-Meyers, a large, family-owned retail furniture store chain operating in small towns throughout the South. He lived in Richmond and his wisdom and experience as a chain store retailer were invaluable as Wards began to grow.

The board that Sam and Hecht assembled was small, congenial, and hardworking. The high quality of its members was a testament to the founders' personalities rather than the size or stature of the business. Nonetheless, members took their roles seriously. They seldom missed meetings, participated actively in discussion, and invested in the company's stock. And they were not shy about expressing their views. Sometimes they would block a management initiative they felt was imprudent or unwise.

A few years later, when I was CEO, I experienced the power of this board. At a two-day retreat in Pinehurst, North Carolina (the same place Ruth and Sam had been headed just before Wards was conceived), the same board refused to approve my 1983 Three

Year Plan, which recommended two new stores in Birmingham, Alabama, because they feared that the growth would overextend the company financially. Instead, they insisted that the management team to postpone the openings at least until the following year. My team was confident that there was no significant risk and that the leases we had negotiated but had not yet signed would

Wards Board of Directors – 1969, clockwise from bottom: Hyman Meyers, Morton Wallerstein, Sam Winokur, Frederick Deane, Sam Wurtzel, Bill Rivas, A.L. Hecht, Alan Wurtzel

be impossible to duplicate a year later. Still, we accepted their decision. While we thought we understood the business better, we appreciated the fact that, collectively, the board members had a lot more business experience.

Undisciplined Pursuit of More

In 1965 Wards raised a million dollars by selling 55,000 shares of preferred stock, further diluting the founders' interests. The stock offering and Wards' favorable earnings in its licensed departments enabled the company to embark upon an ambitious acquisition program. As Hecht told a local reporter, "We are like the universe. We never stop expanding."[52]

One of Sam's goals was to build a large chain of conventional TV and appliance stores. As a public company Wards could now acquire other businesses without having to pay cash. Known today as a "roll-up strategy," Wards could issue stock in exchange for the stock or the assets of a privately held chain of mom-and-pop stores. If the owner was approaching retirement and had no family in the business, the transaction gave him and his heirs liquidity in the form of Wards stock. Plus he could negotiate to stay on as a well-paid manager for some years. If Wards bought the private company at a lower multiple of earnings than its stock was currently trading for, the transaction increased Wards' earnings per share and hence its stock price, benefiting both Wards shareholders and the seller. This was a win-win for both parties, at least on paper.

Despite its strengths in sales and management, however, Wards in the 1960s lacked discipline in strategic planning. When asked to prepare a budget for the bank, Sam, Hecht, and Ross would sit down for a few hours and, "on the back of an envelope," come up with a sales forecast. Unlike expenses, which they budgeted and tracked in minute detail, there was no effort to budget sales or gross margins by month or by merchandise category or to anticipate changes in product mix or margins.

By the same token, there was no recognition that their roll-up strategy had many pitfalls, including the fact that once they'd been paid, the former owners had a lot less incentive to maintain previous profit levels. Even more fundamentally, Sam never seriously questioned whether the future of small local chains was secure or if they were subject to the same loss of market share as the Wards TV stores were experiencing in the face of the new discount store competition in Richmond. Always the optimist, he believed that whatever a store or business did last year, it could do better this year and next.

The newly created firepower of a public security, combined with the weaknesses of not having thought through a long-range strategy, meant that Wards was poised for what Jim Collins described nearly fifty years later as the "undisciplined pursuit of more." [53]

Carousel Stores

Wards' first undisciplined move was to purchase in 1965 a 120,000 square-foot discount store in Richmond that had been built and operated by Two Guys From Harrison, a fast-growing New York–based discount chain.

Partly because it was too far away from the Two Guys main trade area, the Richmond store was poorly supplied and not doing well. Although his only experience with discount stores was as a licensee, Sam believed that because he was living in Richmond he could run it better. He changed the name to Carousel, replaced all the department operators, and reopened in 1966. The store did okay, but Wards lacked the capital to build a significant chain of Carousel stores. If only to spread the cost of local advertising, Wards needed a second Richmond store. Sam did manage to open a second store three years later, but that was the financial limit of the company's capacity to expand this new business. Although profitable, strategically it was a dead-end street.

Hardware/Houseware Departments

Later that same year, Wards made another undisciplined move. It acquired Murmic, a Connecticut-based chain of six hardware/houseware licensed departments with combined sales of $3 million. Wards had no expertise in hardware or housewares, but now that the company owned a discount department store, Sam reasoned he needed to operate more than just the TV and appliance departments. That was the industry trend, as bigger discount store chains "went vertical" and began operating more and more of the previously licensed departments. Seriously underestimating the complexity of entering a whole new category of goods involving a whole new group of suppliers, Wards was left with a problem when, less than two years later, the Murmic management departed and Sam had no experienced hardware/houseware merchants to take their place. He attempted to build a new team, but the six original departments, plus the two he added in Carousel, never made any money and were eventually liquidated.

Joining the AMEX

From the time it went public, Wards was an "over-the-counter stock," listed in the "pink sheets." In those days, before faxes or the Internet, such stocks traded "by appointment." That is, if someone wanted to buy or sell the stock, he needed to contact a broker, who would call one or more of the known market makers to see if there was a bid to buy or sell. Generally the spreads between the bid and asked prices were large. Being traded on the New York Stock Exchange or even the American Stock Exchange would lower trading costs and increase the company's visibility and prestige, but initially the company did not qualify.

Between fiscal 1965 and 1968, Wards doubled its sales from $13 million to $26 million and its earnings from $450,000 to nearly $800,000. Drunk on its own success, it announced that it would achieve sales of $100 million by 1973.[54] Wards was now big enough to be listed on the American Stock Exchange. In 1968, on one of the most upbeat days of his life, my father took my mother and me to New York to witness Wards Company's first trade on the American Stock Exchange. Sam felt like a true American capitalist!

Unfortunately, however, joining the AMEX further facilitated undisciplined expansion by providing the company with a more desirable currency for acquisitions. Fortunately for me, it also created the need for in-house counsel.

Enter Alan

I joined Wards in December 1966 as vice president for legal affairs. The company had come a long way since the summer of 1949, when I, still in high school, had worked on rooftops installing TV antennas. Subsequent summers, while in college, I had driven a delivery truck or supervised the warehouse.

For seventeen years the business had been a part of my life. It was often, but not exclusively, the topic of dinner table conver-

Sam and Ruth Wurtzel at Americans Stock Exchange

sation. In the early days Sam would hold "executive committee meetings" with Ross and Hecht at our house every other Sunday after supper to review business strategies that needed more thought and discussion than they could fit in during the normal workday. Sometimes I sat in, but while I found the meetings interesting I never had any desire to join the business, nor did Sam urge me to do so.

Following college my next stop was Yale Law School. Complex legal questions fascinated me and I became caught up in the law and the *Law Journal*. After law school I moved to Washington, D.C., to clerk for a federal appeals court judge and subsequently joined Fried Frank, the small Washington office of a New York–based law firm, where my legal work was primarily representing Native Americans. While the work was both challenging and satisfying, I did not see it as the focus of my career. As today's young people might think of Teach for America, I thought of it as a wonderful way to help people in need, but not a long-term calling. In January 1964, I took a two-year leave of absence to become the legislative assistant to newly elected U.S. Senator Joseph D. Tydings, of Maryland.

Meanwhile, I had followed the fortunes of the family business, and, once in practice, occasionally did some legal research for the company, but I gave no thought to becoming part of it. Then one day, while I was working on Capitol Hill, Sam told me that he was looking for an in-house lawyer to pursue his roll-up strategy and handle some acquisitions. He wondered if I knew anyone from law school who might be interested.

My two-year commitment to Senator Tydings was almost up, so when Sam asked me to help him find a lawyer, I began to think that instead of going back to the law firm, becoming house counsel for Wards might be my next step. I considered my father a master at managing people and working collaboratively with others—two areas in which I felt less secure. Maybe I could hone those skills by observing him.

I knew that working in a family business could be a mixed

blessing. It could open up opportunities for the boss's kid that might not be otherwise available, but it also had the potential to exacerbate normal family tensions. My only sibling was an artist with no interest in business, so that potential complication was not an issue. But fathers and sons are often in competition. Business issues can complicate family relationships and vice versa.

A few weeks after Sam's initial inquiry, while I was visiting my folks in Richmond, we had a further conversation, and when I said that I would consider becoming in-house counsel myself for two years my father's face lit up. I wondered at the time if his request to help him find a lawyer wasn't simply a ploy to sound me out without proposing directly that I do it. He was clearly capable of that kind of deviousness. So Sam and I agreed that in December 1966, when my job in the Senate was over, I would move to Richmond to be Wards' in-house counsel for two years, at the end of which time I would return to my law firm in Washington.

The two-year limit reflected my reluctance to change careers from law to business, but within a few months I discovered that business was both more interesting and more challenging than being a lawyer. Business up close was a lot more complex than it had appeared from afar. More important, it had an unavoidable accountability that the law lacked. As a lawyer you can do a great job but lose the case for a whole host of reasons beyond your control: having the wrong client or a bad judge, or just being on the wrong side of the case law. As a businessman you may lose money for a few years as a result of changing economic or market conditions, but after the cycle passes, if you are still not profitable, you need to make changes in your business model or find a new business. You cannot continue to blame factors beyond your control. I liked that challenge and the accountability.

After I had been at Wards for six months my father suggested that if I learned the business and he was satisfied that I could run it successfully, he would retire as CEO in 1972, when he turned sixty-five. I accepted the challenge. Meanwhile, I had a lot to learn. Fortunately, I had some excellent teachers. Sam was endlessly patient with my questions and challenges about what we were doing and why. By and large we got along very well, although, inevitably, we did compete. In the early stages the competition was benign. He was excellent at doing arithmetic in his head, mentally computing percentages faster than I could put pencil to paper. So I took to using a slide rule. Handheld calculators had not yet been invented.[55] Pretty soon I could compete, at least in multiplication. As I gained responsibility and business experience, our competition became more serious, and we began having disagreements over business strategy. For example, in the early 1980s, when Sam was already retired as CEO but still chairman of the board, Zodys, a chain of stores in which we were operating TV and appliance licensed departments, went into Chapter 11 for the second time. Sam wanted to get out immediately, but because the chain was still an important profit contributor, I thought we should bide our time and leave when we could better afford it.

Fortunately, we had a mechanism to resolve such disagreements. His two closest friends, Sam Winokur and Hyman Meyers, were also on the board, and they were smart, fair-minded businessmen. I would go to them and lay out the issues. They would then speak to Sam, and almost invariably his objections would evaporate. As long as he did not have to admit to me that he had changed his mind, he could back down gracefully.

Outside the business we shared many interests, especially his three grandchildren and foreign travel. Sometimes we travelled together as a family, and we regularly had many enjoyable meals in each other's homes. Toward the end of his life, Sam told others that he was very proud of what I had accomplished, but he still had difficulty telling me.

In addition to my father, the top management team, who ran the business day-to-day, was equally generous in sharing their time and expertise. Surprisingly, they did not resent my joining the team. Having the boss's son come into a business can be at best a disruption and at worst a threat. Fortunately, none of these people saw themselves as a future CEO, so they didn't perceive me as potentially usurping the throne.

My first assignment at Wards was to supervise Carousel and the seven hardware/houseware departments, both of which Wards had acquired shortly before I arrived. I knew nothing about either, but common sense and what I had learned in law school about asking questions and digging deeper helped enormously.

The challenge of running Carousel was to find the optimum combination of licensees for the different merchandise categories in the store. In the hardware/houseware business, the problem was hiring a team leader and qualified buyers who could put together assortments in many subcategories (such as tools, kitchen gadgets, and gifts) and promote them to produce profitable sales. In the end, finding and keeping talented buyers we could afford in a business with sales well under $5 million proved impossible, and we liquidated the division.

Meanwhile, Sam was anxious to get back to growing by making acquisitions.

Custom Hi-Fi

The best and most enduring of Wards' acquisitions was Custom Electronics in May of 1969. Custom was a Washington, D.C.–based company that operated nine licensed hi-fi departments in discount stores (in many of which Wards also had licensed departments selling TVs and appliances), plus four conventional audio stores in regional malls in Washington, D.C.; four small discount audio stores called Dixie Hi-Fi; and a mail-order business. Its sales of $4 million nicely complemented Wards electronics sales.

The merger made strategic sense. The synergies were obvious. In a short time we combined the hi-fi departments in the discount stores with our TV and appliance departments, thus eliminating costs. We also began carrying hi-fi equipment in our own conventional stores. Because the audio vendors were an entirely different set of suppliers, Wards needed Custom's specialized knowledge to buy and sell hi-fi equipment successfully.

Ted Roussil, the principal owner, was a smart, likable guy who understood that hi-fi was becoming a mass-market product. He wanted to grow but knew he lacked the discipline to manage a larger operation. He loved hi-fi and hated accounting, and he especially hated having any limit on his ability to buy as much as he wanted of a "good deal." While he chafed at financial discipline, he taught Rivas, Rexinger, and Bruckart the hi-fi business, and that made us millions in the years ahead.

The Mart

Less than a year later, in fiscal 1970, Wards made the worst acquisition in its history. The Mart was a forty-year-old business with four large stores, all in Indianapolis, that sold TVs, appliances, furniture, sporting goods, and other miscellaneous hard goods. The owner, Joe Rothbard, was a larger-than-life character, highly regarded in the industry as a first-rate TV and appliance merchant. He headed National Appliance and Television Mer-

Custom Hi Fi mall store – circa 1975

chandisers, the most effective buying group in the country, composed of ten or so large Midwest TV and appliance dealers. Sam saw this as a "must-do" deal. Bringing Rothbard into the company would be a feather in our cap and would show the industry that our roll-up strategy was working.

The problem was that the Mart was ten or twenty years behind the times. Rothbard also had trouble passing up a "good deal." As a result, in addition to TVs and appliances, the Mart warehouse was full of old furniture, sporting goods, and unsellable junk. To make matters worse, it was full of ineffective old-time retainers whom Joe could not bring himself to fire.

More and More

Later that same year, Wards announced three more acquisitions of independent TV and appliance dealers: Franks, in Fort Wayne, Indiana; Certified TV, in Norfolk, Virginia; and Woodville Appliances, in Toledo, Ohio. All were small and none worked out. In the process we learned that small, family business are idiosyncratic. Their systems, people, and approach to the market are generally one of a kind. Trying to fit such organizations into a larger, more disciplined company is generally not worth the effort. It is better to build from scratch.

As if that were not enough, for fiscal 1970 the company made three other significant expansion moves. It arranged to build a second Carousel store in Richmond; it took over the automotive departments in both the Carousel stores and added them to its hardware/houseware division; and it acquired fourteen, soon to be twenty, TV and appliance departments in Zodys, a West Coast discount chain based in Los Angeles.

Zodys was the most interesting of these new ventures and had the most potential. After a long-standing prior licensee went bankrupt, Zodys' management had selected the appliance division of Westinghouse Electric Corp. to run their TV and appliance departments. Westinghouse had sold a lot of product through Zodys' previous licensee and wanted to protect its market share in LA. But it soon became clear that a manufacturer trying to be a retailer is caught between a rock and a hard place. If Westinghouse sold its products at list price in a discount store, it failed to attract buyers. If it offered discounts, it antagonized its full-price retail dealers. As a result, they threw in the towel, and we bought the inventory and store fixtures from Westinghouse on very favorable terms, including significant financing. The departments, despite Zodys' corporate problems, made good money for many years.

Fiscal 1969 was Wards' best year for sales ($37 million) and earnings (almost $700,000, or 1.8 percent) since the company was founded. The following year sales continued to grow, but earnings began to reflect the erratic and undisciplined nature of the expansion and dropped precipitously to 0.6 percent. After

Zodys department store in Los Angeles – circa 1970

that, they got even worse and did not recover until 1976.[56]

As a result of these helter-skelter acquisitions the business had become too complex to manage. The operations outlined in the 1970 annual report included:

- Fifty-seven licensed TV and appliance departments (including audio in some locations) in nine different discount chains from coast to coast
- Twenty-one freestanding TV and appliance stores (some of which included furniture) in five different markets under five different names and merchandising strategies
- Four hi-fi stores and a hi-fi mail-order business
- Two mass-merchandising stores and two gas stations in Richmond
- Eight hardware/houseware licensed departments and two automotive departments

Of the lot, only the Custom hi-fi business and the TV/appliance licensed departments were solidly profitable. The Carousel stores and the original Wards TV stores made a little money. All of the other divisions Wards had acquired with its newly minted public stock lost money.

For the first five years of my employment I was part of Wards' growing problem. By helping to negotiate the post-1967 acquisitions, I facilitated the expansion program. I did not understand that fitting these pieces together into a coherent management structure was all but impossible. At the time, so much growth was exciting and looked sensible to me, to the board, and to the rest of the management team. In retrospect, it was a near disaster. We came within a hair's breadth of having to file for bankruptcy.

Train Wreck

How could this happen? Sam Wurtzel was a very smart man. He was also a visionary and an excellent salesman. Visionaries, however, often see the forest of the future while stumbling over the trees currently at their feet. To sell effectively, salesmen have to believe their pitch, and, too often, they drink their own whiskey without noticing its side effects.

Sam had deluded himself into thinking that he could manage this hodgepodge of small businesses with the same management techniques as used by General Motors. He admired Alfred Sloan, who had assembled, largely by acquisition, the biggest and most profitable business in the world. GM had six operating divisions (Chevrolet, Pontiac, Buick, Cadillac, Oldsmobile, and a locomotive division). Each had its own management and its own P&L. The divisions competed in the marketplace against other brands and against one another.

Sam believed that if GM could manage six distinct businesses, so could he. By giving his division presidents bottom-line responsibility for profits, he believed he could hold them accountable for the results, just as GM did. What he failed to realize was that GM's size and profitability enabled it to attract much higher-quality executives to manage a multibillion-dollar division than he could attract or afford for a division doing $5 or $10 million. And rather than six separate operations he had twelve.

To compound the problem, his acquisition targets were essentially friends and acquaintances in the industry, not the result of a systematic search. Before making an acquisition, we reviewed the projections of the company we hoped to acquire but did not dig deep or hire independent accountants to review the books. Believing that almost any acquisition could increase earnings if bought at the right price, we gave very little thought to the strategic and personality fits necessary to achieve success. In short order we paid the piper.

Habits of Mind

The events of Chapter Three demonstrate the following Habits of Mind that lead to success or failure.

Be Humble, Run Scared: *Continuously doubt your understanding of things. Business success contains the seeds of its own destruction. Worry about what the competition knows that you do not. Andy Grove, the legendary cofounder of Intel, got it largely right in his book* **Only the Paranoid Survive***.*

In our enthusiasm, we (including me, Sam, and the rest of the board) failed to appreciate the difficulty of acquiring an assortment of small, informally run businesses. Everything a business does is a reflection of the personal style of the owner. Fitting these disparate, idiosyncratic businesses into a larger corporation required a lot more time, patience, and capital than we imagined. We should have been far more skeptical, indeed scared, of our ability to manage this explosive growth.

Evidence Trumps Ideology: *In business, as in politics, decisions are too often based on unproven assumptions about what works and what doesn't. We all need operating assumptions about human nature, the economy, and the like, but when things do not work out as planned, we need to determine whether our assumptions were based on evidence or ideology. Evidence about the real world trumps ideological assumptions every time.*

Sam's belief that he could acquire mom-and-pop TV and appliance businesses around the country and roll them up was not necessarily a bad idea. But it was untested. Instead of buying one or two and waiting to see how that would work out, he went full steam ahead and nearly wrecked the company. These acquisitions also flew in the face of underlying business trends that were making locally dominant TV and appliance dealers obsolete in the face of new competition from discounters and mass merchants like Sears Roebuck and Montgomery Ward. This was a strategically inconvenient fact we ignored in the haste to grow.

Boldly Follow Through: *Big ideas require bold leadership and attract loyal followers. The effort comes to naught if the execution is tentative or not well disciplined.*

Sam's vision of starting a retail TV business in Richmond was a bold idea. His roll-up and diversification strategy was another big, bold idea, especially for its time. It attracted independent TV and appliance dealers who wanted to convert their locked-in equity into a stock that could be traded on the AMEX. But the execution was awful. Wards did too little due diligence and made too many disparate deals without pausing to see how the first one or two worked out.

Lessons Learned

The events of Chapter Three demonstrate the following Lessons Learned that lead to success or failure.

Making acquisitions on the basis of trust and friendship, without deep due diligence, is a recipe for disaster: When acquiring the Mart and Certified TV, Sam did not think it was necessary to "look under the covers" too deeply. He had known the owners for a decade or more and believed they ran a "good business." Besides, they were going to stay in place and continue to run the stores. In fact, they were not used to receiving direction from the outside. And now they had the liquidity that had been denied them as a private company. As a result, the relationships soured almost as fast as the businesses failed.

Making multiple acquisitions without a viable plan to manage them is an obvious mistake: Sam thought he understood what was required because he made the analogy to General Motors. But he failed to dig deeper and realize that the practices of a multibillion-dollar corporation were not directly applicable to a small enterprise like Wards.

ALMOST GONE
(1971-1977)

PART II

Chapter Four

RUDE AWAKENING

If you owe the bank $100 that's your problem.
If you owe the bank $100 million, that's the bank's problem.

—J. Paul Getty

When written in Chinese the word "crisis" is composed of two characters—
one represents danger and the other represents opportunity.

—John F. Kennedy ,address, 12 April 1959

Transitions are difficult to date. Did the American Revolution begin in 1773 with the Boston Tea Party? In 1775 with the Battle of Bunker Hill? Or in 1776 with the Declaration of Independence? Hard to tell.

Likewise, the Good Years for Wards Company (1949 to 1970) morphed into the Almost Gone Years (1971 to 1977), during which time Wards continued its madcap expansion, nearly went bankrupt, found its footing again, and resumed its forward progress.

The Real World in the '70s

Inflation had been growing since the late '60s as the government pursued the Vietnam War without raising taxes. When President Nixon implemented a wage-price freeze in 1971, he acknowledged what was already apparent: Stagflation was casting a gloomy shadow over American industry.[57] Compounding the problem, the 1973 Arab Oil Embargo caused the cost of oil to skyrocket, making transportation and consumer goods significantly more expensive.

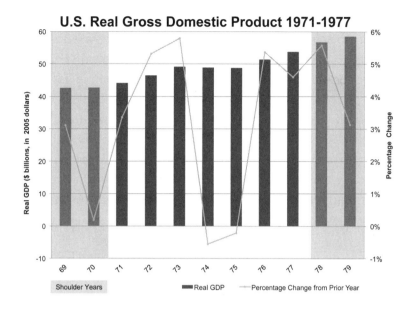

U.S. Real Gross Domestic Product 1971-1977

Shoulder Years | Real GDP | Percentage Change from Prior Year

Two years later, the 1973–75 recession ushered in what was at the time the longest economic downturn since the Great Depression.[58] The economy was nothing short of dismal. As inflation rose, ultimately hitting 12 percent in 1974, Americans experienced a significant decline in real income.[59] Consumers stopped buying. Businesses, struggling to survive lower demand and rising costs, laid off workers. Unemployment rose to 8.5 percent.[60] Double-digit interest rates effectively terminated capital spending and dramatically raised the cost of home mortgages, pushing the economy into an even steeper downward spiral.

Stagflation was changing American life in other important ways. People searching for job opportunities moved in large numbers to the South and Southwest, known as the "Sunbelt." Low-cost air-conditioning now made hot summers bearable and new highways and airports lifted small communities out of isolation. Additionally, a more favorable business environment, including right-to-work laws that limited union organizing, enticed many companies to move their factories, and sometimes their headquarters, to the South.[61] The West Coast also held an alluring promise of

U.S. Population by Age Group 1971-1977

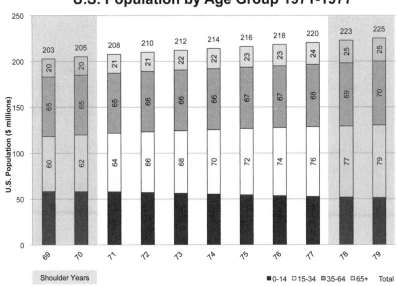

well-paid employment. Silicon Valley became emblematic of the West Coast lifestyle: high tech, high risk, and high growth. By 1975, it was home to one hundred thousand engineers.[62] By the 1980 census, more than half the still fast-growing U.S. population lived in the South and West.[63]

Another lifestyle change, also accelerated by the recession, was the rapid entry of women into the workforce. A decrease in the marriage rate and an increase in the divorce rate since the 1950s created a large pool of single women needing to support themselves. In addition, families that previously had been able to subsist on one income were now struggling to make ends meet, so more married women were also entering the workforce. As a result of these trends, by 1975 women made up 40 percent of the civilian workforce, up from 35 percent a decade earlier.[64] Their separate incomes entitled women to a bigger voice in deciding how the family spent its money, creating new marketing opportunities and challenges for American business.

The troubled economy also began to separate the strong retailers from the weak. The unprecedented rise of discounting in the

1960s and the slowdown in the economy in the '70s left most markets overstored. With lower sales and higher costs cutting into profit margins, retail executives sought new strategies to improve productivity. Point-of-sale registers that tracked both cash and inventory, the UPC (Universal Product Code), and related scanning equipment that captured data from a price tag were introduced during this period.

Economic instability also fostered other changes in the retail landscape. The convenience store was born. Some newer formats, like Kmart, Walmart, and Target thrived, while many industry pioneers, such as Korvette and Woolco, disappeared.[65] At the same time, several new formats emerged as entrepreneurs tried to fill the void left by fallen giants. Catalog showrooms, led by Best Products and Service Merchandise, provided a low-price alternative to discount stores. By the 1973, the stock market valued the publically owned catalog showrooms at $1 billion. Fifteen years later they were all but gone.[66]

Other formats that emerged survive to this day, including the off-price apparel chains Marshall's and T.J.Maxx. Many big-box category killers, such as Toys "R" Us and Levitz Furniture, emerged in virtually every category of goods. Price Club, an innovative warehouse format requiring paid membership, opened in one of Howard Hughes's recycled airplane hangars in 1976 and achieved unheard-of sales. It expanded and was quickly copied by Sam's Club and BJ's. When Price Club faltered, Costco scooped it up. As a result of these innovations, the retailing landscape was becoming extremely diverse and highly competitive.[67]

Consumer Electronics and Appliances

The grimmer the recession became, the more that Americans wanted to escape into the world on their televisions—and in color. Despite hard times, more than 42 million color sets were sold between 1973 and 1977.[68] Household penetration rates soared from 36 percent in 1970, to 68 percent in 1975, to 83

Consumer Electronics Factory Sales 1971-1977

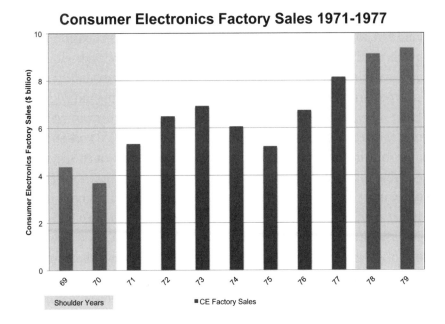

percent by 1980.[69]

The first personal computer was introduced in 1975. Initially offered for $400 through electronics hobbyist magazines as a do-it-yourself kit for amateur programmers, it was an instant success, selling thousands in the first month. By 1979, a Silicon Valley–based firm named Apple had devised a disk drive system as well as graphics and spreadsheet programs that, for the first time, would make the personal computer useful to nonprogrammers. Although they were clumsy by today's standards, they paved the road for the consumer computer revolution.[70]

Despite a dramatic decline in housing starts and home sales, the appliance industry avoided a major decline. Freezers and microwave ovens, which had not yet gained significant market penetration, sold well as families resolved to save money by freezing and reheating leftover food.[71]

Despite innovative new retail formats and exciting new products, however, the early '70s were a tough time for electronics and appliance manufacturers and equally tough for retailers.

Creating a Strategic Plan

When I became CEO of Wards in April of 1972, Rick Deane, with the support of the rest of the board, told me that my first task was to develop a detailed five-year plan. "I do not want something on the back of an envelope," he said. "Make a thorough study of the opportunities," he directed, and return to the board in six months "with firm recommendations based on solid research."[72]

At the same time, Hyman Meyers was advocating for the company to radically narrow its areas of concentration. He felt that Wards had too many divisions and sold too many types of merchandise in too many types of stores. He believed that in order for the company to build a successful big business, management would have to concentrate on just one business model and one line of merchandise.

To reinforce his point, he told a story that has stuck with me. His company, Heilig- Meyers, had an opportunity to purchase three furniture stores in Myrtle Beach, South Carolina, at a cost that would be recouped from the cash they generated in just three years. They were perfect additions to his fifty- or sixty-store chain in all respects but one: Because Myrtle Beach was a resort community, 10 to 15 percent of the merchandise sold in these stores was unpainted furniture, and Heilig-Meyers did not carry unpainted furniture anywhere else. For that reason, Hyman decided it would be too big a distraction from the core business. For him, simplicity and uniformity were more important than even this attractive acquisition. In order not to complicate his business, he passed up a sweetheart deal.

Of all the good advice I received from the board over the years, creating a long-range plan and simplifying the business were clearly the best. They forced me to think systematically about the purpose and nature of strategic planning, about the outside world, about retail trends, and about Wards' strengths and weaknesses.

My premises for strategic planning were simple, almost self-evident:

- The world is constantly evolving. To be relevant and effective, strategic decisions need to be made with an understanding of the environment in which the company operates.
- For retailers, that environment includes demographics and consumer trends, the economy, available technology, competition, and the economics of the business model.
- Once made, strategic decisions must be monitored and regularly reviewed so that the decision maker holds himself accountable for his decisions and for the process. This enables him to learn from the inevitable mistakes.
- As the external world changes, strategies will need to be revised. Businesses that lose touch with changing external realities are doomed to fail.

Wards' first plan focused on operational issues and opportunities. It projected sales and earnings for the next five years, but not balance sheets or cash flows. We soon modified our planning to add these tools in order to better project inventories and achieve higher rates of return on capital. We also quickly moved to writing a three-year plan rather than a five-year plan. Our crystal ball was too cloudy to see more than three years out.

We also went to planning *every other year*. One year did not provide enough distance. By skipping a year we would have enough perspective to take a step back and reflect on why certain outcomes were different from what we had projected. In addition, the CEO needed to be intimately involved and personally responsible for the planning process. Doing this thoughtfully is too time-consuming on an annual basis. Also, updating a multiyear plan every year with next year's budget and adding a new year's budget at the end, as many companies do, can too easily become a mechanical, rather than a thoughtful, exercise.

We wanted to involve the vice presidents and the heads of each division in the process, not only so that we could benefit from their input but also to increase the likelihood of their embracing the plan once it was adopted. The board would have ultimate approval, but only after searching questions and extended discussion during which adjustments were made, generally over the course of a two-day retreat.

The 1973 Plan was brutally honest and self-critical:

> Our greatest single weakness has been our inability to develop and stick to sound operating and accounting procedures. The continual failure of our inventory and accounting systems to record accurately what goods we have on hand and what our earnings are has created serious problems in controlling our business internally and creating credibility in the investment and lending communities.[73]

Relevant Trends

The plan then asked, "What is the anticipated environment in which the company will operate five and ten years from now?" It highlighted three trends that seemed relevant.

Recruiting store management

> Stores are open nights and weekends. It is challenging to recruit and retain individuals willing to devote the time and effort necessary to manage a small retail store.

Growth of the suburbs

> Middle America has moved from the farms to the cities and from the cities to the suburbs. "Today most middle-class Americans are afraid to go downtown, especially at night. Today's downtowns are the enclosed regional malls. They offer selection and entertainment. With the construction of circumferential highways around and through most of our cities, they also offer convenience, parking space and relative safety."[74]

Consumerism

> "Like it or not, Ralph Nader is here to stay. Truth in lending, Truth in Advertising and ultimately Truth in Merchandising will all affect the retail environment of the future....The consumer of the future will increasingly insist on fair and honest values and high quality after the sale service." [75]

The plan next examined long-term developments in retailing and focused in some detail on several emerging retail formats that sold our type of merchandise:

1. The catalog stores, such as Best Products
2. Home improvement centers, such as Lowe's
3. Specialty retailers, such as Lafayette and RadioShack
4. Non-store selling—primarily by mail or phone
5. Warehouse showrooms, such as Levitz and Kennedy & Cohen

After reviewing the options, the plan determined that "the furniture warehouse showroom is the revolutionary retailing concept that has the greatest applicability to our business." [76]

Basic Principles

The plan described the basic principles of the warehouse showroom as:

Selection

> "Kennedy & Cohen's newest showrooms run 18,000 sq. ft....four times the size of our largest Wards TV store. [They offer]...far greater [selection] than the average TV and appliance retailer." [77]

Carry home convenience

> "Up to 60 percent of the sales of these warehouse showrooms are carried home the day of the sale. [M]any people seem to want it "now" and are willing to tie it on

the roof, stuff it in the trunk, or rent a trailer to get it home today." [78]

Location convenience

"Levitz and its followers have followed the same real estate strategy as the closed malls," generally locating in the suburbs, at or near the intersection of an interstate highway and a major artery. [79]

Selling the sizzle

"To a large extent, the success of warehouse showrooms is dependent upon selling the customer on the concept of buying from a warehouse. Levitz and its followers are generally not cheaper than their competition (especially if the extra charges for delivery, etc., are added to the take-with price) but they have convinced the public that they buy in bulk, have selection, excellent sales assistance and after the sale, service and satisfaction." [80]

The plan concluded: "[W]e believe the warehouse showroom will attract the big middle slice of the market."[81]

Strengths and Weaknesses

Having settled on the warehouse showroom format as the best option going forward, the plan then moved on to analyze the company's strengths and weaknesses.

"Our greatest strength has no doubt been the creation of an able, dedicated, hardworking, loyal management team, from the store level up. Virtually all of our key operational people grew up in the business."[82]

Other strengths included merchandising:

"There is probably no more talented team of major appliance and audio buyers in the country."[83]

Weaknesses were spelled out:

> "One of our basic weaknesses in the past five years has been our unwillingness or inability frankly to catalog our strengths and weaknesses, and to develop a plan to capitalize on the strengths and correct the weaknesses."[84] Also "our inability to develop and stick to sound operating and accounting procedures…inadequate attention to distribution expense and…stretched financial resources."[85]

Out of all this came the following conclusions:

> For the foreseeable future, expansion would have to be financed by closing older stores to open new ones and by the annual depreciation reserve. Within that constraint, we should:
>
> • Expand the audio business by opening more Dixie Hi-Fi stores.
>
> • Open a warehouse showroom in Richmond under the name Loading Dock and, if it works, open more as we can afford them.
>
> • Exit all the licensed departments except Zodys. Stay in the Zodys stores so long as they are profitable. Be prepared to open warehouse showrooms in LA when financially feasible.
>
> • Close two Wards stores in Richmond and get out of the furniture business at the Mart. Otherwise, stand pat in Toledo and in Indianapolis to see if they could grow profitably.
>
> • Sell the Carousel stores and exit the hardware/houseware and automotive businesses.

While not as radical as Hyman Meyer's recommendation to consolidate to one business, this was a dramatic simplification.

Peter Drucker, the highly respected management consultant and author of *Management by Objectives*, observes that too often "managements 'navel gaze' and look for problems or solutions only within their own organization."[86] A viable strategic plan needs to focus first on the external world to determine **what** to do before focusing inward on **how** to do it. Our plan surveyed the economy, social changes, and retailing trends in order to put the decisions to be made in a broader context.

- It was totally honest and self-critical.
- It reviewed our various operations in detail, looking at the hard numbers and assessing the risk/reward ratio of changing or not changing each retail format in question.
- It projected sales, earnings, and the investment required to be sure these financial projections were actually feasible.
- It created a framework for holding ourselves accountable for the forecasts we made and for our fidelity to the plan.
- Fortunately, the plan was completed before the economic tsunami hit.

Wards Hits the Fan

The first four years of the 1970s had been difficult for Wards. Overexpansion, compounded by high unemployment and inflation, adversely affected earnings. Although sales increased from $48 to $68 million, Wards was able to eke out only minimal profits ranging from $265,000 to $550,000—less than 1 percent on sales and barely above breakeven.

I became CEO in early 1972, just as the recession arrived. The only "silver lining" was that it is possible to learn more from adversity than from success. This was my postgraduate education.

As we continued to focus on digesting the many acquisitions we had recently made and closing especially unpromising stores, our biggest challenge was cash. While most of the acquisitions were largely for stock, they all required cash investments. In some cases we needed to build inventory; in others our plan to liquidate unwanted inventory proved stubbornly slow. Some stores required remodeling and others needed to upgrade their data processing equipment. To conserve cash we eliminated unproductive operations and concentrated on inventory control, expense reduction, and management realignment.

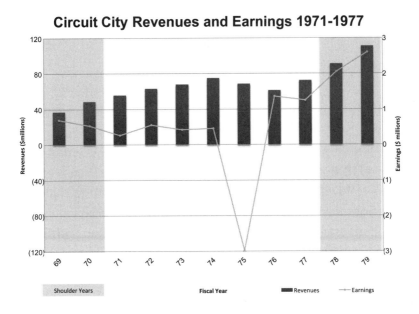

Circuit City Revenues and Earnings 1971-1977

The 1973 Plan called for shedding the unprofitable operations previously acquired, including most of our licensed departments, while simultaneously adding inexpensive-to-open and quickly profitable Dixie Hi-Fi stores. It also, proposed that we commence construction of a long-planned distribution center plus a showroom and corporate offices in Richmond. Despite our profit struggles and unheard-of interest rates, we were able to negotiate a $3 million line of credit that allowed us to move forward with this ambitious plan. In fact, we were assured by our investment banker that interest rates were declining and that, in a quarter or two, we could permanently finance the project by issuing industrial revenue bonds.

The crisis came to a head in 1975. Following a disastrous Christmas selling season Wards' largest landlord, National Bellas Hess, filed for bankruptcy, with all the rest of our discount department store landlords following in the next nine months.

When the prime interest rate ran up in the spring of 1974 to an unaffordable11.5 percent,[87] we decided to delay issuing the bonds that were to permanently finance our new warehouse and offices. And when Zodys, where we planned to remain, filed for

reorganization that November, any hope of an industrial bond un-
derwriting vanished. Although Wards was able to pay its bills,
it was in default of several financial covenants in its bank loan
agreement. We had violated the cardinal rule of corporate finance:
One should not finance long-term assets with short-term borrowings—even for a few months.

Although we consulted bankruptcy counsel, we were determined to avoid Chapter 11 if at all possible. Our first task was to
persuade the banks to hold their fire while we restructured. We
immediately consulted Morris Goldstein, an experienced financial consultant who had recently joined our board. My very able
chief financial officer (CFO), Ed Villanueva, and I flew to New
York for an emergency meeting with Morris, who advised us to
take the initiative and advise the banks of our default before they
discovered it for themselves. He also counseled us to develop a restructuring plan to get back into compliance and devise a monthly
reporting plan to keep the banks fully informed of our progress
and at bay. Fortunately, the five-year plan we had recently completed provided us with a road map to show the banks how we
could land on our feet.

By being up-front about our problems, we gained credibility and some time to work out our restructuring. Our two lead

Artist rendering of The Loading Dock and distribution center – circa 1974

banks, both in Richmond, insisted that we report sales, payables, and cash balances on a weekly, rather than a monthly, basis. Otherwise, they supported our restructuring plan. They each had $3 million to $5 million (equivalent to $21 million today) at stake and wanted to keep us alive so long as there was hope of repayment.

The out-of-town banks were another story. Wards had bank accounts in every city where we did business into which we deposited the cash we received on a daily basis. One of the ways Wards financed itself was to use these short-term deposits to leverage relatively minor lines of credit from each of the depository banks. Sam thought it was smart to spread the risk and not be beholden to just a few banks for credit.

As it turned out, those banks, where Wards had credit lines of $100,000 to $500,000, were not nearly as flexible as the local banks whose investments in our future were much larger. Ironically, the least flexible was Morgan Guaranty, where Sam had opened an account because it made him feel like a real American capitalist to have lunch in the private, walnut-paneled dining room at the venerable bank J.P. Morgan had founded. The lesson I took away was that if you are in default and owe a bank a little money, they own you. But if you owe them a lot, you at least have some leverage. See J.P. Getty quote at the beginning of this chapter.

Do It Yourself Reorganization

To implement our now-accelerated Five Year Plan we needed, first and foremost, to purge our unprofitable acquisitions. Between November 1974 and May 1975:

- We closed twenty-seven TV and appliance licensed departments in discount department stores around the country. We decided to remain in our twenty-nine Zodys departments, at least temporarily, because their profit contribution was too big to close them immediately.
- We sold the two Carousel Department Stores in Richmond for a

profit of more than $500,000 and freed up some working capital.

• We also dramatically reduced overhead by eliminating two vice presidents, dozens of middle managers, and hundreds of store level personnel.

At the same time:

• We also made significant personnel shifts. I asked Bill Rivas to move to Los Angles and direct the growing West Coast business from there. Dan Rexinger was put in charge of the audio business and the East Coast TV and appliance stores. Walt Bruckart was moved to LA to merchandise the Zodys division and build a buying office there.

• Despite the strains and the layoffs created by the divestitures, morale remained high. It had been a close call and our stock price had dropped precipitously, but we were alive and proud that we had not been forced to declare bankruptcy.

Habits of Mind

The events of Chapter Four demonstrate the following Habits of Mind that lead to success or failure.

Confront the Brutal Facts: *The worst person you can fool is yourself. Ignoring or denying reality does not help it go away. Once you understand the issues, be bold enough to take decisive action.*

The first strategic plan pulled no punches. It identified the company's long-standing internal weaknesses, even at the risk of embarrassing my father and the accounting staff. In 1974, when Wards was facing bankruptcy we took the initiative to inform our banks before they discovered we were in default under our loan agreements.

Maintain a Current Road Map: *If you don't know where you are going, any road will take you there. Regular strategic planning based on how the company relates to its external environment, including the economy, compe-*

tition, and the customer, is essential to success.

Having a strategic plan in place made it far easier to convince our lead banks that we could make the adjustments that would allow us to weather the storm, and it was a good guide for management at all levels, who would be involved in implementing our turnaround strategies.

Boldly Follow Through: *Big ideas require bold leadership and attract loyal followers. The effort comes to naught if the execution is tentative or not well disciplined.*

With the strategic plan in hand, we began to implement a radical restructuring that included closing stores, selling divisions, reducing staff, and simultaneously opening nine new hi-fi stores and a major new warehouse and corporate office complex, including a warehouse showroom—which would be our prototype for the future.

Lessons Learned

The events of Chapter Four demonstrate the following Lessons Learned.

Know When to Hold and When to Fold: We needed to decide where the future of the company lay. Given the fragility of being a licensee, where the success or failure of the store was not in our control, exiting as many licensed departments as possible made strategic sense. The Mart and many of the freestanding chains we had acquired were no longer viable for the same reasons that we had decided to get out of mom-and-pop stores and into warehouse showrooms.

Business strategies have a limited shelf life. When external conditions change, the business needs to change. It is better to take the initiative and fold your cards rather than be the victim of circumstance.

Strategic Planning Is Vital: The most critical lesson we took away from this period was the importance of strategic planning on an ongoing basis. Strategic planning means that the CEO must take a careful, thoughtful look at the social, economic, and competitive contexts in which the business operates to help determine **what** to do. The CEO also needs to be brutally honest about his organization's strengths, weaknesses, and required resources, in order to determine **how** to do it.

The plan needs to be grounded in solid projections for the P&L, the balance sheet, and cash flow over the period it covers. Having initially drawn up a five-year plan, we determined that, for the future, three years was about as far as one could see into the future with any hope of accuracy. We also decided that strategic planning every year (as compared to annual budgeting) would tend to become mechanical and shallow. Doing it every other year would give us some distance and perspective on what had been accomplished and what had changed in the external environment.

Mind Your Bankers: Another painful lesson was the importance of maintaining good bank relationships. In times of adversity there is more security in being an important debtor to a handful of banks who have, relatively speaking, a lot to lose, than in being a minor borrower at many banks, some of which might prefer to take the loss and move on. In all cases, it is important to keep your banks informed of upcoming trouble and to be as up-front as possible while making it clear that you intend to do whatever is necessary to repay the loan.

Chapter Five

BUILDING THE TEAM

*The best executive is the one who has sense enough to pick good men
to do what he wants done, and self-restraint enough to keep from meddling
with them while they do it.*

— Theodore Roosevelt

Besides being difficult to date, transitions are also hard to execute. Taking over from my father as CEO was no exception.

The process began at a board meeting in August 1967, a little less than a year after I had arrived at Wards. Sam announced Hecht had decided to retire in March 1968, at the end of the current fiscal year, and that he (Hecht) was going to sell 75 percent of his stock in a secondary offering. Sam also announced that he (Sam) planned to retire in the spring of 1972 when he turned sixty-five.

Some observers in the business had the feeling that Hecht was being "pushed aside" while others felt that his job performance had slipped. Although things appeared amicable on the surface, an underlying tension had developed between the two longtime friends over business strategy. Sam was still driven to build a big business while Hecht, who was ten years older, had always been more risk-averse and content simply to make a good living. Sam wanted to create a monument. My arrival gave new impetus to his expansion ambitions, and although he never spoke about what happened between them, even to me, it seems likely that his acquisition determination precipitated Hecht's decision to retire.[88]

Ten months after Hecht left the company, Marty Ross, longtime treasurer and CFO, also resigned. A short newspaper article in the Richmond paper stated that Ross had quit "because he had differences of opinion as to management policies."[89] As the business grew, others had assumed some of his earlier responsibilities for planning and support operations and he resented being confined to financial matters. In addition to sharing Hecht's more conservative approach to expansion, he also may have expected that he would run the business after Sam and Hecht retired, and with my coming on board that seemed less likely.

Who Gets on the Bus

With the founding generation gone or about to retire, Sam and I needed to reassign some duties and bring in new senior management. Fortunately, there was ample talent available. Bill Rivas, Dan Rexinger, Ed Villanueva, and Walt Bruckart, each of whom had at least five years with the company, became the "four horsemen" who would help me take the company from $50 million in sales to $1 billion.

Bill Rivas was a native of Vermont and had served in the Air Force as an airplane mechanic during the Korean War. He was discharged in Florida in 1961, and he and his wife were making their way back to Vermont by bus when they ran out of money in Richmond. After a short stint working at Best Products, another Richmond retailer on the way up, Bill applied for a job as a salesman at Wards.

Rivas was not a college graduate, but what he lacked in formal education he more than made up for in common sense and emotional intelligence. Bill's greatest strength was his love and understanding of people. He had the ability to size people up, determine their hot buttons, and play to their strengths. He focused on morale and knew how to get the best out of subordinates. He described managers or salesmen as having their "dauber up" or down. If it was down he worked hard to figure out a way to get it back up and put a smile on their face.

Within six months of his coming on board, Sam sent him to Norfolk as assistant manager of Wards' new licensed department at National Bellas Hess. Eighteen months later he was promoted to manager. In 1965, Rivas returned to the home office to assist Hecht as a merchandise manager. In quick succession he became general manager of the Wards TV stores in Richmond and then manager of seven licensed departments. In 1968 he was promoted to vice president and was soon elected to the board and its executive committee.

After graduating college, Dan Rexinger, a native of Buffalo, New York, joined an executive training program at a local department store. Then, realizing that he could earn more money by selling, he quit the training program to become an appliance salesman. Hecht, who was in Buffalo recruiting store personnel in connection with a new licensed department, got Rexinger's name from several vendors. At Hecht's invitation, Rexinger went to Richmond to meet Sam and take a battery of psychological tests that Wards was then using to get a deeper understanding of an applicant's management potential. He was hired in 1962 to be the assistant manager of Wards' new licensed department in Buffalo. Five months later he was transferred to Norfolk and soon after that to Mobile.

In 1966, Sam called him and asked, "Rexy, how would you like to come to Richmond and take a merchandising job?" Rexinger was delighted with the offer but reluctant to move because he and his wife were waiting to adopt a child in Alabama. When Sam put on his social worker cap and explained that he knew people in Virginia who could help them retain their place in the adoption line in Alabama even if they moved, the Rexingers agreed to come. Before long Rexinger was a general manager for merchandising and advertising, and in 1969 he was made a vice president of Wards and a member of the executive committee.

Rexinger was a cooler character than Bill. He sometimes affected a Humphrey Bogart wise-guy attitude but beneath his "hard shell" was truly a warm and caring person. He, too, attracted great loyalty among his subordinates and, equally important, was a great team player. He and Rivas had traded responsibilities

Bill Rivas – circa 1970

Ed Villanueva – circa 1970

Dan Rexinger – circa 1970

Walt Bruckart – circa 1980

within the organization so often that they could finish each other's thoughts. While they sometimes disagreed, they settled any disagreements privately and never jockeyed for position. Their goal was for the company to win, believing that with company success their contributions would be recognized. They encouraged cooperation rather than competition throughout the company. Their approach of "no silos, no egos" defined the company culture for many years.

Ed Villanueva joined Wards in late 1967 after responding to an ad for an assistant controller that appeared in the *New York Times.* A graduate of Manhattan College and a CPA, he was, at that time, working for S.D. Leidesdorf, a large New York accounting firm, and had already decided that he wanted to make a change. He had honeymooned in Virginia, and he and his wife had liked the idea of living in Richmond, so he answered the ad and was invited to interview. He and Sam Wurtzel hit it off.

Villanueva very quickly showed his abilities as a financial forecaster and accounting manager and, in the summer of 1968, he became director of budgeting. One of the company's problems had been an inability to maintain accurate inventories or to produce financials that were not subject to material correction. Ed's demonstrated ability in those crucial areas, in addition to his material improvements to the budgeting process, got him promoted to Corporate Controller, the top accounting position. By 1971 he was named Treasurer and Chief Financial Officer.

A quiet, reflective, thoughtful person with a razor-sharp financial mind, Ed had the ability to see around corners and anticipate the financial issues we would be facing six months or more down the road. I was more the optimist and risk-taker, Ed the more conservative realist. We were a good balance for each other, and for fifteen years I never made a serious decision without his advice and support.

Walt Bruckart grew up in a small town in southwestern Pennsylvania, where his family ran a grocery store. As a youth Walt did every grocery store job there was, from sweeping the floor to ordering the merchandise. After a year of college, he was drafted into the army. Upon discharge he drifted from job to job for several years before joining the leading local department store, where he was assigned to the TV and appliance department. After a few years he was running the department so successfully that he sensed it was becoming too large a part of the store's business, and that this was making the owner uncomfortable. As a result, he said, "I saw the writing on the wall," and began looking around for a new opportunity.[90]

A supplier told him he should apply to Wards because "they are as crazy as you and just as intense." In 1968, after the usual series of interviews in Richmond, he was hired and assigned to a group of five licensed departments in the Carousel stores in Akron and Canton, Ohio. Fifteen months later Wards took over fourteen Zodys departments in California and Walt was asked to move to Los Angeles to be the local buyer.

Walt is one of the smartest people I ever worked with. He was shy, quiet, and a great listener. He marched to his own drummer and shared little about his life outside of work. But he worked like a Trojan. On his desk was a sign: "Success in life is 10% inspiration and 90% perspiration." He kept in his head hundreds of brands and models, their wholesale cost and retail price, and figured out how the mix of merchandise could work together to create a "program" that made sense to the consumer and profits for the company.

Who Gets off the Bus

At the same time that we were building the team, we also needed to eliminate two longtime executives who did not fit the new organization. Both had been raised in the old "bait and switch" school. One ran the freestanding Wards TV stores and the various licensed departments in Richmond and the Tidewater region of Virginia. The other was the vice president for merchandising.

Both resisted the new consumerism policies and, more important, neither could be trusted to give a straight answer. One of my gurus in those days was Peter Drucker, who stressed in his various writings that integrity in an organization is essential. One thing that always stuck in my mind was his test of integrity: Ask yourself, "If I had a son or daughter, would I be willing to have him or her be mentored by this person?"[91] These two VPs flunked that test.

Once the decision was made to remove the VP of merchandising, there was no question that we would bring Walt Bruckart to Richmond to fill that job. It was one of the best decisions Wards ever made. Walt went on to become the premier TV and appliance merchant in the country, universally respected by vendors and competitors alike. He also had that indefinable merchant prince's instinct for knowing what customers would want. In a significant show of confidence, manufacturers would invite him to view a drawing or a mock-up of a planned new product and solicit his opinion as to its strengths and weaknesses.

He was tough as nails as a negotiator but worked hard to figure out what was important to each of our suppliers and how their interests could be made to fit with Wards' objectives. He never forgot a favor or reneged on a commitment. As a result he got excellent pricing, early information on future products, and the first opportunity to purchase high-demand items. Under his leadership, merchandising became one of Wards' cardinal strengths and key competitive advantages.

Creative Hires

Building on Sam's belief that employees will rise to a challenge, I began hiring obviously bright and hardworking people for middle-management positions that roughly matched their interests despite their lack of retailing experience. They included a college history professor who became head of strategic planning;

a staff member of the Virginia Government Reorganization (Little Hoover) Commission who became the chief merchandising allocator, responsible for inventory turns; and an out-of-work lawyer who ran the real estate department, in charge of scouting and acquiring locations for new stores.

In addition, and also based on the belief that ability trumps experience, we began to move people from one job to another to find the best fit. If someone was capable and honest, but was not working out in a particular job, their supervisor or a vice president would try to determine where in the organization that person might be more effective. Sometimes I would sit with the individual and ask, "If you could have any job in the company, what would you most like to do?" Generally the answer led to a discussion and together we found a "home" where the employee could be both productive and successful. We began to call it "putting square pegs in square holes and round pegs in round holes."

Sam was right. Hiring bright, hardworking people is an important way to build a team, and often more cost-effective than bringing on someone who had a lot of relevant experience but less growth potential. In general, finding the right job for the right person was mutually beneficial. Occasionally, however, it became clear that in order to be fulfilled or effective, a particular employee would have to move on.

Develop a Learning Culture

Sam believed in a learning culture. He paid for employees to go to school. He taught at industry seminars and was an avid and keen observer of what was happening in the marketplace. But he did not systematically study how his competitors operated. This changed under my watch.

Although the acquisition of the Mart had been a financial disaster, its owner, Joe Rothbard, made a significant strategic contribution by persuading Wards to join National Appliance and Television Merchandisers (NATM), a buying cooperative he headed. The organization had its origins in the late 1940s when an informal group of Midwestern appliance retailers, many of them World War II veterans, began to exchange product pricing information and transship among themselves. They were known in the trade as "The Forty Thieves." I dubbed Rothbard "Ali Baba."

Sam and Hecht had, of course, been aware of NATM and had been asked to join, but they found the group too undisciplined for their taste. After we acquired the Mart, Rothbard urged me to reconsider. At first, Rivas, Rexinger, and Bruckart were opposed. They all thought we had more to teach than to learn. But the more we debated the pros and cons, the more convinced I became that we had little to lose and possibly much to gain. So in 1974, shortly after being named CEO, I decided, with the unenthusiastic consent of Sam and the other key executives, to join NATM.

At that time, members of the organization had combined purchases of about $100 million. The group had an office in New York run by a capable executive director, Saul Gold, a former buyer for Allied Stores, and, more important, a buying committee, composed of the top merchants among the NATM members who met with manufacturers, primarily at trade shows, to negotiate prices on specific, commonly purchased brands and models.

By the mid-1980s NATM's fifteen members were responsible for collective purchases in excess of half a billion dollars annually and had aggregate sales of $1.5 billion, accounting for 9.2 percent of all US brand-name television sales and 8 percent of all US branded audio sales.[92] Wards alone accounted for 2 percent in each category. Because as a group NATM was able to commit to large purchases, it received exceptionally low prices and access to desirable goods in short supply. NATM was also able to negotiate with manufacturers to build models called "derivatives" that were just slightly different and available only to its members. This was important to both the manufacturer and the seller because the derivative models had unique model numbers and could, therefore, not be compared head-to-head with a similar model other dealers carried. Bruckart, the one-time skeptic, soon became a leader on the buying committee, where he made a significant contribution but also learned a lot.

Almost as important as preferred pricing, NATM provided Wards an excellent opportunity to learn how other successful retailers of appliances and electronics ran the nonmerchandising aspects of their businesses. Since its members were initially in non-competing markets, we could have long and frank discussions about credit, service, sales training, compensation, advertising, site-selection, inventory controls, data processing, and so on.

Over time, as members expanded into one another's territory, the group began to fall apart. While it lasted, however, it provided an enormous boost to our knowledge and profitability.

Managing Execution

The success of a retail store chain depends on its ability to have store personnel execute company policies every day, in every transaction in every store. Because we were selling products that were readily available at many other outlets, it was vital that we consistently provide a positive customer experience. As far as the customers were concerned, the store personnel they dealt with *was* the company, which meant that every employee, no matter how low on the ladder, had to represent the company's values. As the company grew, this goal became more and more challenging to achieve.

Sam and Hecht had gone a long way toward developing management training as well as merchandising, budgeting, and financial control systems to address this challenge. Rivas and Rexinger devised another method called "The Swing." Every fall, top store management executives would conduct a rapid-fire, store-by-store inspection to ensure that every location in the company was ready for Christmas.

Jim Gillum, Dan Rexinger, and Bill Rivas would each charter a private plane and, for a week or two, swing through three or four stores a day. Armed with a checklist, they and their team, which included each store's district manager, would inspect the smallest details regarding merchandising, pricing, cleanliness, signage, and, most important, the sales people's knowledge of the selling strategy for key categories of goods. As needed, they dealt with personnel issues. For store managers, "The Swing" was a source of great pride (if they were ready) or great fear (if they were not). Many "career decisions" were made during this process. The Swing was a superb teaching opportunity and a key contributor to the company's superior execution year after year.

Another technique for developing strong managers was to train them to think like senior executives. Every January, following the all-important Christmas selling season, each store manager was asked to provide his district manager with monthly sales and gross margins estimates for the next fiscal year and to project payroll and any other key variable expenses that he or she could control. Every division prepared month-by-month, line-by-line, merchandise-category-by-merchandise-category budgets for each store and, at all-day meetings, often over several days, they presented their budgets to me and the other members of the executive committee. We then went through them with a fine-tooth comb, challenged any expense that seemed out of line, and reviewed every sales assumption. Typically the store managers' sales forecasts were too optimistic and the expenses not tight enough, but by the end of several days, discussion of numbers inevitably led to discussions of personnel, which led to discussions of strategy. The division personnel attending the budget session felt that this was a team effort and got a sense of how top management looked at various strategic and tactical issues. Once the budget was approved, the store operations team had the authority and the responsibility to "make it happen." The budget, adjusted at six-month intervals, was the principal vehicle for measuring and enforcing accountability as well as rewarding performance.

Compensation policy is a critical element in building a business. It is the most tangible way to signal to employees at every level what the financial goals of the organization are and what behavior will both advance the company's objective and benefit them personally. Constant adjustments are needed to keep incentives aligned with a company's changing objectives.

Excessive emphasis on confidentiality can become an obstacle to this overarching objective. In my experience, even if you attempt to keep compensation information confidential there are no secrets. The SEC requires that the earnings of the top five employees of a public company be shown to the world. Pay and bonus information at lower levels inevitably gets out, especially if you have a participatory budgeting philosophy. [93] It is best to be discreet, but open enough on a "need to know" basis to enable supervisors and managers to participate, as they should, in compensation decisions.

From the beginning Sam had made a point of paying at or above the market. As the company grew in size and geography he did surveys to determine competitive wages for lower level jobs in the various markets. Executive pay was more subjective, but as we grew, we recruited both directly and through headhunters and paid as needed to be competitive. Annual reviews at budget time were the opportunity to correct inequities and make wage and salary adjustments.

In building a team, there are two principal considerations for setting executive compensation: internal and external equity. External equity is both more obvious and more objective. There is a market price for vice presidents of finance, technology, and store operations, just as there is for secretaries and truck drivers. Finding the market price and paying at or above it takes some work, but is not rocket science.

Internal equity is a lot trickier. The first question is: What is the right differential between the CEO and his or her immediate reports? You often see in proxy statements that the CEO is making twice as much or more than the person directly below. That is the wrong way to build a team because it says, in effect, that the CEO is twice as important as the second in command. At Wards,

I kept my salary no more than 20 percent higher than the salary of my top associate. My direct reports appreciated that, and it set a pattern for compensating their reports.

The second question in internal equity is the degree of pay differences among senior managers. Two senior vice presidents, each earning hundreds of thousands of dollars in base compensation, can get their noses out of joint if the differential between them changes by even a few dollars. "How come Joe got a $10,000 dollar raise and I only got $7,500? What are you trying to tell me? Or him?" I have served on the boards of companies where all the senior managers were paid the same to maximize internal equity, but that creates the very real possibility that those with a higher market value could easily be attracted away. In my experience the best way to deal with these issues is for the CEO to put together proposed pay raises for the entire executive team, including him or herself, show it to the team, generally one-on-one, and explain the reasoning behind the changes.

Transparency and honesty go a long way toward soothing hurt feelings. If everyone understands that what they may view as anomalies are for the good of the team as a whole, they can generally accept them.

This brings me to my last point: bonuses. The best way to align the values of the company with the behavior of employees is an active and material bonus system. Other than hiring and promotions, designing, redesigning, and adjusting incentive systems probably took up more of my time than any other personnel issue.

For managers and other salaried personnel, annual bonuses were based on a percentage of base salary. While the percentages varied by level of management, they too reflected relatively modest differentials between my subordinates and me. When it came to equity compensation (stock options), I felt it appropriate for me, as the one who made the ultimate strategic calls, to take a bigger differential. This was easily accepted since the value of my options was dependent on the company's performing well. In every case except that of top management, where bonuses were based solely on meeting corporate profitability objectives, bonuses had two components: 80 percent based on the profits of the company or the division to which the executive was assigned, and 20 percent on the achievement of individual goals set by the executive and his supervisor. This split was also designed to affect behavior and prevent someone from getting a "free ride" based on the results that others created.

Some employees, however, were not on straight salary. Salesmen were on commission, and their bonuses were based on total sales, sales of higher-margin products, and sales of extended service policies. Repair technicians were paid based on jobs completed but lost their compensation for a repair if the product was returned within thirty days. Again, the idea was to influence behavior and balance productivity with quality work. For hourly workers there was no formal bonus system, but if, and only if, the company had a good year, everyone got a week's pay as a Christmas bonus.

Store managers had the most complex set of incentives, with both monthly and annual bonuses. Monthly bonuses accounted for roughly a third of the manager's total compensation, more than enough to get attention. Sales and margin targets for bonus purposes were reset monthly to keep them realistic, based on the trend of the past few months. Our goal was to keep the rabbit close enough to the hound that the hound would win two out of three months. Annual bonuses focused on longer-term objectives such as merchandise shrinkage and employee turnover.

In addition to sales and margins, however, we often had several other targets, depending on the issue of the month. Sometimes you felt like you were making soup: a pinch of this and a dash of that to get the emphasis among a store manager's multiple tasks appropriately focused. Managers in general were highly responsive to these incentives.

At the non-store supervisor and executive level, every manager, from the shipping dock foreman to the CEO was rewarded, as a percentage of base salary. Eighty percent of these bonuses were generally based on the financial results of the company (if they worked at headquarters) or of the operating division (if they worked for a division), and 20 percent on achieving individual objectives that had been set with their supervisor at the beginning of the year. Bonuses were significantly increased for beating the earnings target and were reduced pro rata for missing the target. According to this formula a high-performing division could pay bonuses even if the headquarters did not.

So how does this complex system of bonuses build a team? First of all, having a transparent formula rather than unbridled discretion reduces suspicion and improves trust. Second, it means that everyone is motivated to put his shoulder to the same wheel. The Christmas after we moved into our first big warehouse in Doswell, Virginia, for example, the incoming freight trucks were lined up waiting to be unloaded. The distribution department could have been upset that the merchants had not staggered the delivery dates to smooth the warehouse work flow. The merchants and operations guys could have replied, with some credibility, that the new warehouse was inefficient and still experiencing start-up pains. Instead of pointing fingers, however, both groups, plus a lot of other executives, showed up after normal business hours and on Saturdays to get through the freight "bulge" and turn it around to the stores in time for Christmas. They all understood that their bonuses were at stake.

The bonus system, in other words, was designed to reduce the interdepartmental politics inherently typical of any large organization and reward everyone who could influence results for pulling together to achieve budget objectives.

In fact, Wards had precious little "office politics." It is easy to say and the boss is often the last to know, but I truly believe that with few exceptions, we created a real team. People pulled together to achieve the budget that the entire senior management and several levels below were an integral part of developing. It was a matter of both pride and pocketbook to bury your differences and work together to get the job done.

Management Style

Sam's style had always been both authoritarian and paternalistic. He genuinely loved people. If someone had a problem he would patiently hear them out, offer advice, and, if necessary, loan them money, meet with their spouse, or open doors to medical treatment or psychological therapy. But he did not look to his subordinates for advice on how to run his company. He was twenty to thirty years older than most of his senior managers and held himself a bit aloof. They typically called him "Mr. Wurtzel" or "Mr. Sam" as a mark of respect.

I was the same age or younger than most of the senior management. But I was also a lawyer. My style was to question everything and to debate the things that did not make sense to me. I was also stubborn. Like a dog with a bone, I would continue to argue long beyond the point of usefulness.

One day, after I had been there a year or two, Rivas and Rexinger asked to meet with me at the end of the day. Basically they told me that I needed to change my style. I was too arrogant, too sure of myself, and too much the "prosecutor" in seeking information. Rivas later put it, "Alan did not have a lot of patience. If you were competent, Alan liked you. But he wasn't real tolerant if you had a lot of problems, where his father would want to save you." I have never forgotten that conversation. It was a brave thing for them to do, and I admire them for their courage and willingness to try to teach a "young dog" to behave properly. I have tried to heed the lesson they taught me, not always with success. But the partnership I had with the "four horsemen" lasted until I retired in 1986, and those of us who are still alive continue as friends to this day.

Over time I developed my own management style, which focused on an executive committee composed of the key executives who reported to me. All decisions were made by consensus...up to a point. That point came when we began to repeat ourselves. I firmly believe that better decisions come out of healthy debate.

Sometimes we could not agree and found ourselves repeating the same old arguments. If it was a big decision, I would put the issue down for review at a future meeting, and if, after some time, there was still no consensus and no new information or arguments forthcoming, I reserved the right, as CEO, to make the decision. As long as everyone felt they had been heard, they would loyally support the decision—even if they had lost the debate.

Habits of Mind

Curiosity Sustains the Cat: *The world is constantly changing. Be open and curious and strive to learn from others. Continuously try to understand the market and the changing economic, demographic, and other relevant forces at work that impact your business. Study your competitors. They may have insights and practices worth emulating or refining.*

By joining NATM we got the opportunity to learn what our peers were doing and to copy the best of what they did. Although, on balance, we ran a much bigger and better business than any of them, each did something we could learn from.

Mind the Culture: *Create a caring and ethical culture where employees can make mistakes without fear of adverse consequences. Beware of employees who are more concerned about their own success than the success of the business. Understand, exemplify, and reinforce the company's positive history and culture.*

No one can build a big business singlehandedly. You need a strong and effective team. To build a team, you need to carefully monitor who gets on the bus, who gets off, where they sit, and how you pay them.

Creating a team is a long and patient process of building trust and mutual respect. Our creative hiring process and bonus-based compensation system ensured that we had talented employees with incentive to work together to achieve Wards' success regardless of their job or their individual background and prior experience.

Encourage Debate: *Learn from dissent. Involve senior staff and the board of directors in an open process to find the best answer. Create a board that will raise thought-provoking questions and challenge management to justify its plans.*

Open and frank communication with subordinates is critical to gaining support and maintaining loyalty. Most people care more about being heard and seriously consulted than they do about winning a debate on any particular business point.

Chapter Six

GROWING AGAIN

A bend in the road is not the end of the road ... unless you fail to make the turn.
— Author unknown

With the disaster of near bankruptcy averted, a strategic plan we could believe in, and a loyal and talented management team, we were ready to focus on creating the future.

Audio Stores

In the mid- to late 1960s, audio components (receivers, tuners, speakers, turntables, and tape recorders) were emerging as mass-market products. Riding the crest of the lifestyle changes taking place in the '60s and the immense interest in popular music stimulated by Elvis, the Beatles, the Rolling Stones, and other popular bands, home audio equipment became a prized possession, especially for young males. Fortunately, audio components were a natural fit with Wards' core television business.

Wards' 1969 acquisition of Custom Hi-Fi turned out to be both a strategic coup and our salvation. The key asset was Ted Roussil, the company's highly respected founder. He knew the audio business and its distinct channel of domestic and overseas manufacturers, and over the next five years he taught Dan Rexinger, Bill Rivas, and Walter Bruckart how to wheel and deal in that world.

He was also an exuberant, if somewhat undisciplined, entrepreneur. Rivas and Rexinger would recall years later how, on their first visit to Custom, they discovered that the store housed in the home office building, which also did the largest volume of business, did not use a cash register. Roussil and his employees just put the money in a cigar box and counted it when the box was full.

At that time, the manufacturers controlled retail pricing for most consumer electronics products. Under the Robinson-Patman Act, manufacturers could establish a "fair-trade" price for its products, below which no retailer could sell. However, the District of Columbia and a handful of states exempted themselves from this anticonsumer law.

Although he lived and did business in nearby Maryland and was not covered by the District of Columbia exemption, Roussil had established a substantial mail-order business under the name Dixie Hi-Fi, through which he sold audio equipment at well below fair trade prices. He also transshipped to other audio dealers in violation of his franchise agreements. Pretty soon he opened other Dixie Hi-Fi stores in Maryland and Virginia.

So long as the orders were large and payments were made on time, most manufacturers looked the other way and treated Custom as if all its stores were covered by the DC exemption. While Roussil was occasionally shut off, he could generally get reinstated with a stern warning and an insincere promise not to do it again. As a lawyer, I had qualms about Wards' violating the law but rationalized continuing Roussil's practices in the belief that these laws were anticonsumer and poor public policy.

Customers typically heard about the Dixie Hi-Fi stores through word of mouth or through Roussil's mail-order catalog. To save 20 to 30 percent on a $1,000 stereo system, customers would order by mail or, to be sure the deals were legitimate, drive from as far away as Philadelphia and North Carolina to pick up their merchandise in Maryland.

The Dixie stores, typically located in somewhat seedy, low-rent neighborhoods, attracted young, mostly male, audio buffs. The windows were painted yellow and stenciled with brand-name logos. They had an illicit look that was reminiscent of a speakeasy or an "adult" bookstore. Inside the store was a service counter similar to what you would find at an auto parts wholesaler. The stores were small, averaging five hundred square feet of display space and two thousand square feet of stockroom. Displays were minimal and most of the merchandise was not plugged in or operable. Customers generally came in knowing what they wanted by brand and model number.

Dixie's low prices and broad selection of top brand names generated enormous traffic, and with very low rents, scanty fixtures, and almost no advertising, they generated excellent profits and a high return on investment.

The 1973 Strategic Plan recommended opening more Dixie Hi-Fi stores on the East Coast and in California. Between 1970 and 1976, Wards opened twenty-four Dixie stores that averaged $800,000 in sales and 12 percent pretax profits annually. They had an enormous impact on our ability to survive.

All good things, however, come to an end, and near the end of the decade the government decided to interpret the pro-trust Robinson Patman Act not as a stand-alone law, but in conjunction with the antitrust laws that encouraged price competition. As a result, the government ceased enforcing the Act.[94] This allowed everyone to begin discounting hi-fi equipment, so the Dixie formula no longer worked. By 1982 all the Dixie stores were closed, and we needed a new strategy to replace the lost cash cow.

At the same time, the conventional Custom Hi-Fi stores were also adversely affected by the demise of the fair-trade laws. With everyone now discounting hi-fi, the rents Custom Hi-Fi was paying for its mall-based stores were no longer feasible. In some malls the rent ran as high as 6 percent of sales, generally greater than the store's net profit.

Circuit City Electronics Stores

As shown on the chart on page 98, the improving demographics of audio customers were even more important than the volatile economics of the 1970s, as shown on the chart on page 95. In the years 1970 to 1977, while the U.S. population grew by 6 percent, the number of fifteen- to thirty-four-year-olds grew by nearly 20 percent, comprising more than one-third of the population.

These changing demographics, the continued decline of audio prices, and the end of the recession resulted in an explosion of demand from young families and single women. These customers didn't want to travel to second-class neighborhoods to shop in tiny stores with yellow painted windows that looked like dirty bookstores. In addition, the merchandise was also changing. Tabletop TVs, now called "portable TVs," were quickly becoming so small and so inexpensive that people were putting them in almost every room, including kids' bedrooms, kitchens, and second homes. Also coming to market were a myriad of new electronic toys, including hi-fi cassette recorders and players for home and car, boom boxes, video tape recorders, and video players. Based on this product proliferation, we decided that we should close our no-longer-profitable audio stores and open new "all electronics" stores to replace them.

Before we opened these stores, however, we needed a new name. "Wards" was not an option. After the Second World War, Montgomery Ward had dropped the "Montgomery" in their advertising and began calling itself simply "Wards." Like David with a slingshot, Sam sued the giant Montgomery Ward in the mid-1950s. He thought that Wards was his name, but, unlike Solomon, this judge divided the baby. He awarded Sam the Wards name to use only in Richmond and Petersburg, Virginia. In all the rest of the world Montgomery Ward could call itself just plain Wards.

With Wards not available and the Custom and Dixie names tarnished, we consulted the W.B. Donor advertising agency for assistance in choosing a name for the new stores. Believing that there was likely to be a long succession of new electronics products coming on the market, Donor suggested Circuit City.[95] It had a futuristic ring and was broad enough to encompass any product that needed to be plugged in or turned on.

With the new name and the new strategy, we closed the seven Custom and four Dixie stores in and around Washington, D.C., and launched six Circuit City stores in April 1977. The new stores were about six to seven thousand square feet, bright, well located, had attractive operating displays for every brand and model, and were staffed by salespeople who were well groomed, well trained, and wearing company blazers. In short, Circuit City stores were places where families and single women who did not know the item they wanted by model number would feel comfortable buying hi-fi equipment and other small electronics.

Circuit City Electronics store – 1977

Warehouse Showrooms

While the new Circuit City electronics stores were immediately successful, we did not think they were the ultimate format. During the yearlong preparation of the 1973 Strategic Plan we had studied the concept of warehouse showrooms pioneered by Levitz Furniture. Levitz had built large showrooms where customers could see furniture in roomlike settings. To enter the showroom, however, they needed to walk through a large warehouse with boxes of sofas, chairs, and tables piled on twenty-foot-high racks whose purpose was to impress them with the company's quantity, selection, and implicit buying power.

The first warehouse showroom for TV and appliances, founded by Melvin Landow, had opened in Miami in 1966 under the name Kennedy & Cohen.[96] As in Levitz stores, customers walked through a large warehouse full of merchandise, past windows opening onto a functioning service department, and into a large (ten-thousand-square-foot) showroom with multiple brands and a large section of TVs, appliances, and other consumer electronics. Compared to the Wards stores at 3,000 to 5,000 square feet, or a licensed department at roughly 3,500, this was a vast expanse of merchandise. Salesmen were dressed in ties and blazers, and it all looked very professional. Kennedy & Cohen was an immediate success, and Landow rapidly expanded to ten other cities.

For the retailer, large warehouse showrooms, as compared to multiple smaller stores, required fewer managers, offered greater scheduling flexibility, and facilitated better training opportunities for sales personnel. Having sales, warehousing, and service under one roof also eliminated duplicate displays, increased inventory turnover, and improved operating efficiency. For customers, the warehouse showroom's advantages included massive selection, immediate pickup, and a convenient location near a major highway, as well as free parking, discount pricing, the security of dealing with a large company, and the visual demonstration that the company maintained trained staff to service what it sold.

The key members of our team visited most of Kennedy & Cohen's warehouse showrooms and were impressed by what we saw. The biggest weakness was that, despite its professional appearance, it was a high-pressure, bait-and-switch operation. It was said that Kennedy & Cohen "sold everybody once but nobody twice." It was also a high-cost operation, with high advertising and selling expenses. Always the egotist, Landow wrote a book, *Your People Are Your Business: A Manager's Manual for Making Millions*

The Loading Dock

in Merchandising.[97] When he filed for bankruptcy a few years later, one wag suggested he should write a sequel on how to **lose** many millions in retailing.

By the fall of 1973 Wards broke ground for its own warehouse showroom in the West End of Richmond (where we still had the right to use the Wards name), with occupancy expected in the spring of 1975. The showroom, to be called Wards Loading Dock, would replace the four original Wards TV stores in Richmond. In addition to the 12,000-square-foot new store, the 133,000-square-foot building would also house a major warehouse and distribution center for our Eastern operations as well as our corporate offices and a service department. As hoped, the new Loading Dock was a big success. First year sales were $3 million, equal to that of the four Wards TV stores it had replaced. Profits ran 6 percent of sales, far higher than the old conventional stores. We were now ready to grow the concept. Our 1976 Three Year Plan noted that "we want to explore how we could make an impact [with Loading Docks] in Los Angles without overextending ourselves. If that were not possible, we see the opportunity to add Loading Docks within a few hundred miles of Richmond."

In the end, we concluded that adding warehouse showrooms in Los Angeles at that time would be too big a financial undertaking. We would need a minimum of six stores to cover the market and defray the very high costs of advertising in the *Los Angeles Times* and on TV. Instead we decided to grow closer to home. In 1974, prior to opening the Loading Dock, we added a warehouse showroom as a licensee in a large regional furniture store in Norfolk and a second one a year later in Hampton, Virginia. These provided excellent, low- cost opportunities to experiment in operating a large store, but being a licensee was not how we wanted to position the company in the long term.

Refining the Consumer Offer

With the two new retailing concepts, Circuit City electronics stores and the Loading Dock warehouse showroom, up and running we could focus full time on the consumer offer as a whole—that is, what we were providing our customers in terms of merchandise, location, ambience, service, price, and satisfaction.

The core values that Sam and Hecht had formulated in the early days had carried the business a long way. But the lack of attention to strategic planning had run the company into the ditch. In the process of restructuring, we embraced and maintained all of their core values regarding the treatment of employees and suppliers. But now, in a different era, it was necessary to update their policies regarding the consumer offer.

Consumerism

When Wards entered the licensed department business in the early 1960s, the company had to move to a one-price policy. At least in theory, discount stores did not allow negotiated pricing. At the same time, however, charging different customers different prices for the same merchandise continued in the Wards TV stores and the other conventional stores Wards had acquired.

In 1972, a year or so before becoming CEO, I concluded that neither bait-and-switch advertising nor negotiating prices was any longer acceptable or profitable. There was something sleazy and distasteful about trying *not* to sell an advertised item and even more so in charging a passive and uneducated customer more than a smart, aggressive one. Besides, I believed we would make more money by selling at fixed low prices, turning our inventory faster, and making more sales per salesman, than by trying to milk every customer for the highest price they would pay. Sam, although somewhat skeptical, agreed.

Rivas and Rexinger, after some resistance, also agreed. We held many a meeting trying to persuade the "old school" merchants and store operators, especially in the Wards TV stores, that we needed to change. Those who objected had to be "reeducated" or terminated. To tell the truth, the skeptics were right in a sense. In the small neighborhood stores a one-price policy actually lowered margins without increasing sales. But once we opened the Circuit City stores and the warehouse showroom, our new pricing policies and consumerism stance became essential to growing the business—and they did.

Clarity of Mission

As we abandoned bait and switch, we also needed to clarify our core marketing policies for customers and for employees. We needed something short, simple, and easy to remember. It became the 4-S policy: *Savings, Selection, Service,* and *Satisfaction.*

Savings meant that if, within thirty days, you could find the same item at another store for less, we would refund the difference plus 10 percent of the difference. It was a convincing offer to back up our claim of low prices that we rarely had to make good on, and when we did, we did so cheerfully and at very low cost.

Selection meant that compared to any competitor we had the largest selection in the product categories we carried. Customers in the Circuit City stores and the showroom were confronted by a thirty- or fifty-foot-long TV wall with 60 to 120 sets stacked four high and all tuned to the same channel. In the warehouse showroom we initially had refrigerators and freezers stacked on racks two high simply to make an impression.

Service meant good service during the sale by a knowledgeable salesperson as well as service after the sale by capable technicians.

Finally, we guaranteed *Satisfaction,* remembering that customers may not always be right, but a complaint is an opportunity to make a friend.

The 4-S policy was printed in our ads, on customer receipts and shopping bags, on wallpaper in the stores, and on the salesmen's blazers. It became a mantra that everyone, from cashier and stock boy to vice president, knew and supported. I used to joke that I would have it tattooed on every employee's forehead (or backside) if I could.

In the late 1980s we added a fifth "S": *Speed,* reflecting our commitment to making the entire transaction—from selection to checkout to receipt of the goods—as smooth and as swift as possible.

Having a clean, clear, and consumer-friendly set of core values as well as an easy-to-remember mission was essential to our success. The value of this approach is illustrated by an incident my wife still remembers. One evening, well after I had retired, we were in India having a drink on a veranda and struck up a conversation with a couple from California. When they learned I had worked at Circuit City they told me that once, when the husband was hospitalized, his wife had gone to Circuit City to purchase a TV for when he came home. The set she chose was a large table-top model that was too heavy for her to carry into the house and too small to qualify for free delivery. So the salesman had offered to bring it to her house after hours and set it up. "Circuit City made a customer for life," she said. I have heard similar stories many times. Service above and beyond what is expected, like a well-handled complaint, is truly a way to make a friend.

At no point did we put profits at the core of our philosophy. Rather, our mission was to give the consumer a better deal and still make money. To be successful, as we said on many occasions, "We need to buy it better, sell it better, deliver and service it better, and account for it better than our competitors." If we did all those things better, the profits would follow.

To a certain extent this was an irrational, contradictory set of expectations. How can you sell it cheaper, provide better service, and still make a profit? On paper you can't, but as Collins and Porras point out in their book *Built to Last,* great companies are not immobilized by the "Tyranny of the OR." They go on to find the "Genius of the AND." A successful company, for example, can be both "highly idealistic and highly profitable." It can focus on the big picture and the small details. Inspirational goals can attract and motivate people to achieve those goals even if they are contradictory. That is why we were able to provide customers both the lowest price *and* the best service, and still prosper.

Ready to Grow

By 1977, when the dust from all of the openings and closings had settled, Wards emerged as a dramatically simplified company. It had two basic businesses, each with two flavors. The TV and appliance business was reduced to three warehouse showrooms on the East Coast and thirty-two Zodys departments in LA. The "audio" business had ten stores selling portable consumer electronics. Six were in DC, called Circuit City, and four were in Richmond, called Sight and Sound. In addition, there were still twenty Dixie Hi-Fi stores open in the Mid-Atlantic, the Midwest, and the West Coast. We were on the way to Hyman Meyer's goal of just one business.

The restructuring was working. By the mid-1970s, Wards was the leading independent retailer of TVs and appliances in the nation. For the fiscal year ending March 31, 1977, the company had sales of $72 million and net operating profits had rebounded to nearly $1.2 million before one-time expenses (called "extraordinary charges"), nearly double the previous high. We had restructured the balance sheet. We had permanently financed the warehouse showroom, and office complex and negotiated a new $5 million revolving line of credit. Our net worth had grown to $7 million from a low of $4.1 million and working capital was a healthy $10 million.

Wards was ready to grow again.

Habits of Mind

The events of Chapter Six demonstrate the following Habits of Mind that lead to success or failure.

Chase the Impossible Dream: *Do not be limited by what Collins and Porras, the authors of* Built to Last, *call the "Tyranny of the OR." Be willing to embrace the "Genius of the AND." Two worthwhile goals that seem mutually exclusive can inspire an organization of "ordinary" employees to achieve extraordinary results.98*

In building a compelling vision a company can, and often should, embrace mutually contradictory goals. Customers, like the rest of us, are not purely rational beings. They want the best quality **and** the lowest price, the highest levels of service **and** a quick shopping experience. Aspiring to these somewhat contradictory goals challenges the organization to think outside the box and ordinary employees to perform extraordinary feats. Making a profit is important, but meeting customer needs is critical to long-term success.

Keep it Simple and Accountable: *Develop a clear and well-articulated set of policies for dealing with customers, suppliers, and employees. For any organization to succeed it is essential that each and every employee internalize the company's goals and values. Employees should also be held accountable and incentivized to pursue those goals and values every day.*

The 4-S policy was simple and easy to remember. If we could deliver on Savings, Selection, Service, and Satisfaction, we could meet all significant consumer expectations.

Focus on the Future : *Manage for the long term and not the short. Don't let short-term earnings swings divert a long-term strategy. Ignore the skeptics and short-term market swings. If things go well, the value of your company, whether public or private, will respond over time.*

In the dark days of 1974–75 it was necessary to both contract and expand. At the same time we shed our losers, we needed to create some winners. Having a strategic plan enabled us to move in both directions simultaneously and persuade our lenders that there was hope we would emerge a strong, profitable company.

THE GREAT YEARS
(1978–2000)

PART III

Chapter Seven

RAMPING UP

*In preparing for battle I have always found that plans are useless,
but planning is indispensable.*

—Dwight D. Eisenhower

Twenty-two years is a long time in the history of any company.
Between 1978 and 2000, Wards Company changed its name to
Circuit City Stores, Inc.; changed CEOs; created an innovative
and successful $2 billion used-car business; increased its elec-
tronics and appliance sales from $91 million to $10.6 billion; and
increased earnings from $2 million to $327 million.

These enormous increases in the company's sales and earnings
were driven by rapid store growth, improved financial strength,
and continued investment in people, technology, and distribution. Most importantly, they occurred in an extremely positive
environment for electronics and appliance sales, including the
development of exciting new products and unprecedented price
declines in consumer electronics.

The Real World, 1978–2000

As in any multidecade period, the economy between 1978 and
2000 had its ups and downs. The first few years were difficult. The
continuing stagflation of the late '70s left nearly a third of the nation's industrial capacity idle.[99] Then, in 1980, inflation hit a jaw-
dropping 13 percent[100] and unemployment reached 9.7 percent.[101]

In 1981, however, Ronald Reagan's inauguration ushered in a
long period of growth. Businesses were now free to expand and

U.S. Real Gross Domestic Product 1978-1986

merge without much fear of government regulation or antitrust enforcement.[102] In fact, the economy was launched on a twenty-year path of unprecedented expansion. Between 1980 and 2000, the real gross domestic product (GDP) of the United States grew by 92 percent [103] and real per capita income by 44 percent;[104] average household debt rose by a whopping 232 percent[105] and real personal consumption expenditures by 102 percent.[106] Following a brief recession in 1990–91, America enjoyed an unbelievable nine-year period during which the real GDP grew every single month[107] and unemployment dipped below 5 percent [108], while inflation hovered between 2 and 3 percent.

Known as the "New Economy," this exceptional prosperity flew in the face of prevailing wisdom that an economy could not sustain both high growth and low unemployment for an extended period without significant inflation. This New Economy was distinct in three significant ways.

First, its success was directly tied to the rapid rise of technology. The NASDAQ Composite Index, a measure of high-tech stocks, rose more than tenfold between 1990 and 2000, until the tech bubble burst in mid-2000. By 1998 the economic contribution of the Internet ($301 billion) had surpassed both the long-established energy and telecommunications sectors.[109]

A second defining characteristic was technology-enabled productivity. In the business sector, the widespread introduction of computers allowed output per man-hour to double every five years between 1985 and 2000.[110] For any business hoping to remain competitive, computers were no longer optional.

Increased use of technology, in turn, heightened the demand for skilled workers. In 1950, 40 percent of the jobs in the United States required skilled labor. By 1997 that number had grown to 75 percent.[111] This shift put a premium on education and training and improved the incomes of the better educated.

Finally, the new economy was increasingly part of a global marketplace. The Internet erased barriers to communication and the spread of information, allowing corporations to market, manufacture, and source talent almost anywhere in the world. While this created problems for inefficient or high-wage American industries like apparel manufacturing, it also created a worldwide demand for hard-to-duplicate American products and services, such as Boeing airliners, IBM computers, McDonald's franchises, and Coca-Cola.

In the two decades between 1980 and 2000, the U.S. population also grew 24 percent, from 225 million to 280 million.[112] With higher divorce rates and young people marrying later, the number of households grew even faster.[113] For TV and appliance retailers, this was a scenario made in heaven. The '80s were especially positive. Baby boomers, born between 1946 and 1964, were coming of age. In October 1984, *Fortune* magazine observed:

> With the oldest boomers now approaching 40 and the youngest just leaving college, the generation is now entering its prime years of earning—and spending. The boomers are a mouthwatering market…because they're maturing into the most affluent generation the U.S. has ever seen.[114]

By the 1990s, the children of these early "boomers" typically had families of their own. In fact, some of their offspring were al-

U.S. Population by Age Group 1978-1986

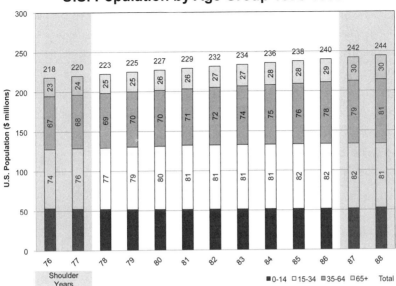

ready entering their teenage years. And not only were teens growing in number, they also represented a substantial increase in buying power. Because baby boomers had waited longer than previous generations to have children, they were better established financially by the time they started a family. This fact, paired with boomers' tendency toward two-income households and, possibly, guilt about their absence from home, encouraged parents to spend more money on their offspring. In many cases TVs and other electronic devices became the family babysitters.

From 1994 to 1999, annual purchases by twelve- to nineteen-year-olds increased by half, from $99 billion to $153 billion.[115, 116] In addition, tech-savvy teenagers increasingly influenced their parents' and grandparents' purchases of cars, computers, and home entertainment equipment.[117]

All this prosperity and fecundity had important ramifications for American retailing.

The first suburban enclosed mall was Northgate Shopping Mall,[118] which opened in Seattle in1950.[119] By the mid-'80s, there were more than 26,000 shopping centers of all kinds and 811 regional and superregional enclosed malls.[120] In fact, malls accounted for more than 45 percent of all retail sales. Surveys showed that Americans were spending more time in malls than anywhere else except at their home, job, or school.[121] In short, Americans were beginning to "shop till they drop[ped]."

While all this was going on, the changes in income distribution occasioned by the Reagan tax cuts had significant implications for the retail industry. Tax cuts designed to spur economic recovery favored the rich, while increases in Social Security taxes and Medicare fell disproportionately on the less affluent. Correspondingly, the fastest-growing retail formats of the 1980s targeted not only the most affluent but also those at the low end of the earnings spectrum.

For example, the enormously popular warehouse clubs that offered deeply discounted prices in a no-frills environment with little to no service appealed directly to shoppers with limited discretionary spending. The success of industry pioneer Price Club inspired many imitators, including Walmart's Sam's Club, Costco, and Zayre's BJ's Wholesale Club.

At the same time, Tiffany & Co., FAO Schwarz, Nordstrom, Abercrombie, and other chains that targeted the upper middle class began expanding in this period, and specialty retailers, along with big-box "category killers" that carried large assortments of merchandise at generally low prices were also drawing middle- and upper-income shoppers away from traditional department and discount stores. Moderately priced specialty stores—Toys "R" Us, Waldenbooks, and The Gap, for example—that appealed to both moderate and higher-income customers also began taking market share.

Closer to home, Wards' success as a consumer electronics specialty retailer was attracting a lot of attention and more than a few copycats. When the company first went public in 1969, it was the only publicly owned retailer in this segment. Except for RadioShack, which, in 1975, was spun out of Tandy Leather, Wards remained the lone publicly owned specialty TV and appliance retailer until the early 1980s. Then, in rapid succession, Silo (Philadelphia), Highland (Detroit), and others jumped into the public pool and began swimming to new markets. By 1986 there were twelve such public companies and more coming on stream every year.[122] One of these, Best Buy, started in Minneapolis in 1982 and within a decade was rivaling Circuit City for leadership in this segment of retailing.

By the early '90s, traditional retailers were losing market share to big box specialty stores with large selections in their chosen fields.[123] Just as supermarket chains replaced mom-and-pop grocery stores, Home Depot and Lowe's began to supplant local hardware stores, Staples and Office Depot drove local stationery stores from the field, and giants like Toys "R" Us revolutionized the retail toy business. In 1992 the big-box chains accounted for 15.5 percent of the discount industry, and in just six years that number had grown to a 20.2 percent share. [124]

Another important retail development of this era was the expanded use of information technology. By the early '80s, machine-readable bar codes and Universal Product Codes, or UPCs, allowed firms to gather data, easily and inexpensively, at the point of sale and identify hot sellers, stagnant merchandise, and products that were nearly out of stock. Retailers like Walmart were able to improve productivity by as much as 2 percent per year,[125] and those who used technology most effectively were able to leave their competitors in the dust.

Electronics and Appliances

In the 1980s, all other retail segments paled in comparison to the dynamism, visibility, and product proliferation of consumer electronics. Confirming the rubric that it is better to be lucky than smart, I often thanked my lucky stars that Sam had decided to go into the retail electronics business and not the retail shoe business. Between 1980 and 1986, factory shipments of consumer

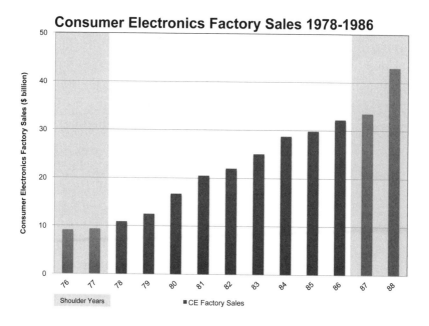

Consumer Electronics Factory Sales 1978-1986

electronics nearly doubled, from $16.7 billion to $32 billion.[126] Products that had been invented barely five years earlier enjoyed explosive growth. Between 1981 and 1985 Americans purchased 70 million color TVs, 27 million videocassette recorders, and 123 million portable audio players (aka "boom boxes").[127]

Wards' 1980 annual report featured a two-page discussion of "Merchandise for the 80s." It recalled the product advances in the prior ten years, including hi-fi cassette recorders, cassette players for home and car, portable stereo radios, CB radios, and pocket calculators, while noting dramatic price-to-performance reductions in basic hi-fi components and color TVs. Looking forward, it predicted that many more electronics products, including home and office telephones (now that consumers were free to purchase them rather than renting them from the telephone company) and video games, would reach significant market penetration.[128]

The blockbuster among all these products was the videocassette recorder, or VCR. Sony introduced the Betamax player in 1975. Touted as the first affordable, reliable, easy-to-use VCR, the device initially experienced slow growth. Consumers were confused by the battle between Sony's Betamax and JVC's VHS format. But then JVC outmaneuvered Sony by persuading most other manufacturers to adopt its VHS format, and VCR sales took off, doubling each year between 1980 and 1985.[129] During that time, Americans bought a staggering 27 million VCRs,[130] and VCR penetration grew from 1 percent of television households in 1980 to nearly 70 percent by the end of the decade.[131] To meet the demand for movie videos, grocery and drugstores began renting tapes and a whole new industry of video rental stores emerged, selling and renting more than $1 billion in tapes in 1984 alone.[132]

VCRs were only part of the home entertainment growth story. By 1980 almost 20 percent of American homes were connected to cable TV, and for rural areas the satellite dish was just over the horizon.[133] Equally exciting, a convenient new audio format, the compact disc, boosted sales of hi-fi equipment for home and cars. As the price of CD players dropped below $300, sales jumped more than twentyfold in the three years between 1983 (35,000 units)[134] and 1985 (850,000 units).[135]

By 1985 personal computer prices had fallen below $2000, fueling rapid growth from two million units in 1982 to three million in 1985[136], and a household penetration rate of 14 percent.[137]

Big screen and projection TVs exhibited new life as prices dropped and performance improved. Consumers increasingly purchased big screens worthy of displaying their VHS tapes, cable TV programs, and video games. And each purchase stimulated another, as individual components could be linked to form a comprehensive home entertainment system.

As the chart on page 154 shows, during the early 1980s the consumer electronics industry grew at an astounding rate of 20 to 25 percent per year.[138, 139]

Largely as a result of this growth, in fiscal years 1984 and 1985, Wards' same-store sales grew a mammoth 41 and 37 percent, respectively. We were truly in the right place at the right time.

Sales increases did not, however, automatically translate into higher profits. In the rush for market share, manufacturers and many retailers slashed prices to rock-bottom levels. The average price of a VCR dropped 11 percent between 1983 and 1984 alone.[140] Put another way, between 1967 and 1983, the price index for consumer electronics remained flat while the general consumer price index increased 300 percent.[141]

Price deflation is a double-edged sword. While it obviously stimulates demand, it poses serious challenges to manufacturers and retailers. If the price goes down 50 percent, each product has to sell twice as many units to make the same sales dollars. While higher volumes do leverage fixed costs, they also dramatically increase variable costs. Double the unit sales require more transportation, more storage, and more selling and cashier time to generate the same sales dollars, resulting in lower profits.

In the appliance industry, as in the larger economy, consolidations, and mergers had a field day. Industry rivals sought to fill out their product lines and offset price deterioration with economies of scale. By 1986 almost 80 percent of the $11 billion major appliance industry was in the hands of four manufacturers: Whirlpool, General Electric, Maytag, and White Consolidated.[142] Sears remained the dominant appliance retailer with its Kenmore brand (made by Whirlpool) and a 30 percent market share.[143]

Fortunately, consumption-crazed yuppies demanded the latest and greatest appliances, including ice-in-the-door refrigerators and microwave ovens. Household penetration of the latter soared from 8 percent in 1978 to 61 percent in 1987.[144]

These were, indeed, heady times for electronics and appliance retailers in general and for Wards in particular.

Superstore Expansion

By 1978 the stars had aligned. We had recovered from our overexpansion of the early '70s. We had restored our balance sheet and embraced new systems to improve productivity. The only legacy remaining from those years of rampant expansion were the Zodys licensed departments in California. They were not a part of the future we envisioned but were too profitable to close immediately. The company had embarked on a far simpler growth strategy that would concentrate on the Circuit City stores, which sold electronics only, and the Loading Dock warehouse showroom stores, which sold electronics and appliances.

Notwithstanding lingering stagflation and high unemployment, the six original Circuit City stores that Wards opened in Washington, D.C., in April of 1977, did well from the start. In the first year, their sales were 31 percent higher than the six Dixie Hi-Fi and Custom stores they had replaced. That same year we also added three new Circuit City stores in the Carolinas, for a total of nine, and in 1978 we added ten more. By 1980 we had thirty-six all-electronics Circuit City stores, almost all located in the South.

These five- to six-thousand-square-foot stores could be created by remodeling some of the larger existing Dixie stores or be fitted into readily available retail spaces. They could be rented, despite our weak balance sheet, on five-year leases with one or more five-year options to extend.

The larger warehouse showrooms, carrying console TVs and appliances, required a custom designed "build to suit" store and much longer-term leases. In the early to mid-'70s our balance sheet was not strong enough to build or lease more than a few such stores. We added a second Loading Dock in Richmond in 1979 and several years later, as our balance sheet improved, we announced three new warehouse showrooms for Raleigh, Durham, and Greensboro, North Carolina. They opened in 1981, replacing or, in Raleigh's case, supplementing the smaller Circuit City electronics-only stores we had opened in those markets a few years earlier.

To avoid confusion, yet still benefit from the positive image of the earlier, smaller Circuit City stores, we decided to call these new, much larger showroom stores Circuit City Superstores. At the same time we also renamed the two Loading Docks in Richmond so that all our warehouse showrooms would be Circuit City Superstores.

The superstores were all freestanding buildings, typically 34,000 square feet, located on three acres of land that included a two-hundred-car parking lot and a truck loading ramp. The building contained a 12,000- to 14,000-square-foot showroom; a 15,000-square-foot adjoining warehouse; and space for customer credit, sales training, and administrative functions. Initially they also contained a "nursery," where parents could let their kids play while they shopped. In addition to being a nice feature to brag about in our ads, the nursery enabled the salespeople to make their pitch without the distraction of young children. (Unfortunately, the nurseries were discontinued—deemed too expensive to staff—shortly after I left the company.) A few years later we added automobile bays in the rear of the store to install car stereos.[145] This enabled us to become a one-stop destination for car stereo equipment.

The stores, designed on the premise that a compelling retail offering is partly drama, were big and bright, with many custom-

Race Track Concept

built displays. As you entered you saw a 100-foot-long wall of portable TVs, four rows high and all tuned to the same channel. The selling space was laid out like a racetrack, to encourage customers to circulate throughout the store and see the full range of merchandise.

At the center was a circle of counters displaying small goods: Walkmans, radios, phonograph needles, headphones, and other small and easily pilferable products. Salespeople were behind the counters to assist customers. Around the outside of the "track" were console TVs and, in later years, computers and other, larger electronics products. On the perimeter walls were floor to ceiling shelves with tabletop TVs all tuned to the same channel as well as row upon row of audio components (receivers, tuners, and turntables), all hooked up and ready to demo. In a room dedicated to speakers, salesmen could switch back and forth between any two speaker sets with any tuner to demonstrate the differences as the music played. Yet another room was dedicated to car stereo, where custom-made displays enabled customers to compare the sounds of different combinations of speakers and tuners. At the back of the racetrack was a large display of refrigerators, stoves, washing machines and dryers, and freezers.

Instead of a central checkout counter there were multiple sales terminals strategically located around the selling space so that customers required the assistance of a salesperson to make a purchase. Each section had well-trained, dedicated sales personnel, all dressed in company blazers, ready to help. Few goods were available for the customer to pick up on the sales floor.

Since every electronics product on display was hooked up and operational, the displays required power and, in many cases, antenna connections. Smaller goods needed to be operational yet restrained to prevent theft. Management spent many hours and many more dollars designing and building these single-purpose fixtures. The downside was that, as the merchandise changed in size or type and new categories were added over the years, redesigning and modifying the specialized fixtures became a logistical challenge and a financial headache.

By the time we opened the superstores, we felt it unnecessary and impractical to show the customer a functioning service department, as had been standard in the initial Loading Docks. The stores did, however, accept carry-in merchandise to be repaired at company-owned-and-operated service facilities and returned to the customer at the store. We also continued to do in home repairs for major appliances and console TVs.

Superstore Rollout

Many of our peers made the mistake, as we had earlier, of jumping around to any attractive market regardless of geography. But we had already learned the hard way that stores in far-flung locations could be difficult to manage and expensive to service. So as we rolled out the superstores we began with markets close to home. Our parameters became any southern city with a population of more than three hundred thousand within widening radii of our Richmond distribution center. As we filled in the markets within a three-hundred-mile radius, we would build another distribution center roughly six hundred miles away that would serve stores within its three-hundred-mile radius until the two circles touched.[146] By systematically growing in concentric circles we saved on distribution and supervision expenses.

By the end of 1983, we had eight superstores in five metropolitan markets in Virginia, North Carolina, and Tennessee. The superstores and the seven associated Circuit City stores in the same markets were cranking out $100 million in sales per year. In addition, there were thirty-one Circuit City electronics-only stores located in Washington, D.C., and in other markets, mostly southern cities, whose sales totaled another $100 million-plus. Also, by that time our licensed departments in the Zodys stores in California had grown to thirty-nine and their sales to $73 million.

As a result of this expansion and the unprecedented demand for new electronics products, the company, despite difficult economic times in the early '80s, produced good growth in sales and earnings. Between fiscal 1978 and 1984, sales grew from $91 million to $356 million and profits from $2 million to $12 million. Toward the end of that period, return on stockholder equity averaged a very respectable 27 percent.

Once again Wards had caught a retail wave, not unlike the one Sam and Hecht had surfed when they rolled out thirty-seven TV and licensed appliance departments in discount department stores in the early 1960s. The difference was that this time we were not dependent on the financial health or merchandising strengths of a landlord.

Restoring the Balance Sheet

A decade earlier, Wards had nearly succumbed to the 1973 recession because we were financially overextended. We'd learned a lesson the hard way, and as soon as we were able, we made several important moves to clean up and strengthen our balance sheet. In 1977 the company converted a long-term $800,000 subordinated note it had issued in connection with the Mart acquisition to a $450,000 short-term note and some stock. A year later, the company redeemed the preferred stock it issued in 1965 to facilitate the first expansion into licensed departments.

As a result of these changes and several years of good earnings, shareholder equity doubled, from $7.1 million in 1977 to $15 million in 1981. But the big move was yet to come. In 1981 we decided to acquire a bankrupt chain of eight electronics stores with a $41 million loss to carry forward.

The Lafayette Acquisition

As the name implies, Lafayette Radio Electronics Inc. started during the early days of radio, initially selling "do-it-yourself" kits to hobbyists. Gradually, the business expanded to carry a whole range of imported electronics parts and finished private-label consumer products, not unlike RadioShack today. Most of the goods were sourced in the Far East from nonbranded manufacturers using the Lafayette label.

At its peak in 1976, Lafayette comprised a chain of 119 company stores plus hundreds of franchised dealers all over the country and a sizeable mail-order business. Sales totaled $99 million. As hi-fi became more of a mass-market item, however, private label goods began to lose market share to brand names like Sony, Panasonic, and JVC. That, and the end of fair trade, which allowed retailers to discount branded products, cut deeply into Lafayette's business.

The final nail in their coffin was a spike in citizens band (CB) radio sales in the late '70s. For a few years this was the hottest selling electronics item in America, especially among truck drivers. Then, at about the same time the demand from truckers was largely met, the government decided to increase the available CB channels from twenty-three to forty. As a result, Lafayette's considerable twenty-three-channel inventory was worth almost nothing and its many pending orders for forty channel units tightened the financial noose around its neck. By 1977, Lafayette was hemorrhaging cash. The company tried desperately but unsuccessfully to borrow money, find a merger partner, or restructure. On January 2, 1980, Lafayette filed for bankruptcy under Chapter 11.

I had followed Lafayette's troubles in the trade press, but had otherwise paid little attention until September 1980, when Sam, then serving as chairman of the board, called to say he had heard that the chain was down to eight stores, all in and around New York City, and that it could be bought for almost nothing. I was not much interested until he added that they had a $40 million tax loss carry-forward. This would enable us to avoid taxes on up to $40 million of future earnings, potentially a big boost to future net worth. Going into New York was not part of our plan, and given our earlier failures, I did not favor growth by acquisition. On the other hand, if the stores were well located and the Lafayette name still had positive resonance, the tax loss could cover a lot of marketing and remerchandising expenses. Besides, all Lafayette's senior management personnel were going or already gone, so we would not be taking over and trying to retrain an existing organization, as we had so unsuccessfully tried to do in the past. Finally, Lafayette did not carry TVs, and our recent experience in transforming Custom and Dixie stores into Circuit City stores by adding video products gave us hope that we could quickly add significant volume to the Lafayette base business.

So I called Bob Greenberg, the CEO of Lafayette, and arranged to meet him early in the next week. Time was of the essence. The banks had given Lafayette an ultimatum: come up with a plan to reduce its debt by September 30 or close all but one of its stores (to preserve the tax loss). Within a few days following my visit, we had sketched out a plan to lend Lafayette $2.1 million, half to reduce its bank debt and half to buy goods for the upcoming Christmas season. This would give us some time to enter into an acquisition agreement.

At my initial meeting with Bob, I learned that Lafayette, as part of its Chapter 11 reorganization, had sublet forty vacated stores at a substantial profit. In those days, the bankruptcy laws allowed a debtor an extended period to either renounce its leases or keep them and sublet to others at a profit. Many of the Lafayette leases had been made years earlier when retail rents were much lower. As a result, the $2.4 million purchase price, which we paid in stock, was more than offset by the $4.2 million in sublease income we stood to earn over the next five years.

Although the transaction is easy to summarize after the fact, buying a company in bankruptcy can be tricky and potentially risky, at least for a novice like me. I worried a lot about the many possible pitfalls. During the prior four years many other potential buyers had kicked the Lafayette tires and decided to pass. Hadn't they seen that the sublease income would pay for the chain and that the tax losses could provide a good return even if Lafayette did not flourish in the tough New York retail environment? I worried that they knew something I did not. But perhaps it was just a matter of being in the right place at the right time. I got to Lafayette only days before the banks were about to close them down. Earlier, their expectations and their terms had been higher. And, possibly, my legal training may have better equipped me to weigh the risk/reward ratio.

Nonetheless, at the board meeting we held in New York to approve the transaction I had butterflies in my stomach. Most of my senior management was less than enthusiastic or outright opposed, and as board members they freely expressed their opinions. Their major point was that the New York market was totally different from the southern markets we were used to. Recruiting and managing people would also be different. Shrinkage (loss of merchandise through shoplifting, internal theft, or sloppy bookkeeping), would be higher, vendors would be less flexible about accommodating the new Southern kid on the block, and the competition would be both rougher and less predictable.

The rest of the board saw, as I did, that there were broader isssues than just merchandising and store operations: The tax loss would be a significant strategic advantage, and they felt that our team was smart enough and dedicated enough to learn and master the New York retailing scene. We also had excellent legal advice about how to minimize the risks. In the end, the board voted in favor of the acquisition, and their support enabled me to squelch the butterflies and take the risk.

Financially, the acquisition worked out well. Lafayette never made (or lost) any serious money, but the tax loss shielded more than $39 million in profits from income taxes. At the then-current tax rates (45 percent), the Lafayette losses saved us nearly $18 million in taxes over the next four years. As a result of continued strong earnings and no taxes, our net worth increased from $13 million in the fiscal year that ended March 31, 1981, to $70 million for the fiscal year ended in 1985. That, plus $19 million raised in a 1984 stock offering, brought our net worth to $89 million.

From a store operations standpoint, however, my management

team had been right and the acquisition failed—for interesting reasons. Between 1981, when we completed the acquisition, and 1986, when we departed the New York market, we remodeled all eight of the Lafayette stores we had acquired and added seven more. Average store sales increased from roughly $1 million per store to $4 million. But despite the growth in volume we were still only breaking even.

As senior management had predicted, New York turned out to be a very difficult market. Lots of dealers were selling lower-priced "gray market" goods, that is, goods made for markets other than the United States and without enforceable product warranties. Other dealers charged the 8 percent New York sales tax and never reported or paid it. Many engaged in bait-and-switch tactics or even more egregious forms of consumer deception. And no matter how hard we tried, our gross margins in New York consistently ran 6 percent below our corporate average. That was the difference between an average pretax profit margin and breakeven.

Our major competitor in the market was Crazy Eddie, a publicly traded company. "Crazy Eddie" Antar ran a chain of old-style bait-and-switch shops with a very creative, madcap advertising pitch ("Our prices are insane!") that aired extensively on low-cost, late-night TV. We countered (not very successfully) with an ad campaign that stressed our "no-haggle" policy. Eddie kept reporting pretax earnings in the range of 8 percent while we were just breaking even. True, Crazy Eddie had more stores and a bigger market share than Lafayette did, but we could never figure out how the company was able to make so much money in such a tough market. It took a while to discover our competitor's secret.

The truth came out after we had left the market in 1986: Eddie's financials were fraudulent. For years, as a privately held family run business, it had under-reported income to save on taxes. When the company went public, the family reversed these "reserves" to show greater earnings. In addition, they falsely inflated inventories, hid expenses, and secretly altered their accountants' work papers.[147]

As the law was closing in, Eddie fled the country to avoid indictment. When the dust settled and the litigation ended, it turned out that in the three years prior to our departure Crazy Eddie had reported $30 million in phantom profits when, in fact, the chain was basically breaking even, just like Circuit City!

Fortunately, when we exited the market we were able to cancel or sell our operating leases at a profit, and a number of talented employees agreed to move to other Circuit City locations. While we hadn't made any money operating in New York, our income from the old Lafayette leases more than covered any expenses or loses we incurred, and the tax savings put us in a whole new league.

California Here We Come

They say that luck comes to a prepared mind. Our first Strategic Plan in 1973 had expressed a long-term interest in opening a chain of superstores in Los Angeles. We already had very significant investments in both financial capital and human talent in the licensed departments in Zodys, but despite the obvious appeal of having a chain of superstores in the largest market in the country, we never seriously considered building a chain of our own. Just to get started, we would need at least six to eight well-located stores to spread the huge expense of advertising in LA, and the prospect of assembling multiple stores in a short period of time was both daunting and financially risky.

On the other hand, we were wary of licensed departments. The 1974 bankruptcies of National Bellas Hess, Zodys, and the other landlords that had been the backbone of Wards' initial expansion clearly exposed the vulnerability of being a licensee. Our concern was intensified in 1983 when Zodys filed for the second time. Although their troubles were in Michigan, not Los Angeles, where the stores continued to do well, the instability was unsettling.

One day early in November 1984 I called the general merchandise manager of the Zodys chain to ask if he knew anyone in LA with electronics merchandising experience whom we might hire. He told me that he was about to leave Zodys to take over the liquidation of a substantial chain of Pier One–type stores in LA known as The Akron.

The Akron's talented and creative founders had retired, selling out to a large West Coast drugstore chain. But the chain lacked the entrepreneurial skill for sourcing products in Asia and advertising them cleverly in the States. So, after losing money for a few years, the drug chain sold The Akron to the Hong Kong Chinese family from whom it sourced most of the goods. The family, in turn, installed their twenty-something son in LA as president, and by 1984, they too had also lost a lot of money and wanted out. At this point, although they did not know it, their major assets were the below-market leases for their eighteen large stores in Los Angeles and San Diego.

For me this was the barbershop conversation that Sam had in 1949 when he learned that the South's first TV station was about to open. I immediately called the general manager of our LA division and instructed him to visit each of The Akron stores, grade them as A, B, or C real estate, and pace off the exterior dimensions to estimate the square footage. I got his report two days later: All but one of the stores were in A locations. Some were A+, located on the parking lots of major regional malls. They averaged 25,000 square feet—not ideal, but enough for a superstore.

Three days later Wards' executive vice president, Rick Sharp (more about him shortly), and I were in LA. In the interim we learned that the rents on The Akron stores were seriously below market. Better still, the Chinese family wanted only enough money for the leases to pay off their bank debt of about $5 million.[148] Within a few hours of landing in LA we made a deal to buy the leases, subject to obtaining landlord consent to the transfers. We figured that the rent savings over the next ten years would be between two and three times the purchase price.

Securing landlord consent was one of the more interesting challenges of my career. Each one was different, ranging from a highly professional real estate manager for the AT&T retirement plan with fancy offices in Century City, to a partnership of three Hasidic families living in middle class houses in Pasadena, to a fifty-year-old hippie living in a mansion overlooking the beach in Malibu. Sharp or I visited every one of the landlords over a two-week period. Each had special demands for their consent. With persistence, imagination, and good luck, however, we were able to satisfy their demands and our needs.

The next challenge was remodeling and reopening the stores in time for the 1985 Christmas selling season. Our very able director of construction, Bruce Lucas, agreed to move to LA, and we engaged an imaginative New York architect to help modify the superstore layout and apply it to the LA stores we had just bought. One of the adjustments she suggested was to create the "red tower" entrance. The thirty-seven-foot-high red tower, which ultimately became our trademark, was designed to make the store more identifiable as one drove by in the unending sea of stores and shopping centers that characterized LA.

In November 1985, one year after that first fateful telephone call, we opened seven Circuit City Superstores in LA, followed by twelve more in 1986. Instantly, Circuit City became the leading TV appliance retailer in the market. Within a few years the previously dominant Federated Group was on the ropes and Pacific Stereo closed its sixty-four stores.

It was a busy time, 1985 to '86. As we opened our superstores in LA, we also exited the thirty-nine Zodys licensed departments and the fifteen Lafayette stores in New York. At the same time we added ten East Coast superstores in addition to the nineteen in LA. Departing Zodys had long been a goal, but we had been held back by the departments' profit contribution and the large investment we had in the talented people in that market. Being able to utilize their talents in a market-dominant chain of superstores was a dream come true.

Exiting Lafayette was emotionally more difficult. We had made great progress, but the cutthroat New York market was so different from our experiences elsewhere in the country that we had not yet figured out how to make a profit and still uphold our values of treating customers and employees fairly. Quitting after less than five years was anathema to us, but if we were to open superstores in LA we needed to free up some cash, shake loose some key personnel, and remove any distractions. Given those needs, the decision was easy.

The short-term impact on our stock price, however, was substantial. Wards stock dropped by 40 percent, from a high of $31 in the fourth quarter of 1985 to a low of $18.63 in the third quarter of 1986.[149] Numerous Wall Street analysts, and even Wards executives with stock options that were now underwater, came to me with concerns about our decision to close Lafayette and open in LA. I told them that if they were in the stock for the short run, they could be right. But, I said, I was not selling my stock and if our decision to leave New York and go to LA was strategically correct, as I believed it was, we would see the stock rebound and grow well beyond what we would achieve on our present course.

The double shuffle, out of Zodys and Lafayette and into the LA superstores, turned out to be a good move. We traded $150 million of marginally profitable sales (Lafayette's $60 million and Zodys' $90 million) for more than $200 million of highly profitable sales in the initial nineteen LA superstores. Fortunately, we were able to transfer all the capable Lafayette people who wanted to stay with the company, as well as sell or move our inventory and sublease the Lafayette real estate, all so as not to lose money on our exit.

Change at the Top: Theory

By 1981 I had been at Wards for fifteen years. I had enjoyed my time with the company enormously and was proud of what we had accomplished. But several things were gnawing at me. First, I felt my learning curve had flattened out. The first time I oversaw the building of a superstore or a warehouse it was an enormous challenge. The same was true for planning our first stock offering as a public company or designing a health benefits or retirement package. In each case, there was a lot to learn. The second and third time, I would refine what we had done previously, but by the time we opened our tenth or twentieth superstore, for example, the process had become pretty routine. The same was true for many of the other issues I dealt with on a recurring basis. Simplifying the company had its obvious advantages, but running a more streamlined company was somehow less interesting and less challenging than furiously restructuring to ward off bankruptcy or buying Lafayette.

Equally, or more important, I didn't feel that I was making a positive difference in the world. Selling electronics equipment cheaper and more profitably than others gave employment to thousands and consumer satisfaction to millions, but I did not believe I was making the world a better place. I had long thought of public service as something that would be more fulfilling, and at age forty-eight I thought it was time to start planning my exit strategy. All of the strategic issues that got the company into trouble in the '70s had been resolved and we had a clear plan, a strong team, and a fair wind at our backs.

From a financial standpoint, the timing also seemed right. I had a large enough nest egg to pursue public service, possibly teaching or doing other, lower-paying jobs without financial strain. And I no longer felt a sense of obligation to run the company. None of my children were interested in joining the business, and by this time the various new stock offerings to raise money for expansion, along with some sales to further diversify our assets, had reduced the Wurtzel family holdings in Wards to less than 15 percent. It was now truly a public company.

Finally, I was beginning to feel that I had a tiger by the tail and it was running me, rather than vice versa. In retrospect, I suspect that my hands-on management style was no longer appropriate to the size of the organization. From the beginning, I had felt I needed to be involved in every area where I could make a difference. Pretty soon, however, in areas such as accounting or merchandising or store operations, I was largely hands-off. I was confident that in these areas we had excellent leadership, better qualified than I, and that my contributions would be marginal at best. In other areas, such as MIS (management information systems), real estate, and distribution, I took a more active role. With hindsight, I now understand that it would have been wiser to hire stronger people for these functions and delegate more authority. But at the time I had not learned that lesson. For all these reasons, I was ready to move on.

Still, I was not going to resign without hiring and training a successor. When I shared my thoughts with various directors, their response was uniform: It would be hard to hire a truly capable person because, given my relatively young age, the candidate would never believe that when the time came, I would actually leave. One day I was having lunch with the CEO of a moderate-sized local business who was a prospective candidate for our board of directors. When I asked, he told me that he would not be available until a certain date three years in the future. And when I expressed surprise that he would know his availability so far down the road, he explained that this was the date he would turn sixty and retire. In order to recruit a successor and prepare the organization for the transition, he said, he needed to set a specific date. Otherwise, they would not believe he was serious.

I got it. I walked back to the office and wrote a letter to my board saying that I was going to retire within the next five years. In the interim, I would find and train a successor. If I failed to find the right person the first time, I would do it again. But I told the board I was serious about making a change and would not run the company indefinitely. They had no choice but to go along.

Improving the Infrastructure

As I searched for the right successor, I continued to focus on running the business. As we rolled out the superstores and ramped up our sales, we increasingly realized that we needed to beef up our distribution systems, our computer-based information systems, and our personnel policies and practices.

At its heart, retailing is about having the right product in the right place at the right price, and having the right level of service to meet or exceed customer expectations. Equally important is getting the goods from the factory to the consumer at the lowest possible cost. Efficiency obviously affects the profits of any retailer, but for retailers who market themselves as discounters and for whom beating the competition's price is an essential part of the offering, keeping costs down is even more critical.

Strengthening MIS

Starting in the late 1970s, IBM and others had been rolling out store POS (point of sale) cash registers that not only kept track of the money but also captured the unique number of each brand and model sold, known as an "SKU" (stock-keeping unit), making it much easier to manage inventory quickly and accurately.

That worked for many retailers. However, at that time, POS registers could only capture numbers and not letters, and I was concerned about possible errors and confusion if our salespeople and cashiers had to translate an alpha-numeric model number they used every day, such as WHI 9170 CPR (for a Whirlpool seventeen-cubic-foot refrigerator in copper) or PAN 3065 M (for a Panasonic thirty-amp receiver), into nine- or ten-digit number that meant nothing to them or the customer.

So I looked around for an alternative. Our MIS director put out a request for proposal (RFP) to which Hewlett-Packard responded, telling us of an entrepreneur who had built, out of readily available components, a cheap, "dumb" point-of-sale terminal that could handle both alphabetic and numeric input. The terminal had no memory or computing power. It connected to a proprietary store controller that could talk to a mid-sized HP mainframe computer in our office. Best of all, it handled data in real time while most POS terminals transmitted sales information only at night. And it did all this quite economically because it transmitted information from six or eight stores on a single dedicated phone line. It sounded like a system tailored perfectly for our needs.

The entrepreneur in question lived in Potomac, Maryland, and his first installation was up and running in a chain of catalog showrooms in the greater Washington area. His name was Rick Sharp, which brings me back to the topic of finding a successor.

I had begun my search by looking inside the company. But of my top management team, only one was interested, and he had some health issues that took him out of the running. So I engaged a major executive search firm. After four or five months we had still not come up with a candidate with whom I, my board, and the senior management were comfortable. One candidate impressed me all the way to the final salary negotiation. He was an older gentleman who had extensive retail experience with some big chains, but when it came to working out his compensation, he was too anxious. I figured if he could not negotiate a good deal for himself, he would probably not do well for the company. So we started over.

Fundamentally, I believe that retailing is not rocket science. If I could learn to be a retail CEO, lots of others could as well. I believed the essential characteristics for success in my job were intelligence, reasonable people skills, willingness to work hard, and ambition to succeed.

Rick Sharp, the point-of-sale entrepreneur whom I had come to know as we worked together to install the MIS system he had designed, met all of these criteria. He had grown up in Maryland, the son of a middle-management executive at the U.S. Department of Agriculture. Following high school, he went to the University of

Virginia but stayed only one year. He was interested in computer science, which the university did not then offer, so he dropped out of UVA and arranged to join the Air Force with the understanding that he would be assigned to Wright Paterson Air Force Base, which housed one of the country's largest computers in an air-conditioned hangar. Early computers were based on vacuum tubes, which generated so much heat that they had to be constantly cooled. Today's cell phone has more capacity than those old vacuum tube computers, but, at the time, the Air Force base was a great place to learn computer science from the ground up.

Following his military service, Sharp went to work as a computer analyst for Blue Cross, quickly showing them how to save millions by increasing the capacity of their existing equipment rather than upgrading or adding new machines. As a reward they gave him a token salary increase. Thinking this was a poor trade-off, Rick struck out on his own, founding a highly successful computer consulting and custom software development firm. His business was soon acquired by a much larger company, and

Richard Sharp – circa 1986

Sharp was not happy being a vice president without an important role to play, so he quit and retired to play tennis while he looked around for new business opportunities. That is when he came to my attention.

Knowing how bright he was and believing that he had the other essential characteristics to be a retail executive, I proposed that he move to Richmond and come to work for Wards. I promised him, as my father had promised me, that if he learned the business I would retire in five years and turn the company over to him as CEO. After he met with the board and the management team, all concerned agreed to my plan. So Rick came on board in 1982 as executive vice president with responsibility for MIS, service and distribution (his natural strengths), and the Zodys stores in LA.

Strengthening Distribution

His first assignment was to study our distribution systems and design one for a large (225,000-square-foot) warehouse we had just purchased in Doswell, Virginia. Since he had never worked on a distribution project, he hired a top-notch consultant and together they designed and installed a state-of-the-art system.

Instead of picking the merchandise off the warehouse shelves for one store at a time, as we had done previously, the new system organized the picking in waves of eight stores. It printed a shipping label for each item, organized by where that brand and model (SKU) was located in the warehouse. A picker systematically went past each stack of merchandise in logical order and picked enough of the identical SKUs for eight stores at a time. He then applied the preprinted store-destination labels and placed the items on a conveyor belt. A scanner read the labels and each box was shunted down one of eight conveyors that took it to the truck assigned to deliver to that store. It was a brilliant system that saved lots of time and labor and reduced picking errors.

Between the new distribution system and the new computerized store controllers that allowed a salesperson to write up the sales ticket on any one of the many terminals scattered throughout each store, we were well on the way to having one of the most advanced integrated supply-chain management systems in retailing. For every item sold, the computer generated a list of what needed to be shipped to each store to replenish its inventory. That, in turn, reduced the distribution center inventory, which at a certain point, alerted the buyer for that category to place an order with the manufacturer to replenish the distribution center's stock.

Knowing what you have on hand and where it is located in real time provides enormous benefits to any retail organization. Merchants can monitor what is selling and reorder just in time. Warehouses and stores no longer need to keep large "safety stocks" on hand. Faster inventory turns mean less inventory on hand, and thus a better return on investment.

Automating this circle, from selling floor to store replenishment to merchandising staff and back to warehouse replenishment, is routine in contemporary retailing, but in 1983, when the

Automated distribution center – from the 1992 annual report

entire system was up and running, it was far ahead of its time. In those days only Walmart was as dedicated to keeping costs low with excellent logistics. An efficient supply chain enabled us to reduce costs below those of most, if not all, of our competitors. That in turn enabled us to deliver on the mutually contradictory promises of lowest cost and best service.

Strengthening Human Resources

Although the personnel policies Sam had established continued to be at the heart of what we believed and did, in 1975 I had reluctantly terminated Larry Yoffy, co-architect of those policies, to save money during our "time of troubles." Larry remained a consultant, and I became, in effect, the VP of personnel, assisted by a staff to carry out the essential functions. As soon as we could afford it, however, we needed to get some professional HR help.

Sometime in 1984 I attended a seminar at the University of Virginia on the topic of Managing Organizational Stress. It was taught by Bill Zierden, a Naval Academy graduate and former "Rickover protégé,"[150] who was a tenured professor at the Darden School of Business at UVA. I was so impressed by the seminar that I asked Zierden if he knew anyone who would be qualified to become our VP of human resources, or if he might be interested himself. To my delight he was interested in moving from academia to a company where he could put theory into practice.

In 1984, we had more than 2,900 employees and were growing fast. Under Zierden's leadership the company scaled up and improved virtually all its personnel practices. Some of Sam's practices had slipped during the lean years. Under Zierden, sales and management training were strengthened and made more rigorous. Coffee Conferences[151] were once again held on a regular basis. Recruiting top talent was emphasized, and a staff was created to assist line management in carrying out their personnel functions on a timely and ethical basis. In order to focus accountability for store results squarely on the store operations team, they, not human resources, retained full responsibility and authority to hire, fire, promote, and counsel employees. HR was there to aid and assist in these functions but did not have the final say.

One of Zierden's important contributions was to open up a male-dominated organization to opportunities for women on all levels from the sales floor to middle management, although putting women in top management positions was still a few years away. [152] Having progressive personnel policies that were regularly implemented and monitored was just as crucial to our success as state-of-the-art MIS or distribution systems

Bill Zierden – circa 1983

A New Name

As a result of this attention to the infrastructure and the new store formats, Wards had come a long way from the early 1970s. Sales for fiscal year 1985 were more than $500 million and earnings were about $20 million. Given the fact that the company served millions of Americans in nearly one hundred stores from coast to coast, it seemed appropriate that the stock trade under the same name as the stores. Therefore, in 1984 the company asked shareholders to authorize a change of name from Wards Company to Circuit City Stores, Inc. At the same time we announced that the company would move from the AMEX to the New York Stock Exchange, two shifts that increased the attention of the financial markets.

Change at the Top: Practice

At the annual meeting in June of 1986 I stepped down as CEO and turned the baton over to Sharp, while I remained on the board as Chairman. By the end of that fiscal year, in February 1987, Circuit City passed the $1 billion mark in sales. The 53 superstores averaged $14.6 million, with some exceeding $25 million. Sales per square foot were a remarkable $1,237.[153] The 37 all-electronics Circuit City stores averaged $7 million. Over the previous five years same-store sales had grown roughly 300 percent, [154] compared to industry growth of 56 percent. And we were adversely impacting same-store sales by adding more than twenty superstores per year, primarily in existing markets.

Earnings for that year were $35 million, and return on equity, which had recently averaged in the low 20s, hit 27 percent. Stockholder's equity rose to $149 million. Earnings per share jumped from the high teens (16 to 19 cents) in the early 1980s, to 99 cents in 1986 and $2.75 in 1988. For the five years between 1983 and 1987, we had the highest return to investors of any company

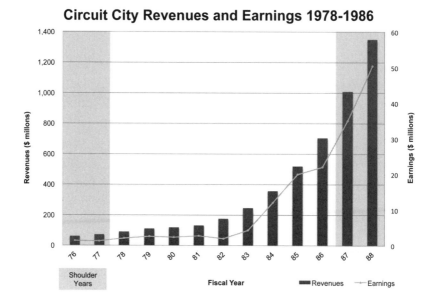

Circuit City Revenues and Earnings 1978-1986

listed on the New York Stock Exchange.[155]

Sadly, one year before we hit the billion-dollar landmark, both Sam Wurtzel and his partner Abe Hecht passed away. Only Sam had foreseen, many years earlier, even when the company was floundering, that it would one day reach a billion in sales. He would have been proud. And Hecht, who was always the cautious one, would have been both surprised and delighted in equal measure. Thirty-seven years after its founding, the company was far and away the largest and most successful retailer of brand-name electronics and appliances in the country, and I left confident that it was in good hands with an open road ahead.

Habits of Mind

Boldly Follow Through: *Big ideas require bold leadership and attract loyal followers. The effort comes to naught if the execution is tentative or not well disciplined.*

Closing all the Dixie and Custom Hi-Fi stores in and around

Washington, D.C., and opening six new all-electronics stores with a new name and a new format was a big idea. Likewise, taking the best of Levitz and Kennedy & Cohen to create a Circuit City TV and appliance warehouse showroom was a big idea that caught the imagination of the public. We were able to make both these formats successful because they met the needs of consumers and we executed them with energy and clarity.

Pass the Torch with Care: *Succession is critical. Most companies cannot withstand successive top management failures. CEOs need to select and groom their successor with care. Boards need to be bold enough to replace the CEO when necessary and to take the time to be sure the right successor is in place.*

The tradition that my father started and I continued—to train a successor and stay on as chairman of the board after retiring as CEO—contributed to seamless leadership transitions. By the time I, and later Sharp, became CEO, we each knew the company well enough to stay true to its culture while integrating our own visions. And just as my father could respectfully share with fellow board members his concerns if he thought I was veering off track, I could do the same when Sharp became CEO.

Focus on the Future: *Manage for the long term and not the short. Don't let short-term earnings swings divert a long-term strategy. Ignore the skeptics and short-term market swings. If things go well, the value of your company, whether public or private, will respond over time.*

While a bit trite, the importance of investing and reinvesting in your business cannot be overstated. In the 1970s and '80s, when we developed state-of-the art inventory management and distribution systems, our NATM peers thought we were foolish to pour so much money into back-office functions. In fact, the improvements to our infrastructure enabled us to grow much faster and more profitably than we would have if we had not been ahead of the curve. Much the same can be said for the substantial investments we made to find, train, and engage smart and committed people at all levels of the organization. As our peers grew, many of them faltered over managing people or inventory at a distance.

Another example of focusing on the future is when Circuit City decided to quit Lafayette and open Circuit City stores in Los Angeles. The stock market did not respond well. Nonetheless, we plowed ahead, believing that if we were making the right strategic move, the stock price would take care of itself. Sure enough, by 1987, Circuit City stock had provided investors the highest five-year return of any company on the New York Stock Exchange.

Lessons Learned

Know When to Hold and When to Fold: Exiting the New York market was both necessary and wise. It was necessary not to be stretched too thin as we entered Los Angeles. It was also wise because long-term prospects to make a decent return in New York were limited. At the time, I was tempted to hang in there and prove that the decision to enter the market had been the right one. In hindsight, five years of breaking even should have been enough to convince me to fold and get out.

Strategic Plans Are Road Maps, Not Straightjackets: Early in this period, having a plan allowed us to focus on rolling out the all-electronics Circuit City stores and then the Circuit City Superstores without distraction or diversions.

Both the Lafayette acquisition and the purchase of The Akron chain in Los Angles were unplanned serendipitous opportunities. The planning process, however, enabled us to understand the contribution the Lafayette tax losses would make to the building of our financial base. The desirability of opening superstores in LA had already been stated in the 1973 Plan. At that time, however, we had not yet seen a path to get there.

Chapter Eight

GOING NATIONAL

Too many people think only of their own profit. But business opportunity seldom knocks on the door of self-centered people. No customer ever goes to a store merely to please the storekeeper.

— Kazuo Inamori

Growth for the sake of growth is the ideology of the cancer cell.

— Edward Abbey

In his first annual report as CEO, Sharp laid out his vision of where the company was headed. Fortunately, he had an excellent economic climate in which to pursue this vision. Gross domestic product doubled between 1987 and 2000. While growth rates fluctuated, the overall gains were excellent.

This strong economy, continued product innovation, and price declines led to unprecedented growth of consumer electronics sales. Between 1987 and 2000, factory shipments tripled from $33 to $99 billion.

Sharp's Vision

While Sharp endorsed the principal strategies of the prior five years, there were some differences in emphasis. First and foremost, Sharp was interested in rapid growth. He believed that the way to accomplish this was for the company to achieve and hold the **dominant market share** in each market in which it operated; to rapidly add **more markets** to get **first-mover advantage**; to provide each customer with a **superior shopping experience**;

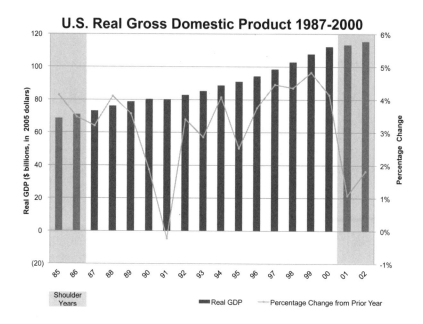

U.S. Real Gross Domestic Product 1987-2000

and to provide **superior credit availability**—all of which were designed to achieve **superior gross margins** while **utilizing technology** to control costs and improve decision making. Each bold-type item above was an important component of his strategy.

Dominant Market Share

Sharp believed that a dominant market share leverages advertising, distribution, and supervision costs. Hence, a "[s]trong market penetration makes us more cost effective....This and other efficiencies permit us to keep our prices low while investing in additional customer services. The result is even better values and deeper market penetration...[that] allows us to achieve above average profitability." This virtual cycle "underwrites its own reinforcement and perpetuation." [156]

Market-related operating efficiency came primarily from advertising, whose cost in those days was generally 5 to 6 percent of sales, or 20-plus percent of gross margin. A larger market share provided a larger sales base over which to spread that cost, as

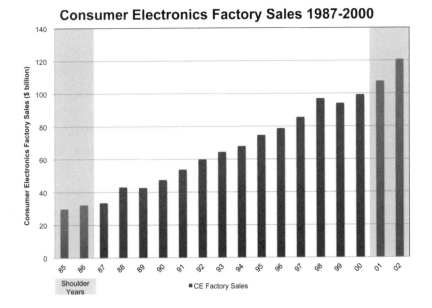

Consumer Electronics Factory Sales 1987-2000

well as greater leverage in negotiating media pricing. To achieve dominant market share, the company needed quickly to optimize the number of stores in each market.

Sharp defined "dominant" as not less than 15 percent of all TV and appliance sales and at least 50 percent more than the nearest competitor in each market, except in major metropolitan centers where there could be two market leaders. Once Circuit City exited Lafayette (NY) and the Zodys stores (LA) and opened Circuit City Superstores in LA, it had a dominant market share everywhere it operated.

More Markets

At the end of 1986, the company was nationwide but not national. It operated stores in eleven southern states and California. But with no stores between the Southeast and California, it served only 13 percent of the U.S. population. Sharp's first annual report laid out a very aggressive growth plan: to double sales in three years. He recognized that the explosive sales growth of the early '80s, driven in large part by VCR, digital audio, and microwave product introductions, had slowed. Accordingly, ambitious growth had to be based on opening more stores rather than dramatically escalating sales in existing stores. While he planned to add stores in existing markets as needed, his primary expansion emphasis was on adding new markets.

In 1987 the company entered San Francisco, Baltimore, and Memphis. In the following three years it added Miami, Philadelphia, and San Diego. At the same time, it replaced the all-electronics stores in existing markets, including Washington, D.C., and Atlanta, with superstores. By 1990 Circuit City had achieved Sharp's initially announced goal of $2 billion in sales. It operated 125 superstores, more than double the number that existed when he took charge, and twenty-three all-electronics stores, ten fewer.

In the ensuing five years (1991–95) sales nearly tripled, from just over $2 billion to $5.5 billion. During that period, the company added 187 superstores, bringing the total to 312. Adding an average of thirty-seven new superstores per year was an aggressive growth strategy. By 1995 Circuit City was in eighty-one markets in twenty-eight states. Except for the upper Midwest (the Dakotas, Montana, Idaho, and Iowa), it was in a major city in every contiguous state except Colorado, Michigan, Connecticut, and New York. New stores in all those states were scheduled for the following year. In 1994, the company announced an accelerated expansion program to add 180 stores in three years, nearly double the previous rate, which would bring the company into every major U.S. market, including New York City. In addition, it planned twenty smaller superstores to serve smaller trade areas.

First-Mover Advantage

This rapid growth was predicated on Sharp's belief that it was important to get first-mover advantage in markets not yet "occupied" by one or more competitors. By being the first big-box TV and appliance retailer in a particular location, Circuit City would have the first shot at prime real estate, dominating the airwaves and print media and establishing a leading market share without the more difficult challenge of having to take business away from a strong competitor. Theoretically, the "first kid on the block" could also intimidate others from entering that market, at least for a time.

In larger markets these advantages were predicated on multiple stores. Multiple stores were necessary in order to spread the very substantial advertising cost, and that put pressure on the company to find the land and build the stores within a short time frame. For a decade or more this aggressive growth plan was highly successful. But what neither Sharp nor I realized at the time was that we were actually creating serious problems for the future.

Downside of Rapid Growth

Real estate decisions are among the most important that retailers make. A multimillion-dollar mistake in the purchase of merchandise can hurt for a few months or a year while you sell out of it. A bad real estate decision, however, lasts for decades. That is why, during the time I was CEO, I personally visited every proposed new location and approved the deal before we bought or leased it. Sharp initially did the same, but as the numbers grew, he needed to delegate more.

Good real estate is not always available when and where you want it. As any developer can tell you, assembling a package of top-flight locations in a particular market can take years. If, in addition, you have parameters as to how much you are willing to spend, the challenge to do it quickly becomes even greater. Given the operating need to cover advertising expenses with multiple stores as quickly as possible, Circuit City sometimes settled for less-than-superior locations. In a new market, for example, we might find one or two A locations right away and then have to add two B locations in order to reach the critical mass we thought we needed to open.

Being more patient and running one or two stores in a four-store market until we found better locations would have made more long-range sense but would have reduced earnings in the short run. By announcing in advance to Wall Street that we planned to open thirty, forty, or fifty stores next year, we had put ourselves under a lot of pressure. Wall Street's relentless demand that public companies show earnings growth every quarter, and that every projection come true, sometimes forced us to make hasty, suboptimal real estate decisions.

In the early days of TV and appliance warehouse showrooms (1980 to 1990), when competition was limited, a key driver in selecting store locations was cost. Sharp and I believed that all Circuit City needed was a destination location, not necessarily at the crossroads of Main and Main, but within easy reach of a regionally accessible interstate highway interchange and, ideally, near a regional mall. Given all the advertising we did, we believed that consumer awareness was high enough, and what we were offering compelling enough, that customers would make an effort to find us. Moreover, our expensive, high-tech store layouts, with every product displayed and operable, and knowledgeable, highly trained sales staff always available, were big expenses that cheaper land could help to offset.

As the race for market share heated up, however, reliance on B locations proved problematic. In many cases, competitors who entered a market five or ten years after we did were able to locate in the newest, hottest mall area that had been totally undeveloped when we built. They were sometimes also willing to pay more. Down the road, as Best Buy's average store sales began to exceed ours, they could afford to pay more dollars and still have the rent be a comparable percentage of sales. And even the locations that were excellent when we acquired them inevitably deteriorated over time as cities and suburbs changed.

The second questionable decision Sharp and I made was to finance the stores with long-term leases. In terms of accounting, a twenty-year lease was not classified as a liability on the balance sheet. In retrospect, we gave that factor too much importance. Whether shown on the balance sheet or just in the footnotes, our longer-term leases were still a financial obligation, and hence seen as a "liability" by any sophisticated lender or analyst. Investors in sale-and-leasebacks liked long-term leases because they did not have to worry about a vacancy for many years, but the inflexibility of these long-term deals often became a problem for us as cities grew and prime shopping areas changed.

Finally, we mistakenly built quite inflexible, high-tech, high-touch stores with relatively large warehouses and relatively compact selling floors. The sales floors were tightly packed with many specialty fixtures designed to display the goods to their best advantage. That approach proved to be shortsighted in two respects. As products proliferated and shrank in size and cost, we needed to move to self-service, preferably with shopping carts. This required a larger selling floor and less warehouse space. To make this change, we would have to, at considerable expense, demol-

Specialty camcorder display – 1997

ish, move, and rebuild the fire wall that separated the warehouse from the selling floor and to light and air-condition the new sales space. In addition, the high-tech single-purpose fixtures became obsolete sooner than we had anticipated as new products emerged and customer tastes changed.

When these problems were identified in the mid-1990s, correcting them would have required a significant capital investment. As we will see, Circuit City in the late 1990s and early 2000s preferred to use its capital to build new stores and repurchase its stock, rather than to reconfigure old stores. Deferring corrective action simply magnified the problem.

Superior Customer-Buying Experience

Sharp believed that the best way to gain market share and maximize profits was to add value to the process of buying and selling all along the chain of distribution from manufacturer to consumer.

First and foremost was value for the consumer. Sharp reaffirmed the company's 4-S policy and raised the ante. He added Speed to Savings, Selection, Service, and Satisfaction. To reinforce our already fierce commitment to customer service, he loudly trumpeted the price guarantee policy ("If you can buy it for less within thirty days we will refund the difference plus 10 percent of the difference") and implemented a "No Hassle" return policy that guaranteed any product could be returned within thirty days for any reason or no reason, plus a "No Lemon" policy, promising a free replacement if the product needed more than two repairs the first year.

To ensure that Circuit City was keeping the promise of its new advertising slogan— "Circuit City, Where Service Is State of the Art"—he implemented an extensive, in-depth telephone survey of 25,000 purchasers per month (300,000 per year) to find out what, if any defects there were in our delivery of the five S's. Any complaint was quickly addressed, the employee involved was counseled on how to avoid such problems in the future, and the customer was advised of the action taken.

Over time, other consumer benefits were added. Home deliveries in larger markets were made available in the evenings and on Sundays. To make good on the commitment to service, Circuit City opened thirty-five state-of-the-art regional service centers, which would efficiently repair a customer's defective merchandise and return it to the store within a week for the customer to pick up. Large appliances and console TVs were repaired in the home by trained Circuit City technicians.

Fundamental to the "high-touch, high-service" approach was a redoubled commitment to sales training. No salesman could earn commission on his sales until he had completed a week of classroom training, two weeks of apprenticeship on the sales floor, and had passed a computerized test of product knowledge and selling skills.

Answer City

Late in the decade, Sharp set up a state-of-the-art telephone service center called Answer City to respond to consumers' questions about their products, including computers and other digital equipment. With complex electronics items, a lot of customer satisfaction or dissatisfaction lay not in the equipment but in the customer's understanding of how to operate it, so Answer City met a strong customer need and eliminated a number of service requests.

By the time the system was ready to go national, however, the company was feeling the pinch of competition. Believing that the cost outweighed the benefits, Sharp discontinued the Answer City. Ten years later, Best Buy acquired a small company called the Geek Squad, which went one step beyond Answer City and, for a fee, sent a technician to the customer's home or office for hands-on installation and instruction. In 2005 Circuit City responded with essentially the same offering and called it Firedog. Answer

City may have been too expensive to maintain, and it was clearly ahead of its time in trying to meet an important consumer need. Had we persisted, it had the potential to become an important difference maker between Circuit City and its competitors, and, like Firedog and the Geek Squad, Circuit City might have been able to charge for the service.

Superior Credit Availability

Credit had always been an issue for Wards/Circuit City. In the early days, before credit cards, my mother supervised the arduous task of bundling customer credit applications with their credit history and their time-payment sales contracts and sending the package to a local bank. Part of her job was to convince the bank to take marginal credits so that Wards could make the sale. By the mid-'60s, consumer credit was transformed by the emergence of large organizations owned and operated by big banks, GE Capital, and other financial institutions. Later on, credit cards replaced time-payment contracts for all but the most major purchases. There is an inherent tension between a seller, who would give anyone credit in order to make a sale, and the lender, who needs to be repaid. Each of the big credit organizations had its own ebb and flow of enthusiasm for buying consumer paper from electronics and appliance retailers. In the late '80s and early '90s, as the economy weakened, lenders became increasingly conservative in extending credit. After being alternately wooed and ignored by GE and then Barclays Bank, Sharp decided that by using computer technology Circuit City could eliminate the third party, extend credit, and manage the losses in-house. He had prior experience running an online system for guaranteeing merchants the validity of customer checks and felt that credit cards were a similar logistical challenge. Despite some trepidation on the part of the board, and especially our local banker, he decided to move ahead with the plan and assigned the project to his new CFO, Mike Chalifoux, who did a brilliant job of setting up and managing the credit operation, in addition to his CFO duties.

In 1990, the company filed for a national credit card bank charter under the grandiose name First North American National Bank. By interfacing with Circuit City's POS system and credit information available from credit service providers, the bank developed a comprehensive online system for credit scoring (in other words, deciding whether and how much to extend credit based on the customer's credit history), authorizing the credit, and billing. Within three years, there were hundreds of thousands of Circuit City customers with private label credit cards and more than $450 million in outstanding credit receivables.[157] The receivables were "securitized" and 90 percent sold to financial buyers, thus removing them from the balance sheet. While Circuit City continued to service the paper, it retained only 10 percent, thus exposing itself to only a small portion of the potential loss.

Strategically, it was an excellent move. Credit approval rates were higher than under GE or Barclays, and the losses were well within projections. Being able to make the credit decision within the context of the product's profitability to the company and importance to the consumer and was a strategic advantage.[158] Circuit City might, for example, be willing the take more of a credit risk on a higher-margin and/or "necessary" product, such as a refrigerator, that the customer would not want to have repossessed for nonpayment.

In 1993, ecstatic over the success of the private label credit card, Sharp and Chalifoux expanded their credit operation to include generic (or unbranded) Visa and MasterCards, useable anywhere. The generic cards had no strategic significance for Circuit City and tied up capital, but they did make use of the credit card bank's expertise, and initially they made money. Within two years, credit card receivables doubled to over $1 billion, and by 2000, they had grown to $2.8 billion.[159,160]

In order to conceal how profitable First North American National Bank was from competitors and Wall Street analysts, and to avoid having to meet the SEC rules for reporting the bank as a separate "line of business," Sharp took the position that bank credit was part of the retail business. He applied the bank profit to reduce general operating expenses, thus inflating the apparent profitability of the stores. For fiscal 1996 and 1997, the only years for which numbers are available, the bank's pretax contributions were 34 percent and 55 percent, respectively, of the Circuit City stores' pretax earnings.[161]

The numbers were so secret that, aside from Sharp and his CFO, none of the operating executives were aware of the magnitude of the bank's earnings. Even the board got to see the numbers only at the end of each year when a piece of paper was quickly passed out and collected, and, starting in 1994, in greater detail every other year as part of the new Three Year Plan.

The only time the bank's profitability was made public was in 2004, after the credit card business was sold. That year, Circuit City disclosed that the generic credit card business had earned $67.7 million, pretax, in 2002 and $26.5 million, pretax, in 2003.[162] The private-label credit business contributed an additional $30 million each year.[163] Taken together, this means the company had been generating somewhere in the range of $55 to $90 million in pretax earnings from the generic and private-label card operations. For five fiscal years, ending in 2004, the company earned an average of $82.3 million pretax. Assuming that the bank profits for those years were comparable to 2002 and 2003, the credit bank accounted for most of Circuit City's profits!

Though my assumptions and estimates may not be perfect, the point is that in the 1990s and early 2000s, the bank's profits were concealing the stores' true operating results. Middle management thought the stores were doing much better than Best Buy, when in fact, without the bank, they were doing no better or worse. In addition to fooling the competition and the Street, the company was, by withholding the bulk of this information from both the board and most senior management, also fooling itself. Like most self-deception, this strategy turned out to have serious consequences.

Superior Gross Margins

In order to pay for all these added values for customers, Sharp and his team believed they needed to maintain and, if possible, improve the gross margins at which goods were sold. During the '90s, many of Circuit City's competitors were reporting lower earnings as a result of eroding gross margins. Sharp was determined not to let this happen.

The principal reason for his emphasis on sales training was his desire to sell higher-margin products. As before, the 1990 Annual Report said, "Our buyers choose those products that supply the best features at each price *while also meeting Circuit City's standards for profitability* [emphasis added]."[164] By this, Sharp was actually articulating a continued commitment to step-up selling and a strong commitment to selling extended service policies (ESPs). In some cases, the bottom line profit on the ESP was as great as, or greater than, the profit on the merchandise itself.

In looking for margin, Circuit City did not, however, compromise on its commitment to be price-competitive. It maintained its long-standing policy of empowering local managers to set competitive prices and meet the price of any legitimate competitor. Nonetheless, Circuit City was generally a price follower: It was rarely the first to lower the prevailing price. On the other hand, the ability to sell more highly featured and higher-margin products was a definite competitive advantage. In addition to better profits, this gave Circuit City access to better brands, better pricing, and more of the intangible "goodies" a manufacturer can bestow, including greater availability of hot new models and/or products in short supply.

These were the policies Sam first established and I had perpetuated. At the time they had made sense for major appliances and big-ticket electronics. But the times were about to change.

Drawbacks to "Margin Mania"

In the '80s and even more so in the '90s, electronics prices were plunging like Niagara Falls. Between 1991 and 1994, after several years of price warfare in PCs, the price of a middle-of-the-line IBM computer fell from about $3,500 to $1,500.[165] VCR prices, which had averaged around $400 in 1986, leveled off at $150 by the mid-'90s.[166] There was also an explosion of smaller, lower-priced electronics products, including portable music players (Walkmans, portable CD players, and, later, iPods), small screen TVs, home phones and answering machines, portable radios, compact stereo systems (boom boxes), video game consoles and games, and prerecorded music in both tape and CD formats. All of these dropped significantly in price after their initial introduction.

They also became very familiar to consumers, who were often buying them for the second or third time. As a result, sales assistance was generally not needed and sometimes unwelcome. Most of Circuit City's competitors treated these smaller, less expensive products as self-service items. They were set out in large floor displays (bulk-outs) from which customers would pick up what they wanted and take it to a central checkout. Sales personnel were available to answer questions, but one did not need to deal with a salesperson to purchase these bulked-out items.

At Circuit City there was no central checkout. Sales personnel handled all sales for two reasons: The system provided an opportunity for step-up selling and for selling ESPs. Even on low-cost items (such as a $129 boom box from Panasonic and a similar one from Sony) there could well be a 5 or 10 percent (or greater) difference in gross profit difference. If so, salesmen were incentivized to sell the Panasonic, knowing that their commission would be higher. They were also well compensated for selling an extended service policy. Both these margin-enhancing opportunities might have been lost or diminished if a customer could pick up a product, as in a supermarket, and take it to a central checkout.

Sharp's preoccupation with margin also manifested itself in product selection. I had long believed that if you were in the electronics business you needed to both carry a full line of the relevant products and be highly price competitive. Back in the heyday of catalog showrooms like Best Products and Service Merchandise, we went toe-to-toe on audio even if we lost money on Pioneer and other promotional brands. We, like any successful discounter, could not take margin *percentages* to the bank, only *dollars*. So selling a reasonable amount at a lower margin was generally better than making far fewer sales at a greater gross profit.

Sharp marched to a different drummer. He tried hard to avoid low-margin goods. For example, the company carried virtually no video game players or games, a big volume category for our competitors. Similarly, Circuit City was slow to carry CDs, and, when it did carry them, its selection was not as broad or deep as others. In the process of avoiding low-margin products, Circuit City made younger customers, to whom games and CDs especially appealed, believe that it was not as relevant as some competitors were.

There was a brief period in the mid-1990s when Circuit City managed to lure CD customers back from Best Buy by selling discs at a super-promotional price of $9.99. However, after 1995, when Best Buy was in deep financial trouble, Circuit City thought it was safe to let CD prices return to their original $11.99 and $12.99 price points. At least one former Circuit City executive believes this move relieved significant margin pressure on Best Buy and facilitated its survival.[167]

Even more important, for most of the '90s Circuit City intentionally deemphasized home computers. Sharp, despite being a computer visionary, was initially skeptical that home computers would ever become a mass-market product. In a sense he knew too much and was too far ahead of his time. He believed that it was a waste of resources for every home to have its own computer. It would be much more efficient to share hardware and software resources online. In that scenario, home computers would be just a keyboard and a screen, with all the software and data on one or more giant hard drives somewhere on the Internet, ready to be accessed online. Essentially, Sharp was foreseeing cloud computing twenty or more years before it became generally available. By the same token, he also thought that CDs would soon be extinct, because music could be more cheaply and easily downloaded over the Internet. Again, he was ahead of his time. That is largely the way people buy music, and many buy movies, today, but it was at least twenty years in coming.

Once it became clear that music and computers were not going away any time soon, Sharp relented and added them to the store mix. But the low margins they afforded were always a bone in his throat. As a result, the limited floor space and inventory dollars Circuit City was willing to devote to them, and to the associated software and peripherals, prevented the company from being a leader in these products. *Discount Store News,* the industry trade publication, described the differences between Best Buy's and Circuit City's 1992 computer presentations as follows:

> Circuit City and Best Buy offer a similar brand selection, with both carrying Apple, IBM, VTech, Acer, and Packard Bell. However, Circuit City, which also stocks AST and Compaq, is primarily in the promotional 386SX business; Circuit City offers a limited selection of software (as few as 25 titles in smaller stores, with a maximum of 250 in larger stores), while Best Buy stocks over 2,000 DOS titles and is testing Macintosh software. In peripherals, Best Buy enjoys a clear advantage, offering a heartier selection...with the expressed intent of increasing its selection still further. By adding these items to its SKU list, Best Buy has greatly enhanced its customer shopping frequency rate—a boost sorely needed among consumer electronics retailers [all emphases added].[154]

The third way in which "margin mania" hurt Circuit City was in the interplay between the credit bank and store operations. For much of the 1990s a principal way to compete in electronics and appliances, as in new cars, was to lower the finance charges. Best Buy and others frequently ran ads promising "no interest" for six, or even twelve, months on specified merchandise. Besides being a good draw, this was a backdoor way to discount merchandise that was otherwise subject to manufacturer's approved pricing (MAP) and could not be sold below the MAP price without the risk of the manufacturer's terminating one's franchise. In order to compete with Best Buy, the Circuit City store operations executives needed to convince the executives running the Circuit City credit bank to eliminate first-year interest charges to the customer, something they were not willing to do unless the stores reimbursed the bank for the lost revenue. When the store operations team calculated what that would cost, they concluded that the resulting gross profit would not meet the company's profit objectives or Wall Street's expectations. While competitive on price, they elected not to compete with credit. Of course, Best Buy also paid its credit provider to offer no interest for a year, but it elected to pay the piper to get the business.

The long-term consequences of these margin-driven decisions became more and more apparent as the years went by.

Superior Technology

Applying the same creative intelligence he demonstrated in the development of his pioneering point-of-sale system and the mechanization of our distribution centers, Sharp began applying technology to every facet of the business in order to reduce costs and improve quality.

Early in his tenure as CEO, he acquired Patapsco, a custom technology development firm that had designed and built the POS controllers for our stores. Soon they were also making switch boxes for the car stereo and audio rooms that allowed customers to mix and match tuners and speakers and played an important role in all our future technology initiatives. As the need arose, Sharp also automated the laborious process of making sales projections by computing "run rates" (the sales pace the store was achieving over a specified number of months, allowing for seasonal variations) and computerized the labor-intensive process of preparing ads by using computer graphics software. In addition, he began collecting customer purchase and repair information so that there was an accessible online record of what each customer had bought, when he bought it, whether he had a service contract, and what the service issues were. In due course, he eliminated the dedicated telephone lines between the cash registers and the home office computer, replacing them with much cheaper satellite communications.

At the end of the '90s, Circuit City became the first brick-and-mortar electronics retailer to sell online and offer immediate in-store pickup. This was a huge advantage in online retailing that many customers utilized and appreciated.

Sharp's Team and Style

After I retired, the "four horsemen," on whom I had relied to run the business, began to drift away: Rexinger and Villanueva in 1988, Rivas in 1991, and, finally, Bruckart in 1995. They were all approaching or past sixty by then, some had health issues, and all had more retirement money than they had ever dreamed of accruing.

Over time, Sharp recruited strong people to supplement the team he inherited, including Jack Fitzsimmons, an engineer trained in Ireland who had responsibility for distribution, service, real estate, construction, and other behind-the-scenes functions; Austin Ligon, a Yale MBA and senior strategist for Marriott hotels, to whom he assigned Corporate Planning; Steve Cannon, a talented lawyer/lobbyist who became general counsel; and Alan McCollough, whom our human resources director, Bill Zierden, recruited from Burlington Industries shortly after I departed. He also promoted some younger, skilled executives, including CFO Mike Chalifoux and Richard Birnbaum, a multitalented long-term employee who was responsible for marketing and store operations.

When Rivas retired, Sharp realized that he needed to add strength to store operations. Until then, Circuit City had always promoted people to this sensitive position from within, but Sharp went outside and hired a top executive from Montgomery Ward, whose style was much more Theory X than Theory Y (See Chapter Two). Although he brought a lot to Circuit City in terms of modern retail store management, he would often give orders rather than ask questions. He sometimes embarrassed subordinates in front of their peers, and he insisted on doing things the Montgomery Ward way before he understood the Circuit City way. He also initiated a competition between store operations and merchandising, telling one buyer, "If you shoot the bear [meaning Walt Bruckart, VP of merchandising], the rabbits will run and hide." In short, he was talented, but his management style ran counter to the Circuit City culture and generated increasing tension and discontent.

Within a few years, Bill Zierden, as VP for human resources, went to Sharp to say that this new executive was creating problems. To his credit, Sharp polled his subordinates, became convinced of the truth of what he had been told, and let the man go. As far as I can tell, no long-term harm was done. It was as if the company had expelled an infection and recovered. But the memory of the incident, or more accurately the lack of collective memory, came back to haunt the company after Sharp departed.

Sharp ran the company through an executive committee composed of the senior vice presidents for each important area. Although very detail oriented, he was relatively hands-off on the small stuff but held each committee member accountable for results in his area. By doing that he created a strong esprit, great loyalty, and a sense of self-confidence. As he said in the 1989 annual report:

> We devote all our time, resources and energy to a single

retail segment. As a result, we are better able to anticipate changing industry conditions and especially design systems, programs and facilities to meet the industry's unique demands....[Our] employees...want to be players on this winning team.

Operationally, he kept merchandising (buying), real estate and construction, accounting, and creative advertising services centralized, while he decentralized human resources and store operations, including advertising strategy and pricing, to strong regional vice presidents.

Next Growth Vehicles

CarMax

By the mid-'80s it became apparent that within five or ten years Circuit City would run out of attractive markets in which to build or add stores. Finding a follow-on strategy was essential. Early in his tenure, Sharp experimented with a few "mini-superstores" in markets not large enough for a full-size store, and with mall-based electronics stores called Impulse that carried small portable electronics. Both were credible ideas but neither immediately clicked, and scaling up these operations did not offer sufficient opportunity to make a real difference to the bottom line of a multibillion-dollar company. Sharp also explored opening a chain of furniture stores as well as a home security business similar to ADT. In the end, however, both these ideas were dropped.

While I was still CEO, Sharp and I had considered overseas expansion as well as other mass-market businesses that would, in time, join the Circuit City Superstores in a "portfolio" of retail businesses. One of the options we considered was a chain of office supply stores, à la Staples or Office Depot. But Sharp, to his credit, wanted to find something that no one else had tried. It had to be a big opportunity and it had to be something that competitors would have a hard time copying.

His next attempt to find a companion business was a home run. As part of the 1991 three-year strategic planning process, he and Austin Ligon, whom he had hired as vice president for corporate planning, set out systematically to evaluate possible new retail opportunities. Their criteria were unmet consumer need, market scale, absence of big box competitors, and a skill set that fit with Circuit City. Ligon prepared mini "white papers" analyzing eight different segments of retailing, including sporting goods, auto service, furniture, and new cars. While new cars appeared to be an almost perfect fit, entering that market turned out to be impossible because of state franchise laws and manufacturers' rules regarding dealer organization. A local Richmond entrepreneur, Ron Moore, who had been doing background research for the white papers, asked what Ligon has subsequently called the million-dollar question: "Did you guys notice that half of all the dollars spent on cars are spent on *used* cars?" The light bulb immediately went on for Ligon, and when he raised the idea with Sharp the next day, the two instantly agreed that this was the Big Idea they had been searching for.

The good news was that the used-car market was huge—$375 billion—and that the industry badly needed restructuring. It was highly fragmented, with 89,000 used-car dealers and no economies of scale. It served consumers so poorly, in fact, that used-car salesmen were almost universally recognized objects of ridicule. Best of all, it utilized many of the same skill sets Circuit City had developed: big-ticket selling, consumer credit, and after-sale product service.

The biggest challenge was that each used car is unique. The merchandise had to be bought one car at a time, at auction, from the public, or from leasing and rental companies. There was no Sony or Whirlpool to create a line of products and no manufacturer's warranties except those remaining from the original sale.

Sharp and Ligon, along with a talented programmer from MIS, began to study the industry to determine if they could design a program that set parameters for how much the company could afford to pay for a used car, depending on its year, make, model, mileage, condition, and market appeal, and still resell it at a profit.

Ligon also researched what the public disliked about buying a used car and set consumer policies that would be attractive. These included:

- One fixed price, generally $1500 or more below the Kelley Blue Book price, with no haggling
- Optional financing on a fully transparent basis
- A 128-point inspection of every important electrical and mechanical system backed by a thirty-day bumper-to-bumper warranty
- A five-day/250-mile money-back return policy
- Transparent pass-through of titling taxes and license fees
- A standing offer to purchase anyone's used car at an appraised value, whether or not he had bought a car from us. The appraisal was good for five days, giving the customer an opportunity to test the market and sell his vehicle elsewhere if that were more advantageous.

These revolutionary policies resulted in immediate customer approval and ongoing consumer satisfaction ratings in the high nineties.

Sharp decided on the name CarMax. The first store opened in Richmond in late 1993. Each store included a large showroom and repair facility (50,000 square feet), typically on fifteen or twenty acres, with room to display five hundred to twelve hundred cars, depending on the size of the market. Most were in suburban locations, on or right off a major freeway. On the lot were no fewer than 350 used cars, every one of which was fully repaired and in excellent condition. Except for a few highly selective older cars, they had to be either no more than six years old or have fewer than 60,000 miles on them.

In the showroom were a number of touch-screen computer workstations that enabled customers, with or without sales assistance, to enter their needs and preferences. The computer then displayed a color picture of each vehicle on the lot that matched the customer's parameters together with its age, mileage, price, location on the lot, and other relevant details. The customer could also print out a fact sheet of each relevant car. This process narrowed the search to those vehicles the customer liked and could afford before he decided which car to inspect and test drive. [168]

With few exceptions, the CarMax salespeople had never sold cars before. Most were young and clean cut, in their twenties or thirties. Many were women. Since they were paid the same whether they sold a Mercedes or a Hyundai, their goal was to sell customers something that would meet their needs, not to "step them up" to a more expensive car.

The price was fixed. You could not buy it a dollar cheaper unless it did not sell for a specific period of time, at which point it would be marked down for everyone. Finally, the customer could finance the purchase at CarMax or though his or her own bank or credit union. Online credit approval was typically secured within ten minutes. All finance charges, titling taxes, and other fees were open and fully transparent. The whole operation could not have been more consumer-friendly, and women, who were often insulted, ignored, or intimidated at other dealerships, especially loved it. The first year the original store did $53 million in sales.

The following year a second store opened in Raleigh, North Carolina, and the year after that, two in Atlanta. All were immediately successful. Smelling an exciting new business model, Wayne Huizenga, whose early successes included Waste Management, Blockbuster, and the Miami Dolphins, offered to buy CarMax. When Sharp refused to sell, Huizenga built AutoNation and competed directly in the Florida market. He also took AutoNation public, giving it access to cheap capital. Sensing a battle for first-mover advantage, Sharp ramped up the growth of CarMax and invested heavily in systems to improve the consumer experience and productivity and reduce costs.

To finance CarMax's growth Sharp elected to create a publicly traded tracking stock—that is, a Circuit City subsidiary whose stock price was linked to the earnings of CarMax and not to the

Circuit City stores.[169] The initial public offering (IPO) sold 22.5 percent of CarMax for $412 million, giving what was then a six-store venture a market valuation of nearly $2 billion! Circuit City was repaid in full for the $175 million loan it had provided to start CarMax, and the remaining $237 million was used to finance Car-Max's growth. [170] This was all the equity ever raised to fund the CarMax business.

DIVX Diversion

The next effort to diversify was a major diversion and serious stumble. In 1995 Sharp received a letter from a prominent Los Angles entertainment law firm asking if Circuit City would be interested in partnering in an exciting new way to deliver movies to the home. Home video was a big business: Sales and rentals of movies for the home were the largest single source of movie studio revenue, generating $16 billion in the States and $30 billion worldwide.[171]

In 1995 DVD recorders and players were still in their infancy. The usual way to view a movie at home was to buy or rent a VHS tape. For the average consumer, buying newly released movies on tape could cost as much as $80. Rental, while more affordable at $3 or $4, was inconvenient, typically requiring the customer to pick up and return the tape within 48 hours. From the studios' viewpoint, rentals were a mixed bag. The studio sold the tape once for, say, $60, but the rental company resold it many times for, say, $4, with all of the "pay per view" profits, once the cost of the tape was recovered, going to the retailer and not the studio. Moreover, VHS tapes were easily copied, and the studios lost billions to piracy.

The proposal Sharp received from the Hollywood law firm had the promise of making home videos easier for the consumer to acquire as well as more profitable and far more secure for the studios. After investigation, he concluded that the system would,

with a lot of technological improvements, afford an attractive opportunity for Circuit City to enter the home video business and
make a lot of money. In fact, the upside was huge.

DIVX, as Sharp named it, utilized the new DVD technology,
which captured a movie on an encrypted compact disk that could
only be played on a DIVX-enabled DVD player. Customers could
buy a DIVX movie in a store (or online) for $4.50, take it home,
and play it on a DIVX player that day, the next month, or whenever
they wanted. They had forty-eight hours after the first play to play
it again and again at no charge. Thereafter, they would pay a "pay
per view" fee or have the option to purchase unlimited replays.
Payments for plays beyond the forty-eight-hour window were automatically charged to the customer's credit card over the phone.

Compared to VHS, DIVX offered superior picture and sound
quality. Even better, the consumer did not have to rent, watch, and
return the movie within a two-day window. From a movie studio's
point of view, DIVX offered an important advantage in that the
content could be encrypted to reduce, if not entirely prevent, piracy.

Developing and marketing the idea would require significant

DIVX player from the 1998 annual report

engineering enhancements and a commitment of several hundred million dollars. In addition, Circuit City would have to persuade its suppliers, such as RCA and Panasonic, to produce DIVX-enabled DVD players; persuade our competitors, such as Best Buy, to stock them on their shelves; and then persuade customers to buy one. Despite the hurdles, however, Sharp thought this was a way to gain a dominant position in the $8 billion video rental market.

To enable Circuit City to introduce the product by the fall of 1998, he devoted himself to solving the technical, legal, financial, and marketing issues. He was challenged as never before, and he seemed to love it. He commuted frequently to the West Coast to deal with the studios. He assigned the most capable and creative members of the MIS team to the DIVX project. To free up his time, he turned over day-to-day responsibility for the Circuit City stores to Alan McCollough, and for CarMax to Austin Ligon.

Within a year of its introduction, however, it became clear that DIVX was not going to fly. The initial problem was the Hollywood lawyers. Despite their strong representations that the studios would embrace this product, they could not deliver the industry. Most studios, including Disney, Twentieth Century Fox, Universal, and Paramount, supported the concept. Warner Bros., however, led a determined opposition, and Sony stayed on the sidelines.

Equally important, the plan for Circuit City to market the DVD discs and players was doomed from the start. On the retail front, Good Guys bought and supported DIVX, but Best Buy refused to support a product sponsored by Circuit City, and others played a wait-and-see game. Some board members had warned that this marketing plan would fail, and they were proved right.

Finally, a group of determined anti-DIVX techies launched a vigorous campaign, possibly inspired and funded by Warner Bros. They argued that once you "bought" the disc you should not have to pay for replays and that the phone connection enabling the charges invaded customers' privacy by allowing Circuit City to monitor what movies they watched and how often they watched them.

All this opposition, plus the general fear among consumers that they might be caught in a "format war" like the one between Betamax and VHS some years earlier, led to the demise of DIVX. Circuit City threw in the towel in June 1999 and, at the end of the day, wrote off $350 million, or $220 million after taxes.[172] For a company with more than $2.2 billion in stockholder equity, this was a significant, but far from fatal, blow.

In retrospect the real cost of DIVX was not so much the monetary loss but the diversion of management's attention from the Circuit City stores at a time when it was most needed.

The DIVX debacle aside, however, Sharp's first seven years had gone well financially. Sales and earnings had reached all-time highs. Both the rapid expansion and the strong emphasis on improving the consumer experience through technology and training were paying off. But beginning in the early '90s, storm clouds were already gathering on the horizon while management was focused elsewhere.

Habits of Mind

Be Humble, Run Scared: *Continuously doubt your understanding of things. Business success contains the seeds of its own destruction. Worry about what the competition knows that you do not. Andy Grove, the legendary cofounder of Intel, got it largely right in his book* **Only the Paranoid Survive.**

Sharp and I thought that our carefully designed superstores and expensive specialty fixtures gave us a competitive advantage over the less attractive and effective displays in other TV and appliance stores. In the end, however, rapidly changing merchandise rendered these purpose-built fixtures quickly obsolete. We would have done better to have less "perfect" but more flexible displays, like those of most of our competitors.

Confront the Brutal Facts: *The worst person you can fool is yourself. Ignoring or denying reality does not help it go away. Once you understand the issues, be bold enough to take decisive action.*

Once it became clear that DIVX was not going to catch on, management quickly decided to cut their losses and shut the project down. Although Circuit City took a financial hit, it was the right decision.

Boldly Follow Through: *Big ideas require bold leadership and attract loyal followers. The effort comes to naught if the execution is tentative or not well disciplined.*

During his tenure as CEO, Sharp made bold moves, launching CarMax and DIVX. CarMax took advantage of Circuit City's core competencies to revolutionize the used-car industry. It changed the way used cars are sold in this country. As the business grew in size and complexity, management spun it off as a separate division and ultimately a separate company.

DIVX sought to transform the way people could buy and watch movies at home, eliminating trips to the video rental store and allowing multiple replays at a low price. In retrospect, DIVX was a major mistake. Not only did it fail to attract sufficient movie studio and consumer support, but also it diverted management's time and attention from the stores at a time when they were slipping.

Encourage Debate: *Learn from dissent. Involve senior staff and the board of directors in an open process to find the best answer. Create a board that will raise thought-provoking questions and challenge management to justify its plans.*

By keeping the credit bank's profits a secret from the board and senior management, Sharp allowed Circuit City to believe that it was doing better than the competition and that we did not have to worry about Best Buy's rising store volumes. Ultimately, these chickens came home to roost, big time.

Focus on the Future: *Manage for the long term and not the short. Don't* let short-term earnings swings divert a long-term strategy. Ignore the skeptics and short-term market swings. If things go well, the value of your company, whether public or private, will respond over time.

The rapid rollout of Circuit City stores to gain first-mover advantage and a dominant market share was an investment in securing the future. The same can be said for the aggressive consumer strategies of evening deliveries, a "No Lemons" guarantee, consumer satisfaction surveys, and rapid approval of in-house credit. They cost money but built for the future.

Lessons Learned

Beware of Too-Rapid Expansion: The unforeseen consequences of too rapid an expansion can hurt in the long run. In its haste to open markets quickly and cheaply, Circuit City sometimes compromised real estate quality to the ultimate disadvantage of the company.

Chapter Nine

TROUBLE IN THE CITY

The most difficult subjects can be explained to the most slow-witted man if he has not formed any idea of them already; but the simplest thing cannot be made clear to the most intelligent man if he is firmly persuaded that he knows already, without a shadow of doubt, what is laid before him.

—Leo Tolstoy, 1897

Pride goes before destruction, a haughty spirit before a fall.

—Proverbs xvi. 18

In the early 1980s, Circuit City had very little direct competition. Its principal national competitors were Sears and Montgomery Ward, neither of which carried brand-name merchandise. There were no national mass merchants or home-building stores, and most of the strong regional TV and appliance dealers were members of NATM, who had a mutual understanding that they would not move into one another's territories. All that began to change.

Gathering Clouds

The explosion of popular new electronics products in the '80s meant that nearly everyone in the business was successful. As they grew, many began to copy the Circuit City expansion model, and by 1990, Highland, Silo, Best Buy, Federated Stores in LA, Crazy Eddie in New York, and many others had gone public. All had sales of more than $500 million, and Silo was doing more than $1 billion. Circuit City, at $2 billion, was still the industry leader.

Also in the '80s, many NATM members, buoyed by their success, began moving into territories beyond their home bases. Highland, centered in Detroit, started expanding south through the middle of the country, with a large presence in Texas. Silo, which had originated in Philadelphia, hopped, skipped, and jumped around the country, pursuing markets of opportunity. Its incoherent strategy ultimately led to its near demise and acquisition by Dixons, England's leading electronics retailer. Lechmere, a Boston-based hard goods store with roots in electronics and appliances, and now a subsidiary of Dayton Hudson, began expanding beyond New England into the mid-South, and Good Guys expanded from San Francisco to the LA market. Finally, Best Buy, which started in St. Paul, Minnesota, was, by the mid-'80s, expanding throughout the upper Midwest. In the late '80s, Sears made a fundamental change in its merchandising policies and, while not downplaying Kenmore, added brand names to its appliance mix and to its LXI electronics offerings. By 1990 more than eight hundred Sears stores had opened Brand Central departments carrying many of the most popular brands.[173] Montgomery Ward replied with its Electronics Avenue, also carrying branded goods. In the '80s Kmart (a spin-off of S.S. Kresge), Woolco (a spin-off of Woolworths), and certain other discount chains also began carrying branded electronics and appliances. All were now direct competitors.

At the time of my departure as CEO in 1986, none of this new competition was a serious threat to Circuit City. It marginally influenced which markets we entered first and had an impact on margins in some markets. Except for appliances, where Sears remained dominant, Circuit City was still "king of the hill" among electronics and appliance retailers. Five years later, however, things had changed. One of the biggest changes was the emergence of Best Buy.

Rise of Best Buy

When Dick Schulze founded, in 1966, his Sound of Music hi-fi store, in St. Paul, Minnesota, he ran it as a conventional audio/video business. By 1981 he had seven small stores, averaging 7500 square feet, in and around Minneapolis. Total volume was under $9 million.

Then, in 1981, a tornado demolished the suburban Roseville store, after which Schulze ran a huge "best buy" sale of the water-damaged goods at sharply discounted prices. The result was an unprecedented demand and a cash bonanza that changed his business strategy and his stores' name forever. According to the official company history, "Schulze had come to realize that there wasn't much of a future in a market glutted with vendors serving a shrinking audience of 15- to 18-year-olds with limited resources."[174] His first step was to add appliances to his audio/video mix.

In 1984 Schulze opened the first Best Buy superstore largely based on the Circuit City model, with some significant differences. Best Buy stores were bigger (54,000 square feet, compared to Circuit City's 34,000-square-foot prototype), stripped-down warehouse showrooms with concrete floors, open ceilings, and fluorescent lighting. The displays were basic, not all the floor models were hooked up and operating, and the stockrooms were minimal, with virtually all the backup product stacked on the floor. Customers picked up all but the largest items and took them to a central checkout.

Best Buy carried a full range of consumer electronics, whether or not the category carried a high gross margin. Accordingly, its display of computers and computer-related peripherals, video games, portable electronics, and prerecorded music was greater than Circuit City's. Although sales personnel were available in the "big ticket" sections of the store, help was minimal in the areas where customers could easily select and carry the item to the checkout.

In 1985, a year after creating his first superstore, Schulze took Best Buy public. The offering raised $8 million and the stock was listed on the New York Stock Exchange. With this money he was able to add 15 more superstores in the next two years. For fiscal 1988 sales nearly doubled to $439 million while profits dropped by two-thirds. The year before, Highland Appliance from Detroit had entered the Minneapolis-St. Paul market, and the two chains were engaged in an all-out war.[175] One Minnesota writer believes that at this point, Schulze, distressed at the unrelenting price war, attempted to sell the business: "Rumor had it that, as Best Buy limped into the fall of 1988, Schulze tried to sell his company to Sears and failed because of his demands for certain perks."[176] Schulze denied the rumors, but I know for a fact that, at approximately the same time, he also entered into discussions to sell his business to Circuit City for $30 million. At the time, Sharp's view was that it was not necessary to spend $30 million when all Circuit City had to do was open a store in Minneapolis and "blow them away." And there were also other issues, including a role for Schulze on the Circuit City board and the large amount of Circuit City stock he would have owned.[177] In hindsight, had Circuit City acquired Best Buy for $30 million in stock or cash, it would have been the best money we ever spent. At the least, it would have eliminated a future competitor.

In the decade 1987 to 1996, Best Buy grew its superstore base from two dozen to 272 stores, an amazing performance for an undercapitalized company with only 24 stores as a starting point. Just prior to opening the first Best Buy store in 1984, Sound of Music's sales were under $9 million. By 1987, company revenues had grown an astounding 32.5 times, to $240 million, and by 1996 to $7.8 billion (867 times). More important, average sales per store began to skyrocket. From fiscal 1986 until 1990, they hovered in the $10 to $11 million range, very close to Circuit City's average. Then, in 1992 and 1993 they hit $13 to $14 million, and, in 1994, $19 million. From there, sales per store quickly climbed to $34 million in 2000, more than tripling average store sales in less than a decade.

As it grew, Best Buy kept on reinventing itself to reflect shifting consumer preferences and changes in the marketplace. At first their warehouse showrooms were staffed, like Circuit City's, with commission-earning salesmen who engaged in step-up selling and a polite but determined effort to peddle extended service polices. Then, in 1989, Schulze introduced the Concept II store, geared to the self-confident shopper, where salespeople were paid by the hour, with no commission. Schulze believed that shoppers had only a limited need for sales help and a strong desire for hassle-free buying, which included no offers of extended service contracts, no waiting for merchandise to be brought from the back room, and no switching from counter to counter.[178] The revamped stores featured well-stocked showrooms averaging 36,000 square feet and more self-help product information. Concept II sales assistants hung out in "Answer Centers," where they were available to answer customer questions. In this format, the sale of extended service policies was difficult, so Best Buy turned a liability into an advantage and began to suggest to customers that Circuit City and other retailers who sold these insurance policies were "ripping them off."

A few years later, in 1992, Best Buy began to beef up their prerecorded music and video departments, often using these products as loss leaders to generate traffic. By 1996, a typical store carried over 80,000 music titles, more than most dedicated record stores. Needless to say, Best Buy was crowded with young people eager to buy the latest, most popular recording or movie at a deep discount.

In 1994 came the Concept III stores, which featured a wide range of home office products, especially computers, software, and peripherals. Because of their large selection, these stores became popular places to shop for computers and computer-related products.

Each time new Concept prototype stores were created, earlier stores were remodeled to incorporate the most productive changes.

Best Buy's rise did not, however, follow a straight trajectory. Their elimination of commissioned salespeople was beginning to give manufacturers heartburn. Those companies, too, wanted to sell their better, more expensive products, so Mitsubishi, Hitachi, and Whirlpool all cancelled their Best Buy franchises. In 1998, to requalify for the prestige brands that they had lost, Best Buy created its larger (40,000–58,000 square feet) Concept IV stores featuring more high-tech products, a home theater, better hands-on displays, and deeper staffing (still hourly paid) for high-tech, high-prestige merchandise. Ironically, they also included point-of-sale terminals throughout the store. Best Buy's president, Brad Anderson, told *Forbes* that the move to larger, higher-tech stores was necessary because, "We could not land some of the products we wanted."[179] Despite these changes and improved access to more prestige brands, however, earnings as a percentage of sales did not improve. For the six years from 1986 to 1992 Best Buy earned only $22.4 million on cumulative sales of $3.4 billion, a return on sales of 0.66 percent. Despite these meager returns, however, Wall Street continued to support its growth. In 1986, a year after it went public, Best Buy sold two million shares, raising $33 million net of expenses. For the next five years, it limped along with inadequate capital until, in 1991, it sold seven million shares for $83 million. Finally, in 1994, it was able to raise $320 million with a convertible preferred stock offering.

Understood, but underappreciated by most of the Circuit City management team, was the fact that in the ten years since 1987, when Circuit City embarked on its nationwide expansion and Best Buy was starting to roll out its superstores in number, Circuit City's average store sales had grown only modestly, from $11.6 to $15.5 million per store. In the same ten years, Best Buy grew its average volume per store from $10 million in 1987 to an astonishing $28.5 million in 1997, nearly double Circuit City's figures, and most of the increase was in computers and music.

Then, in 1996, Best Buy's day of reckoning arrived. For the year ended March 31, 1996, Best Buy earned only $1.75 million on sales of $7.9 billion, an insignificant 0.14 percent. The company had borrowed heavily to increase its computer inventories for the

1996 holiday season, just before Intel announced plans to introduce the Pentium chip. Demand for existing computers with earlier generation processors collapsed. In early 1997, saddled with mountains of unsold PCs, Best Buy had to ask its creditors and vendors for an extra sixty days to pay its bills. Its stock tanked, dropping as low as $1.31 per share and ending the fiscal year at $1.54.

Under pressure from its bankers and shareholders, Best Buy engaged Arthur Anderson Consulting to help re-engineer its business. Starting at the store level, Anderson developed a comprehensive set of standard operating procedures for all aspects of Best Buy's business, including merchandising, distribution, and store operations. The management team was also overhauled: Forty new vice presidents were hired, most coming from the outside and replacing much of the company's old guard. Simultaneously, significant changes were made to the product mix by eliminating slower selling product lines. High-touch areas were added to help sell the burgeoning array of digital consumer products, such as cameras, cellular phones, satellite systems, and the fast-selling DVD player. During the makeover, expansion was slowed considerably, and only twelve new stores were opened during the fiscal year ending in February 1998. To gain acceptance and cooperation from the staff on these many changes, Best Buy engaged RHR International, a human relations management consulting firm, which created teams of Best Buy associates to both understand and embrace the changes and then to spread the word to their coworkers. [180]

The effort worked. By June 1998, following a two-for-one split, Best Buy's stock had soared 900 percent from its February 1997 price to a split-adjusted $36 per share. In fiscal year 1999 the company earned $224 million on sales of $10.1 billion, a respectable 2.2 percent, and in the following year, 2.7 percent. Within three years, Best Buy's earnings had recovered.

Of course, they did more than adopt new operating procedures. Reversing course, they again took a page from the Circuit City playbook and concentrated on *selling,* instead of disparaging, extended service policies. They also revamped virtually all their inventory and sales management systems to improve accuracy and inventory turnover. Recognizing the fact that they could never compete effectively with Walmart or Costco on price alone, they looked for ways to enhance their margins. One way they hit upon to do this was to begin offering services, which are much harder to comparison shop than merchandise. These included in-home installation and repair of home entertainment and computer systems. This was the genesis of the Geek Squad, which became a source of additional profit and provided a competitive advantage as products became more and more difficult for customers to install, upgrade, connect to other products, and to operate.

Once again Best Buy had reinvented itself, for the fourth time in less than twenty years. As a result of firm and decisive action the company saved itself from near death and put itself back on the path to becoming the dominant TV electronics and appliance retailer in America.

Response to Changing Competition

At the same time the Best Buy was reinventing himself, many of Circuit City's peers were falling by the wayside. Silo had been sold in 1985 to an English retailer, which in turn sold the Silo stores in 1993. Newmark and Lewis, based in New York, was liquidated in 1992; Highland Appliance, based in Detroit, in 1993; and Luskins, based in Baltimore, in 1997. Tandy's Incredible Universe stores were all closed in 1996, and Lechmere, which had sold itself to a private equity firm, was in 1994 sold to Montgomery Ward, which in turn was liquidated in 1997.

With so many changes in the competitive landscape and such profound changes in the industry, especially in terms of product explosion and price implosion, the '90s were a time for Circuit City to reevaluate its economic model and, if necessary, reinvent itself.

Amidst this industry turmoil, Sharp continued the process of developing a three-year plan every two years and holding a board retreat to discuss it openly and candidly. As he developed a more sophisticated planning staff, the semiannual three-year document, which had always been highly intelligent and analytical, became a weighty tome, at least three hundred pages long, weighing five or six pounds. The length was primarily attributable to careful thinking about the multiple issues impacting a large company in a complex world.

As a result, the Three Year Plans for the last decade of Sharp's tenure as CEO are an excellent window onto how he and his staff understood and dealt with the profound changes taking place in the industry as well as the increased competition from Best Buy and the mass merchandisers. Looking back at these plans reminds me of Elisabeth Kübler-Ross's five stages of grief: denial, anger, bargaining, depression, and acceptance.

1991 Three Year Plan: Denial

Like all its predecessors, Circuit City's Three Year Plan for 1991–93 surveyed the competition, focusing on large national specialists like Highland, Silo, and Best Buy; the smaller regional specialists like Good Guys; and the mass merchandisers like Sears and Montgomery Ward (now Wards).

It noted that "the 'gap' between Circuit City and its competitors has narrowed." Nonetheless, it discounted the competition. Silo was characterized as a poorly managed "spoiler" company likely to be happy with limited profitability. Highland was described as having "an acceptable, but not exceptional, offer to the consumer," and Best Buy as a company with "limited financial and managerial resources, as well as…eroding gross margins… and difficulty sustaining their performance in an increasingly competitive market."

In contrast, the same plan had respect for Good Guys, a San Francisco–based electronics chain with high margins and high levels of service that "proceeded to copy us across the board," and for Sears, whose historically strong position in appliances was deemed to compensate for its "lackluster launch" of the Brand Central electronics format.

With respect to the new competitors, the plan concluded: "While each of these developments is troublesome, none of them individually is particularly threatening to our continued dominance of this business."

1993 Three Year Plan: Anger

Two years later, as GDP contracted and competition intensified, the tone changed. The 1993–95 Plan opened:

> As our industry moved from slow growth to no growth, we simultaneously found ourselves in the midst of a competitive attack in our largest and most profitable market [LA]…and a sudden plunge into a recession whose end is still beyond the immediate horizon.[181]

The anger continued: Good Guys, "the class act among our competitors…*had the temerity* [emphasis added] to enter Los Angeles, our largest, most, successful, and most profitable market."[182] In response, Circuit City launched a "Going to War" strategy designed to neutralize Good Guys' brand image as the "Electronics Specialist." Best Buy also came under attack. Its Concept II store, launched in St. Louis, "may well be losing money," the plan stated, but, at the same time, its pricing policies were creating a "competitive blood bath" for Circuit City.

The plan acknowledged Best Buy as the competitor that, in the near term, would have the most impact on our profitability but did not express any expectation that it would be a formidable opponent for the long run. For the five previous years, Best Buy's earnings as a percentage of sales had averaged a very meager 0.66 percent as compared to Circuit City's 1.75 percent. Under these circumstances it was easy to dismiss Best Buy as "only marginally profitable" and thus likely to join the many other TV and appliance specialty chains that had gone under when the industry slowed down or the competition heated up.[183] The plan also pointed out that a recent stock issue had provided Best Buy capital equal to three times the company's cumulative profits since going public and contemptuously warned Best Buy investors: "Caveat emptor."

By focusing on Best Buy's lower margins and lower profitability as a percentage of sales, however, the plan was ignoring its far higher sales per store and significantly faster inventory turns. Instead, Circuit City attributed its own declining profitability to stalled industry growth and increased competition from discount stores like Walmart and the warehouse clubs.

Nonetheless, for the first time, the company seriously questioned the superstore model. After pointing out that Circuit City's existing or soon-to-be-opened markets accounted for 63 percent of all U.S. television and appliance sales, the plan carefully surveyed the additional markets in which superstores might work and concluded that there were only a couple of years of superstore growth possible beyond the plan's 1995 horizon.

The plan then assessed several alternative formats, including an electronics-only store similar to Good Guys, a self-service warehouse format similar to Best Buy, and a megastore similar to BrandsMart in Florida and Tops Appliances in New Jersey.[184] The thirty-two-page discussion of alternative growth opportunities is commendable for its depth, candor, and thoroughness. In the end, the plan concluded that superstores remained the most profitable growth vehicle. Of the alternative formats, megastores were "clearly...the most profitable" and the plan advised that, "We should seriously consider a test of the megastore format." However, that never happened. And by focusing only on our competitors' bottom lines, the plan failed to ask or answer several all-important questions about the world in which the company was operating: Who were the customers of the '90s? What type of shopping experience were they looking for? Why were Best Buy's average store sales two or three times greater than those of

Circuit City? What did this portend for the future? The concern was more about how we and our competitors looked to investors than about how we looked to our customers.

In short, the plan focused on Wall Street rather than Main Street.

1995 and 1997 Three Year Plans: Bargaining and Depression

The 1995 and 1997 Plans were very similar. Both focused mainly on Best Buy as "our most challenging competition." Both Plans were objective in their comparison of Circuit City and Best Buy, recognizing that each concept had distinct strengths and weaknesses. The 1995 Plan explained, "The Best Buy concept has four economic advantages over Circuit City: higher store volumes, lower labor costs, lower rent and depreciation as a percentage of sales and higher inventory turnover."[185] The major economic advantages of the Circuit City format "were identified as higher margins and ESP [extended service policy] income." Neither plan noted that Best Buy's advantages all trended toward lower operating costs for the retailer while the Circuit City advantages were predicated on higher product costs for the consumer. Nor did they recognize that Best Buy was better meeting consumer expectations by carrying more low-margin products that were in high demand.

As Best Buy ate away at Circuit City's lead in sales, market share, and profitability, the 1997 Plan began to "bargain" for what was the appropriate yardstick of success. The explanation went:

> Circuit City continues to be the leading specialty retailer with a 9.1 percent market share. Best Buy is second with an 8.7 percent market share. Best Buy continues to gain share at a faster pace than Circuit City, but those gains are mostly from growth in PC sales and rapid store expansion.[186]

Comparing national market shares ignored the critical fact that in 1996, when the 1997 Plan was written, Circuit City was in many more markets than Best Buy and had two-thirds more stores (419 versus 251). In the markets they both inhabited, Best Buy had by far the larger share. The plan also noted: "Circuit City has a 9.8 percent market share versus Best Buy's 6.1 percent share *when PCs are excluded* [emphasis added]." Under what twisted logic could one possibly exclude PCs from a market share calculation? They were central to the business, representing 23 percent of Circuit City's sales and 37 percent of Best Buy's.[187]

Being totally candid, the 1997 Plan documented the fact that consumer preferences had shifted toward Best Buy. In 1995, professionally managed consumer research that Circuit City commissioned in Dallas, Chicago, and St. Louis showed the two companies neck and neck in consumer satisfaction with respect to pricing, sales counselors, and "overall visit." By 1997, however, Best Buy was ahead in two out of three markets for all three measures. Instead of trying to figure out how to stop this drift, the plan offered an excuse:

> Best Buy clearly has an advantage on price image. Their name, warehouse style format and aggressive promotions are more effective in conveying their low price image even though we are price competitive on individual SKUs.[188]

Without any evidence, the plan states that "results from the satisfaction surveys suggest that people who purchase at Best Buy have different service expectations than Circuit City customers." In other words, Best Buy got equal or better grades because its customers had lower expectations!

The plan also dismissed Best Buy's store volume and customer satisfaction advantages because "Best Buy's 'Achilles' heel' is their questionable ability to generate a reasonable return on capital and their very thin operating margins." The Circuit City Superstore, it said, "is clearly more profitable."[189] The question that needed answering was why Best Buy was gaining market share. But instead of doing that, the plan changed the subject and continued the complacency. In short, management was depressed but clearly not running scared. To improve its competitive position versus Best Buy, the 1997 Plan proposed more of the same things Circuit City had been doing for years, including greater focus on gross margins, better in-stock positions, and enhanced extended warranty sales.

The only significant innovations proposed by the plan were to acknowledge the importance of emphasizing the sale of computers and to allow certain small electronics items to be taken directly to a central checkout register.[190] But, in fact, it took approximately two years to implement even these small changes throughout the chain.[191]

The 1999 Three Year Plan: Acceptance

The 1999 Three Year Plan was hardly a plan at all. It lamented the industry-wide lack of new product introductions, the falling prices of electronics products, and the popularity of low-margin items as "recent industry trends [that] both hurt our value-added selling format and aided [Best Buy's] self-service offer."

The plan bemoaned Best Buy's lead in volume per store and its growing profitability. It also revealed Circuit City's concern over the consumer perception that "our stores feel less friendly, bright and fun than Best Buy and that they have less variety." Also, it stated, Best Buy's lower price image with customers "has been an ongoing source of frustration for us."[192] Finally, the plan deplored "the paradox...that customers want service when they want it. Too much attention before they are ready for it comes across as pressure. If no help is available when they want it they are unhappy."[193] As a result, Best Buy, it went on to say, is perceived as "a place where customers go to shop. Our store is a place to go for a specific purchase—a mission."[194]

While the plan recognized that consumers preferred Best Buy, it did not offer any solutions. Instead, it explored a wide range of possible responses and then systematically shot each one down. Experimenting with larger stores, more stores per market, simplified sales counselor commissions, and inventory improvements were all dismissed as either counterproductive or not transformational. To overcome the concern that Circuit City stores were "darker and more difficult to navigate," management considered removing some ceilings but nixed the idea "due to the cost ($750,000 per store) and our priority on building new stores." [195]

The plan stressed the importance of the marketing function going forward, which would help convey that Circuit City's pricing was comparable to Best Buy's. But it went on to say that the executive who was recently hired to fill a long-vacant marketing position had been "immediately loaned...to DIVX."

With respect to commissioned sales personnel, the plan pointed out that "our sales counselors are an asset to some customers who value their knowledge, while others feel pressure or have concern that they will be talked into purchasing something they don't really need." Despite the fact that Circuit City was the only one of the top-ten specialty retailers of electronics and appliances that still employed commissioned salespeople, the plan concluded that the company could not abandon the value-added selling approach.

Finally, the plan asked the ultimate question: "whether we should consider moving meaningfully toward their format and try to replace our store base over time." To ask the question was to answer it. "We did an extensive amount of analysis on such an idea a year ago. At that time, we believed that *people would not purchase ESPs [extended service policies] without sales help and we could not mix value-added selling and self-service in the same store* [emphasis added]." [196] A year later, despite Best Buy's success with ESP sales and improved margins, that conclusion remained both untested and firmly held.

In short, Circuit City was stuck in its own belief system. It clearly understood that the world had changed, but it could not bring itself to act on that reality.

Progression

The 1991 Plan dismissed the competition as weak or inept (denial). The 1993 Plan decried the "temerity" of Good Guys and the irresponsibility of Best Buy for where and how they competed (anger). The 1995 and 1997 Plans revealed a hope that if Circuit City could just maintain its superior profit margins, Best Buy would eventually fail to achieve a level profitability that was high enough to attract the Wall Street financing that it needed for growth (bargaining). The 1997 Plan provided contradictory, inconclusive analysis without recommended action (depression). Finally, the 1999 Plan concluded that the strategies that were working for others would not work for Circuit City (acceptance).

How Circuit City Lost its Way

Starting in 1995, Best Buy passed Circuit City in sales per store. In a few short years it passed Circuit City in sales per square foot, profit per store, and profit per square foot. By 1996, it passed Circuit City in total sales and U.S. market share. In 1999, it exceeded Circuit City in earnings.

These relative sales and profit trends demonstrate that customers preferred Best Buy to Circuit City.

As the Three Year Plans make clear, Circuit City clearly understood what was happening. It knew that electronics were becoming commodities, with rapidly declining cost and market appeal based primarily on price. It knew the most enthusiastic customers for electronics were the younger generation and that Circuit City's offering was less appealing to these shoppers. And it fully understood that both Best Buy and the big discount stores—Walmart, Costco, and Sam's Club—were taking portions of their market share.

Nonetheless, at no point in this ten-year planning process did management run scared. It refused to learn from Best Buy's marketing success because Best Buy was, at that point, not a financial

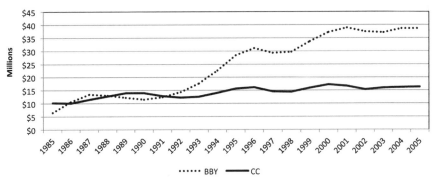

success. By focusing on Best Buy's low profitability in the early '90s, Circuit City's management ignored the possibility of rejuvenation. It believed that Best Buy would enter the dustbin of history, along with many other failed electronics and appliance chains,[197] and continued to insist on the superiority of the Circuit City business model—despite the company's falling market share. Like a rope-bound Gulliver, it knew at some level what it needed to do, but it could not move.

The myopia, however, was not universal. A number of senior and middle managers recognized early on that Best Buy was a serious threat. Bill Zierden and Walt Bruckart visited an early Best Buy Concept I store and reported that it was likely to capture a large market share with its no-frills approach and minimal directed selling. Some years later, Jack Fitzsimmons, senior vice president for Administration, also tried to point out to the executive committee that Best Buy had, in many ways, a better model. His attempt to spell out the advantages fell on deaf ears. While relations within the executive committee remained civil, the mutual trust and respect that characterized the beginning of the decade began to erode. This was a pretty testosterone-heavy, alpha-male group. Their prevailing politics were highly conservative and the views of independent and more flexible thinkers, like Fitzsimmons and Zierden, were not always welcome and were sometimes disparaged.

Contributing to the problem was a change in organization. In 1996 Alan McCollough, a ten-year veteran of the company and Bruckart's replacement as chief merchant, was recruited by another retailer. When he told Sharp he was leaving, Sharp responded with a strong counteroffer and the promise that he would recommend McCollough to succeed him as CEO. In March of 1997, McCollough, in addition to being president of the stores division, was elected president of Circuit City Stores, Inc., the parent company. Although the board did not commit to naming him CEO, all assumed his likely ascension. A few years earlier, Austin Ligon, former senior vice president of strategic planning and integral developer of the CarMax concept, had been named president of CarMax. Now both he and McCollough reported directly to Sharp.

Sharp remained engaged in the CarMax business and was an active participant in Ligon's executive committee meetings. His involvement at Circuit City was, however, significantly different. Although McCollough held regular executive committee meetings, nothing of substance was discussed, and Sharp soon discovered that following the "official" meeting, McCollough and his team would retreat to another conference room to hold the real meeting, from which he was excluded. Although still the CEO, Sharp believed that he needed to respect the authority of his new company presidents and did not confront McCollough on this or other troubling issues.

A third factor contributing to the collective denial of "trouble in the City" was the fact that senior management, with the exception of Sharp and Chalifoux, did not understand that the profits of the credit bank accounted for a major share of Circuit City's earnings. This resulted in senior managers arrogantly (and understandably) dismissing the significance of Best Buy's market share gains. In fact, without the credit bank, Circuit City's earnings were a lot closer to Best Buy's than they realized.

Finally, the store operations executives on the firing line, McCollough, John Froman, and Richard Birnbaum, all knew or sensed that Sharp planned to retire in a few years, and they were in competition to succeed him or at least to move up. Whether out of conviction or desire to please the boss, they all supported Sharp's insistence that the company stick to its step-up selling model.

So why did Sharp, whose analytical abilities are second to none, not see and take decisive steps to deal with the strategic threat from Best Buy? A number of former Circuit City executives who prefer to remain nameless think he was bored, frustrated, and ultimately discouraged by the fact that the consumer electronics business had become a commodity business. It was neither fun nor profitable to compete and lose market share to the likes of Walmart, Costco, and Best Buy.

Others who know him well think Sharp was happier operating as an entrepreneur and an investor than as a manager. That would

Alan McCollough, president 1997 – 2005

explain his preoccupation with conceiving and starting CarMax and DIVX, as well as his corresponding lack of attention to the challenges facing the Circuit City stores in the '90s. Still others believe that through his hands-off approach, he was preparing the organization for his retirement. Whatever the reason, Circuit City lost its way.

Role of the Board

Circuit City never had cutting-edge governance policies. From an outsider's perspective, my father's board would be described today as a board of cronies and retainers. Appearances notwithstanding, the outside directors were, in fact, all outstanding, independent individuals, who agreed to serve not for the money or the prestige but because they knew and respected the principals. They were also investors and were willing and able to stand up to Sam and later to me when they deemed it appropriate to do so.[198]

The board I created over time was technically more independent. Despite their outstanding talents and qualifications, I excluded our lawyer and our banker from the board, but not the boardroom, because of the negative appearance of having company retainers on the board.[199] Instead, I added people whose skills I considered relevant to our task. They included Walter J. Salmon, the leading professor of marketing and retailing at the Harvard Business School; Ted Nierenberg, founder of Dansk Design International, a large designer, importer, wholesaler, and retailer of home furnishings; Doug Drysdale, a tax lawyer with a national reputation; and Richard Cooper, professor of international economics at Harvard and former Under Secretary of State and Chairman of the Boston Fed.[200] The ability to make a positive contribution was the key criterion. Certain directors (but none of the above) were not renominated if they had not a made meaningful contribution to the work of the board.

The Sharp Board

Although Sharp became CEO in 1986, it was not until the mid-'90s that he had an opportunity to play a leading role in determining the board's composition. The board he shaped included Mikael Salovaara, a former Goldman Sachs partner; John Snow, former CEO of CSX, a railroad conglomerate, and subsequently, U.S. Secretary of the Treasury; Jim Hardymon, former CEO of Textron and then a professional board member of 11 listed companies; and Bob Jepson, South Carolina investor, businessman, and founder of the Jepson School of Leadership Studies at the University of Richmond. Their experiences were with much bigger businesses.

Sharp dominated his board to a far greater extent than either Sam or I. He recruited fewer independent thinkers and more former and sitting CEOs, none of whom knew retailing and most of whom had neither the time nor the inclination to challenge his perspective. In fact, Sharp believed that the only important role of the board was to hire and fire the CEO and approve major corporate moves, and his appointees apparently concurred.

When it came to advice and suggestions with respect to operations, Sharp's, attitude, expressed on more than a few occasions, was that he and his management team thought about these issues 24-7 and had considered all the alternatives and pitfalls imaginable. Therefore, it was highly unlikely that a board that met for a day and a half, four or five times a year, could have any useful input or new ideas the management team had not already considered. Needless to say, this attitude raised some eyebrows, especially among the longer-serving directors, but the company was doing so well that none of them entertained the idea that this might be a reason to exercise what Sharp considered their one clear function and fire him.

Nonetheless, the board meetings were open, and, given his restrictive attitude about the role of a board, Sharp was patient with ongoing questions and suggestions. During our discussions about

Best Buy, I was not alone in observing that, "unless we change course, I fear we will soon be 'Avis' and Best Buy will be 'Hertz.'"

Following the 1999–2001 Three Year Plan meeting, I wrote to Sharp:

> The great successes in American retailing have all been based on enabling customers to buy the products they want, in the way they want, at the lowest prices possible....At this last meeting, we disagreed about how to display and sell "commodity" products, including most ACE [i.e. Advanced Consumer Electronics products such as Walkmans, portable music systems, and headphones], low end TV, VCR and some other categories. Clearly, a lot of the public wants to buy commodity electronics on a self-service basis. That's why the discounters (Target, Walmart) and clubs (Costco, Sam's) are displaying and selling more and more and why Best Buy's format gets generally high marks from consumers....I am convinced that if you and your team set it as the objective, you can find a way to run a "mixed" store in which customers who want to pick up an item and take it to a central check out can do so, while those who want help – in ACE or any other department – can get advice.[201]

Sharp disagreed and that was that. When I expressed these views in board meetings, those directors who had retail backgrounds or experience generally agreed, while the rest of the board ignored or dismissed the ideas.

In retrospect, the board did not push back hard enough on the disquieting rise of Best Buy. Nor did the directors insist on full transparency with respect to the credit bank financials. One director recalls that when he challenged the decision not to disclose the profitability of the credit card bank, company counsel offered the opinion that if the company shared this information with the board, it would have to make it public. This was demonstrably incorrect, but silenced further criticism. The company and the board did not appreciate that hiding the bank's profitability from competitors and Wall Street analysts also meant hiding it from our own senior management team.

The board also supported and encouraged Sharp's deep involvement with CarMax and, especially, DIVX. The members did not understand that these enterprises represented a significant diversion of top management's time and attention away from the declining core business.

So why did the board members neglect their duty? There are at least five reasons:

- **Composition.** A board dominated by sitting and retired CEOs is predisposed to support a sitting CEO.

- **Limited Retail Experience.** A board that has limited experience in the business of the company is less equipped to evaluate issues independently and more inclined to accept the views of management. Only three out of twelve outside directors who served in the mid-'90s had retail experience. By 1997 one of them was gone and none of the four directors whom Sharp selected in the late '90s had any retail background.

- **Different Standards.** These were the days before Enron, WorldCom, and Sarbanes-Oxley. The board did not hold regular executive sessions, and the compensation committee that Sharp had carefully selected performed most of the CEO's evaluations. As a result, there were no formal or organized opportunities for the board as a whole to evaluate Sharp or consider whether he was still the right leader. There was a time when our company counsel told the board it would be appropriate to go into executive session to evaluate the CEO, but John Snow, then lead director, responded that "there is no need. We all know he is doing a good job. Just prepare some minutes to reflect that consensus." When I chaired the director search process, I kept Sharp involved, and by the mid-'90s only proposed candidates acceptable to him.

- **Fear of Change.** The board recognized that Sharp was an unusually talented individual. None of us—and I was among the most critical of Sharp's inadequate response to Best Buy—wanted to force a confrontation that would lead to his departure.

- **Self-Preservation.** To be totally candid, all of us, me included, enjoyed serving on the board. On one occasion a few directors went to Sharp to tell him that his dismissive and somewhat arrogant attitude toward director input on substantive issues was not helpful, but the message did not get through. For the skeptical or concerned director, the choices were to quit the board or quit second-guessing management.

As a member of the board, and chairman or vice chairman for most of those years, I hold myself fully responsible for this failure of stewardship.

Sharp's Legacy

Sharp retired in June of 2000 at the early age of fifty-three. He had joined the company in December 1982 and became CEO in June 1986. By every objective measure he departed on a high note. His fourteen-year run as CEO took the company from $1 billion in sales to $12.6 billion; from earnings of $22 million to $327 million; from 4,500 employees to 60,000; and from 69 Circuit City locations to 616, plus 40 CarMax locations. The CarMax locations averaged an amazing $50 million in sales.

Needless to say, shareholder value also soared. Despite some down years in the late '90s, as the company struggled to compete with Best Buy and the mass merchants, profits surged in 2000, the last year of Sharp's tenure. The company's market value went from $4.8 billion when Sharp became CEO to $44 billion when he retired, and the stock was selling near its all-time high of $56 per share. For the five years after Sharp retired as CEO, Circuit City sales, excluding CarMax, remained in the $9.5 to $10 billion range. Earnings, following his departure, however, plummeted from $327 million in 2000 to $155 million in 2001 to $41 million in 2003, and then to a small loss in 2004. Within a year of his retirement, the stock dropped to about $20 per share. In 2006 it peaked at $27 but never got anywhere close to its previous all-time high.

Fiscal Year	Revenues ($000)	Earnings ($000)	Earnings/Sales %
63	5,900	117	1.98%
64	9,300	216	2.32%
65	13,200	451	3.42%
66	22,800	616	2.70%
67	26,800	798	2.98%
68	27,151	458	1.69%
69	37,000	689	1.86%
70	48,600	529	1.09%
71	55,800	265	0.47%
72	63,200	552	0.87%
73	67,900	421	0.62%
74	75,000	457	0.61%
75	68,600	(2,980)	-4.34%
76	61,200	1,360	2.22%
77	72,400	1,250	1.73%
78	91,000	2,050	2.25%
79	111,000	2,600	2.34%

Whether they sensed the drop in stock price coming or not, Sharp and most of his team, riding the general rise in stock prices during the Internet bubble, cashed out $270 million worth of stock and stock options in 2000. By 2003 most of the key players, with the exception of McCollough, were gone. I had sold most of my stock years earlier and left the board in June of 2001.

Habits of Mind

Be Humble, Run Scared: *Continuously doubt your understanding of things. Business success contains the seeds of its own destruction. Worry about what the competition knows that you do not. Andy Grove, the legendary cofounder of Intel, got it largely right in his book* **Only the Paranoid Survive.**

Circuit City's several Three Year Plans during the 1990s reveal both its lack of humility in thinking that it had the only "right formula" and its lack of fear that Best Buy could solve its profit problems. Even as Best Buy surpassed Circuit City in sales and earnings, management insisted on the superiority of the Circuit

City business model and never entertained the possibility that Best Buy might resume selling ESPs or improve its inventory controls. Equally myopic and arrogant, Circuit City systematically ignored or rationalized away massive evidence of the consumer's preference for Best Buy's format.

Curiosity Sustains the Cat: *The world is constantly changing. Be open and curious and strive to learn from others. Continuously try to understand the market and the changing economic, demographic, and other relevant forces at work that impact your business. Study your competitors. They may have insights and practices worth emulating or refining.*

Circuit City was wounded by its failure to respond to changing market dynamics. Declining prices and greater consumer familiarity with electronics made pure price competition from Costco, Walmart, and others a painful reality. Management deemphasized personal computers, computer games and music because of their low margins despite the fact that consumer demand for those products was increasing. And Circuit City realized far too late that Best Buy's Concept II, with big, bright, self-service stores, hands-on displays, and no commissioned sales force, was the way consumers, especially young consumers, wanted to buy electronics and appliances.

Evidence Trumps Ideology: *In business, as in politics, decisions are too often based on unproven assumptions about what works and what doesn't. We all need operating assumptions about human nature, the economy, and the like, but when things do not work out as planned, we need to determine whether our assumptions were based on evidence or ideology. Evidence about the real world trumps ideological assumptions every time.*

In Sharp's mind, the full-service and self-service models were mutually exclusive. Although some members of his staff and some directors argued to the contrary, Sharp was sure that "we could not mix value-added selling and self-service in the same store."[202] He believed that if we let customers walk around with shopping carts and pick up what they wanted, they would buy only low-margin products and, worse yet, not buy extended service policies.

This theory was not tested in a Circuit City store. Outside Circuit City there was a lot of evidence that a mixed floor did work. At the same time Best Buy customers were picking up portable TVs and taking them to a central checkout, other customers were talking to trained sales people about big screen TVs, audio systems, appliances, and other products. Hourly paid Best Buy sales personnel did an excellent job of persuading customers to buy and to insure the product with an extended service policy. To be sure, the product mix was less "rich" with high-margin merchandise, and ESP sales were modestly lower, but the far greater volume produced better profits and a much higher return on investment.

The point is not whether Sharp was right in his belief that self-service and full service were mutually exclusive. The fundamental point is that he did not test his assumption by trying it out in the real world. Unlike Best Buy, which reinvented itself several times in the '90s, Circuit City never fundamentally revisited and reexamined (though it enhanced and tweaked) its format inherited from the '80s. As the competition surged, a wide range of alternative strategies were discussed, debated, and researched. But none was ever tested in an actual store.

No matter how smart you are, assumptions about consumer behavior cannot be verified on a spreadsheet or in one's mind. Only the consumer can tell you if a new or revised retail concept is a good or bad idea.

Confront the Brutal Facts: *The worst person you can fool is yourself. Ignoring or denying reality does not help it go away. Once you understand the issues, be bold enough to take decisive action.*

When it appeared that Best Buy was quickly closing the gap in both sales and earnings, Circuit City at first denied the problem, hoping that Best Buy would fail to get the funding it needed to expand. When that hope proved false, management stewed, studied, and stalled. The board systematically dithered over a whole range of options, but even with the understanding that customers preferred a different shopping experience, Circuit City's directors could not organize their thoughts or galvanize their will to make needed changes or even to experiment with another strategy. Instead, it kicked the can down the road to the next management team.

Encourage Debate: *Learn from dissent. Involve senior staff and the board of directors in an open process to find the best answer. Create a board that will raise thought-provoking questions and challenge management to justify its plans.*

The lack of meaningful debate between management and the board of directors allowed Circuit City to go too long without self-reflection. Although the company was enjoying success at the time, without a skeptical board to question its underlying weaknesses, it failed to deal with changes in the real world and was thus blindsided.

Lessons Learned

Know Your Customers: For any business, but especially for a retail business, success depends on understanding your customers and what they value. Even when you get it right, however, you need to stay alert: consumer needs and tastes are constantly changing. The reason to do strategic planning is primarily to understand the underlying trends that affect your business. For trend waves that are too big to control or influence, it is critical to design a strategy that accommodates or, better yet, surfs those waves to success.

That is what Sam Wurtzel did when he first went into the TV business as the South's first television station opened and again when he began to run licensed departments in newly emerging discount department stores. It is what I did in 1973 when we concluded that small stores were inefficient and that warehouse showrooms were best met the needs of consumers as they moved to the suburbs.

It is what Best Buy did as it developed new Concept I and II stores, switched from commissioned salesmen to self-service, and then shifted its emphasis to computers and in-home technical support. Sharp also "caught a wave" when he conceived and created CarMax as the antidote to the proverbial "used car salesman." It is both ironic and tragic that Circuit City did not apply the same consumer analysis to create comparable updated sales practices for Circuit City as it did for CarMax.

Customers, Taken as a Group, Are Always Right: *The essence of successful marketing is to find out what customers want and give it to them. Consumers were saying loud and clear that they wanted to shop in an open environment with sales assistance if, as, and when they wanted it. They wanted to be able to pick up a product and get out the door without having to listen to a sales pitch for a step-up product or extended warranties. Some wanted sales assistance on certain products. Some were willing to consider extended warranty protection. But no one wanted to be forced to listen to a pitch.*

Despite the fact that Circuit City was clearly losing market share, the management team neither asked itself what customers really want nor tested new strategies that others were finding successful.

Focus on Main Street, Not Wall Street: *Excessive focus on profits and stock price generally results in neither. Business, like love, is often a paradox. Just as you can't force someone to love you, you can't force a customer to buy or to pay a higher price. Circuit City's focus on its objectives of maintaining high margins and a robust stock price rather than on the customer's objectives, left it deaf to what customers were saying and, ultimately, much the poorer.*

You Can't Take Margins to the Bank: *Return on investment, not return on* *sales, is the proper measure of profitability. Excessive emphasis on margins can lead to poor economic decisions. Best Buy demonstrated that Sharp was right. Non-commission sales personnel would result in somewhat lower margins. But it also demonstrated that lower sales costs and higher sales per store could leverage fixed costs to achieve superior returns on investment.*

The critical point that the Circuit City team failed adequately to appreciate is that Best Buy was achieving far higher turnover on its inventory investment. As any retailer knows, the return on inventory investment is the same (two times) whether your margins are 4 percent and you turn the inventory fifty times per year (think grocery stores) or your margins are 100 percent and you turn the inventory twice a year (think hardware stores).

Because publicly owned retailers conceal their true margins by adding extraneous items (warehousing, distribution, and so forth) to the cost of goods, it is impossible to make an apples-to-apples comparison between Circuit City's and Best Buy's (or anyone else's) margins. We know, however, that during the last half of the '90s, Best Buy turned its inventory roughly 6.3 times per year as compared to 4.75 times for Circuit City. Without adjusting for increased selling expenses (which reduce return on investment) or improved leverage on fixed costs (which improve returns), Best Buy would earn the same return on its inventory investment at 15 percent margins as Circuit City would at 20 percent.

GONE (2001–2009)

PART IV

Chapter Ten

GOING

Vision without action is a daydream; action without vision is a nightmare.
— *Japanese Proverb*

Our major obligation is not to mistake slogans for solutions.
— *Edward R. Murrow*

At the June 2000 annual meeting, W. Alan McCollough was elected president and CEO of Circuit City Stores, Inc. McCollough had grown up in the Midwest and, following college, joined the Navy as an operations officer on a minesweeper. After leaving the service he got an MBA at Southern Illinois University and subsequently joined the marketing department at Milliken, the world's largest privately held textile and chemical manufacturer.

As someone without prior retail experience, he was a "creative hire" when he joined Circuit City in 1987. His sharp mind, calm demeanor, and strong work ethic enabled him to rise quickly through store operations to become a division president with responsibility for roughly seventy stores before being promoted to the position of chief merchant upon Bruckart's retirement. McCollough saw himself as a "more technical merchant" than Bruckart. His minesweeper duties had taught him something about electronics, and he loved to tinker with the ever-changing new products and to understand from a consumer standpoint what they were capable of doing. Suppliers appreciated his knowledge and his straightforward manner. Subordinates loved working for him.

In 1997, Sharp made him president of the Circuit City Stores Division. As such, McCollough was responsible for merchandising, store operations marketing, and for dealing with the challenges from Best Buy and the mass merchants. Four years later, as CEO of the whole company, his responsibilities expanded to include CarMax, DIVX, the credit card operations, and the various corporate functions that had previously reported to Sharp.

Turning Point

A lot of systemic problems had been ignored during the last five years of Sharp's tenure. While sales and profits grew and the stock reached an all-time high in 2000, under Circuit City's hood was an aging store base, a failing marketing strategy, an expensive workforce, and an increasingly out-of-date management information system.

The single most important "brutal fact" staring the company in the face was the enormous difference between Best Buy and Circuit City in average store sales: Best Buy, in 44,000 square feet (almost all showroom), sold an average of $37 million per store. [203] Circuit City, in 34,000 square feet (of which only 15,000 square feet was showroom), averaged $17 million per store, less than half its most direct competitor.[204] This sales disparity put Circuit City at a significant disadvantage in terms of dollars available to acquire prime real estate and to purchase a competitive level of advertising.[205] By 1997, as Best Buy grew its store base, its total sales drew equal to Circuit City's, and by 2000 had sailed past, thereby sharply eroding Circuit City's long-standing advantage with vendors. The big question facing the new team was whether Circuit City could stage a comeback and once again rival Best Buy for the lead in the industry or if it was doomed to be second best—or worse.

Some observers believed that by 2000 Circuit City was so far behind Best Buy it could never catch up. The argument was based on the fact that Circuit City and Best Buy had closely tracked each other from the mid-'80s till the early '90s. By 1993, Best Buy pulled ahead and kept on growing while Circuit City fell farther and farther behind. Equally telling, Circuit City's *earnings per store*

Net Earnings per Store 1985 - 2005

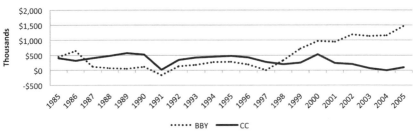

stayed ahead of Best Buy's throughout most of the '90s as Best Buy struggled with inventory management problems and lack of extended service policies. When Best Buy turned those two issues around, its earnings per store took off, doubling and tripling over the next seven years, while Circuit City's earnings declined as it failed to grow sales and come to grips with the changes in consumer buying preferences.

For Circuit City, with a new leader at the helm, 2000 was clearly a potential turning point. If it wanted to catch up with Best Buy it would have to climb out of the hole it had dug. The task was difficult but not hopeless. Although now in third place in consumer electronics, behind Best Buy and Walmart, Circuit City still had sales in excess of $10 billion, some $437 million in the bank, and a profitable business.[206] It also had significant assets it could sell to raise more cash, including one or both bank credit card programs and its remaining interest in CarMax.

Circuit City still had some, albeit limited, time and the money to make the necessary corrections. But management needed fundamentally to rethink the business model and make bold and decisive changes. Other companies have turned themselves around and reemerged in strong industry leadership positions after it appeared to many outside observers that the game was up. IBM and the Ford Motor Company come to mind.

By the late '80s the once-fabled IBM was clearly in trouble. In addition to a bloated workforce, its core mainframe business was being undermined by the PC client/server revolution. Increased emphasis on desktop productivity versus enterprise productivity strengthened the demand for powerful workstations as compared to large mainframes, which were IBM's long suit. When IBM botched the PC revolution and missed the small-server opportunity, it suffered two straight years of billion-dollar losses. In 1993 it reported a massive $8 billion deficit, the largest single-year loss in American history to that time.[207]

For the first time in IBM's 108-year existence, the board went outside, hiring Louis Gerstner, former CEO of RJR Nabisco. Gerstner turned the company around with quick and decisive action. He sold non-core divisions; dramatically shrank the workforce from more than 400,000 employees to 220,000; and recommitted the company to the mainframe business and to providing integrated IT services, including hardware, software, and consulting to its clients. Slowly but surely, IBM regained its footing and its leadership status in the industry.

Ford is a similar story. As early as 2006, Bill Ford, president and CEO of Ford Motor Company, realized radical action was needed. Although the company earned $2 billion in 2006, it had lost $1.5 billion in North America and by that time its sales of SUVs, the mainstay of its domestic business, were plummeting. He created a "War Room," closed factories, laid off thousands of employees, and decided he needed some outside help to implement a "major corporate overhaul."

Within a few months he hired Alan Mulally, a top Boeing executive, and turned the CEO title over to him. Mulally was an unconventional choice. A trained engineer who had headed Boeing's 777 aircraft program, he was not what Detroiters would call a "car guy." At an early meeting, a colleague challenged him: "You know, this automobile business is really complicated." The new chief executive's response was terse: "A car has ten thousand parts and a commercial plane has four million parts in it—and it has to stay in the air."[208]

Mulally continued Bill Ford's program of shedding unprofitable brands and cutting expenses, and, despite a difficult market, he raised new capital. By 2008, when the financial crisis hit, Ford was able to survive without government assistance. Again, bold and decisive action saved the day.

Whether Circuit City could have emulated IBM and Ford and turned itself around is anybody's guess. Personally, I think it was possible to do this and remerge a viable player in the sale of consumer electronics, probably a strong second to Best Buy. But accomplishing that would have required, as with Ford and IBM, clear, bold, and sustained commitment to a viable turnaround strategy. The big question was whether McCollough could envision the decisive action needed and execute a plan to make it happen. And if not, would the board be willing to find a suitable replacement in time to save the company?

The Real World 2000–2005

McCollough, like Sharp, arrived at an opportune time in the business cycle. The economy he inherited began with a stock market bubble. Throughout the 1990s, venture capitalists, investment bankers, and stock market speculators were shoveling dollars at any enterprise ending in "dot-com." In 2001 the speculative bubble burst; the Dow Jones Industrial Average plummeted 36 percent from its all-time high in January 2000 to a four-year low in October 2002.[209] The high-tech-oriented NASDAQ fared even worse.[210] A succession of accounting scandals at Enron, WorldCom, Tyco, and other companies further eroded investors' confidence. Then, the Dow nearly doubled between October 2002 and October 2007, when it reached a new all-time high.[211] Despite these market gyrations, however, the GDP, which had fallen in 1998 to 2000, resumed growing and the meltdown was soon forgotten.[212]

The Federal Reserve's tilt toward cheap money encouraged builders to build more houses and mom and pop speculators to buy second and third houses with little or no money down, for resale or rental at a "guaranteed" profit. Americans went on a shopping spree funded by rising stock prices, reduced savings, and increased borrowings, frequently secured by the the ever-in-

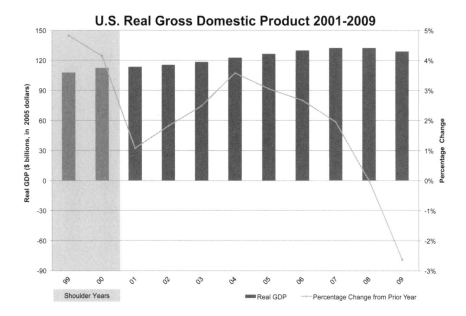

creasing "equity" in their ever-more-"valuable" homes. Between 2000 and 2008, the personal savings rate as a percentage of disposable income averaged 2.7 percent, the lowest level in more than sixty years.[213]

Americans' preference for consumption over saving was, in the short run, good news for retailers. Between 2000 and 2007, retailers enjoyed a 12 percent inflation-adjusted increase in sales.[214] Online retailing demonstrated particularly robust growth. Between 2003 and 2007, this category grew more than 150 percent, from $56 billion to $142 billion.[215] Companies invested in attractive websites to draw web traffic from brick-and-mortar competitors and other e-tailers.

The opening decade of the twenty-first century was an especially great time for consumer electronics. Manufacturing efficiencies drove pricing for virtually all consumer electronic products to previously unimaginably low levels. For example, a standard DVD player, which cost $1000 when it was introduced in 1997, could be purchased in 2003 for under $50, a 95 percent drop.[216] As features improved and prices declined, demand exploded. Cell phone

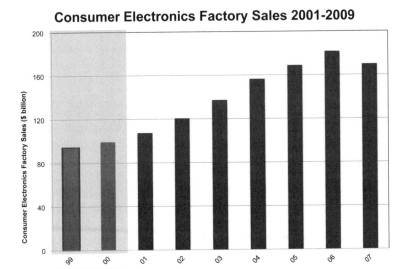

Consumer Electronics Factory Sales 2001-2009

use, for example, more than doubled, from 109 million subscribers in 2000 to 255 million in 2007.[217] Internet users transitioned from dial-up to broadband, which achieved 55 percent household penetration by 2008.[218] Annual personal computer shipments in the United States grew from 49 million in 2000 to 65 million in 2008, a 33 percent increase,[219] and household penetration of PCs reached 78 percent by 2006, up from 58 percent in 2000.[220]

As McCollough clearly understood, exciting new digital products were poised for explosion. For example, portable MP3 player sales, led by Apple's iPod, skyrocketed from $80 million to almost $6 billion between 2000 and 2008.[221, 222] Consumers also thirsted after the latest and greatest in digital television technology. Once Congress allowed satellite providers to broadcast network programming,[223] satellite became a viable competitor to cable, snapping up one-third of the market by 2008.[224] Flat-screen digital TV became the preferred technology as consumers raced to beat the February 2009 cutoff date for transition to digital. In just three short years (2003–06), annual sales of flat-screen TVs grew from just over one million units to more than 17 million.[225, 226] High-definition television sales also gathered speed, as did DVR (digital video recorders) sales.

For Circuit City this price decline was a double-edged sword. While lower prices drove demand for everyone, it was especially advantageous to mass merchants and other low-cost providers. Readily available online product reviews (often provided by Circuit City's and Best Buy's own websites) and an exploding number of magazines devoted to computers and digital entertainment systems facillitated the shift to mass merchants. Such easy access to information empowered consumers to find the product they wanted without the assistance of a trained salesman and to locate (or negotiate) the best possible deals. In 2002, Walmart eclipsed Circuit City as the nation's second-largest consumer electronics retailer.[227] By 2006, full-line discounters' share of the consumer electronics market had grown to 19 percent—nearly double what it was in 1998—prompting *TWICE* (This Week in Consumer Electronics) magazine to declare, "There are no more category killers."[228]

Appliances told a similar story. In the mature appliance industry, with no significant product introductions, manufacturers and retailers cut prices to attract new buyers. Low-cost, low-service retailers like Home Depot and Lowe's benefited. Sears and Circuit City suffered.

The 2001 Three Year Plan

The 2001–03 Three Year Plan that McCollough and his team presented to the board in June of 2000, just as he was about to assume command, was the perfect opportunity to step back and ask: In a market characterized by exploding demand, sharply declining retail prices, higher-tech products, and better informed consumers, is there still a place for a high-cost, high-touch, step-up retailer? Or should Circuit City reinvent itself to be more like Best Buy, or find some other approach that would allow it to surf on, instead of swimming against the waves of change?

The economic, demographic, and competitive environments

described in the 2001 Three Year Plan were right on the money. It identified as macro issues:

- *The current state of the U.S. economy.* It noted that the economy "continues to grow at a record-breaking pace" and that the forecasts going forward were positive.[229]

- *Changing Consumers.* The plan noted that baby boomers in their prime buying years of forty-five to fifty-four would constitute 25 percent of the population over the next few years, and Gen Y, those born after 1979, would represent 41 percent of the U.S. population in ten years. "This is a generation [Gen Y] that has grown up with the computer at home. Their whole world is shaped by technology." Equally important, "Gen Y'ers were "weaned on instant gratification. They exhibit a preference for retailers that allow them to buy into a lifestyle," over "traditional retailers [that] have historically focused almost exclusively on products."[230]

- The plan also described "Ethnicity Everywhere": "Within a decade the U.S. will be the second largest Spanish-speaking country in the world and the Hispanic population will exceed 41 million people." At the time, the purchasing power of this single ethnic group approached a trillion dollars. [231]

- The plan's bottom line was that "there is a mindset change taking place in America characterized by a renewed sense of individualism....Americans believe that they are smarter than average as well as more independent than their parents were at their age, and they wanted to be in charge."[232]

- *Digital Product Cycle.* The Circuit City management believed that "we are in the early stages of what will be considered the most exciting time ever in the history of the consumer electronics industry."[233] The plan correctly forecast big opportunities in digital television, digital set-top boxes, and wireless communications.

- *Best Buy.* The plan did the same detailed analysis of Best Buy as Sharp's plans had in the '90s. This time, however, the results were even less favorable for Circuit City.

U.S. Population by Age Group 2001-2009

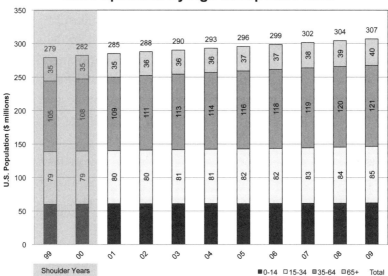

- Circuit City and Best Buy had comparable shares of the U.S. market for most merchandise categories. However, Circuit City was in more markets with a lot more stores.[234] When the plan compared their respective shares in the top fifteen markets they both served, Best Buy was ahead in fourteen.

- The plan noted that, with the help of Arthur Anderson, Best Buy had recently caught up with Circuit City in the sale of extended warranties. Best Buy was also able, by virtue of its far higher sales per store and by investing in technology, to turn its inventories 7.1 times compared to Circuit City's 5.0 times: a 40 percent more efficient use of capital.[235]

- Also worrisome, Best Buy was beginning to focus on selling more sophisticated (and expensive) digital products, an area in which Circuit City had enjoyed a clear lead. And it was improving its website and threatening to catch up with Circuit City in e-commerce sales.

- Further analysis showed that the average Circuit City store had higher gross margins but Best Buy had lower operating expenses. The store operating profit percentages were in the same ballpark:

4.3 percent for Best Buy and 5.1 percent for Circuit City.[236] The big difference was in the dollars. With the average Best Buy store turning twice the volume, its profit per store was $1.6 million, compared to $1 million for Circuit City's.[237] Because the Circuit City stores were more expensive to build, and because Best Buy had higher inventory turns, the plan estimated that Best Buy's internal rate of return on invested capital[238] after five years was 92 percent compared to 40 percent for Circuit City.[239]

The plan identified the issues well. However, in response it only proposed aspirational goals, without clear strategies to accomplish them or the metrics to know if they were achieved. The key initiatives were:

- *Fully Integrated Marketing.* The plan stated, "Nothing is more important than the Circuit City brand." It described a new image-building ad campaign that was currently on the air with Circuit City's new signature tagline ("Imagine That") and declared that the phrase was "intended to communicate the spirit of discovery—our aspiration for the consumer's in-store experience...Discovery encompasses three themes: Empowerment, Potential, and Wonder."[240]

- *Reinvent Our Store Format.* The Circuit City "Store of the Future" would be "bright, open and inviting" and "created around how customers want to shop," including "shopping carts for merchandise and small children." The "more familiar product categories will be self-service, leaving our more knowledgeable commissioned sales counselors in areas where they are needed most."[241]

- *Learning Culture.* Circuit City's knowledgeable sales counselors "have traditionally offered a tremendous competitive advantage in selling advanced products."[242] To maintain this advantage, Circuit City proposed to outsource training by engaging DigitalThink to provide web-based, comprehensive in-store training for all store managers and sales counselors.

- *World Class Supply Chain.* Improved supply chain management will be a "critical competitive front for us."[243] It will lead to higher turns, fewer markdowns, and lower logistics costs all along the chain.

Whether McCollough understood Circuit City's dire straits is not clear. If he was running scared, he wasn't letting on.

Need for a Credible Plan

The plan never asked the hard questions. Its aspirational goals sounded good, but what did they mean in operational terms? How do you create an atmosphere in which "customers want to shop," or make more familiar categories self-service if you do not make significant changes in the stores? And if you do make significant changes, what changes are needed? What would they cost? How long will it take? The hard questions were not asked, much less answered.

Web-based learning and improved supply-chain logistics were also superficially appealing ideas, but there was no discussion of whether online teaching is effective for sales personnel or what investments in hardware, software, or personnel were needed to improve inventory turns and in-stock positions.

The financial metrics of the plan especially lacked intellectual credibility. On the one hand, the plan projected comparatively modest store growth: seventy-five new stores, plus forty-five relocations, over the next three years. On the other hand, it projected staggering sales increases: from $10.6 billion in 2000 to $16.8 billion in 2003, a 58 percent increase in just four years. For the prior four years, Circuit City same-store sales had been basically flat.

Now, despite the serious competitive threats and the dramatic declines in retail prices, the plan projected incredible increases in mostly same-store sales. Moreover, these sales would be at higher gross margins than in the recent past. This would lead to the tripling of after-tax profits, from an all-time high of $327 million in 2000 to $1.13 billion in 2003.[244]

In retrospect, a number of those involved in creating the plan said that it was not intended to be a serious road map for the company, but was made to satisfy the board's expectation of being presented with a three-year plan every other year. One of the major contributors was told to "pull her punches" for the board.

So far as I can tell, no one on the board challenged these fantasy projections. Even worse, this was the last comprehensive three-year plan Circuit City ever made. From that point on, the board would deal with the key issues of store design, real estate, sales compensation, and MIS one at a time. That is far different from having a systematic three-year view of fundamental market and competitive trends, as well as an honest analysis of internal strengths and weaknesses that leads to a comprehensive plan.

Addressing the Strategic Issues

To his credit, for the balance of his tenure as CEO, McCollough attempted to address the key issues identified in his plan. Here is how it played out.

Marketing

The plan stated that "nothing is more important than the Circuit City brand.[245] It determines how we treat our associates and our customers; draws traffic to the store; defines the in-store experience; identifies our customer-service standards; measures our post-sale service; and ultimately determines the percentage of customers coming back to our stores."[246] The plan boldly and correctly stated that the company needed to "re-launch our brand to heighten relevance with a younger consumer" and to "create a consistent message of who we are and why choose us versus Best Buy."[247]

From the beginning, McCollough promised "significant attention to marketing programs"[248] and made two important additions to the marketing management team. He hired Ann-Marie Stephens, formerly with Procter & Gamble, as VP for strategic planning, and a year later, Fiona Dias, who had worked at both Pepsi and P&G, as senior VP of marketing. Besides adding gender and racial diversity to the (previously) all-white, all-male top management ranks, these unusually talented hires signaled a shift in marketing thinking.

The new team identified the core customers as *"those individuals who value leading edge technologies and the sales assisted service we provide* [emphasis added]." [249] This definition reflects McCollough's preoccupation with high-tech digital products, often at the expense of more familiar bread-and-butter electronics. It also clearly indicates Circuit City's intention to skew its marketing to the early adapter and high-end segments of the market and diminishes the importance of customers looking for value or are buying yet another standard product for another room or another home. As such, it ran counter to the trends that were fueling the sales of Best Buy and the mass merchandisers.

Stephens and Dias did extensive demographic, psychographic, and competitive research to see what consumers wanted that other retailers were providing. There is no doubt that their experience at major consumer products firms was long overdue and sorely needed at Circuit City. Research about the customers and what they wanted was critical to rethinking the store design and staffing model, to configuring Circuit City's top-rated e-commerce website, and to determining its advertising strategies.

On the other hand, the package-goods approach to marketing does not easily transfer to the retail-advertising context. The focus of the new TV ads was on high-tech digital products that were exciting but not unique to Circuit City. Customers could buy these products anywhere. This emphasis on "touchy-feely" product-centric advertising comes out of the package goods manufacturing industry. The manufacturer's job is to create demand for products—especially new products. Therefore, manufacturers' advertising typically focuses on the unique features and consumer benefits of their product. Price is generally not part of a manufacturer's pitch.

From a retailer's point of view, all electronics and appliance products are, in a sense, commodities. Every TV and refrigerator is identical to every other TV and refrigerator of the same brand and model. They can be purchased in a host of stores. Retailers, especially low-margin retailers, each with a minor market share, cannot afford to entice the public to desire a product. All they can afford to say is: "If you want this product, buy it from me." As a result, retailers typically concentrate their advertising on price, shopping convenience, and a sense of urgency (say, a "three-day sale"), and not on the product's features or benefits. It is therefore dubious whether Circuit City's vague new advertising slogans, "Imagine That" and "Just What I Needed," motivated customers to shop or buy at Circuit City. In fact, Circuit City's sales did not respond to those campaigns. Instead, its market share declined over the next five years.[250] Adding package goods marketing experience gave a healthy infusion of talent and new ideas. But in the end, the new advertising did not make a strategic difference.

On the other hand, the consumer research enabled Stephens to make a significant contribution to store design and staffing and Dias to take a relatively new website to an industry-leading market share.

Store Redesign, Relocation, and Staffing

Store design and store staffing are as intertwined as a handshake. A store is a sorting mechanism, like a train station or an airport. Customers enter the front door with different interests and leave with those desires satisfied or not. The store layout and the store staff are the intermediaries between a customer's success and failure in finding what he desires. It is frustrating for the customer and inefficient for the retailer to provide full service in a store designed for self-service and vice versa.

Design Conundrums

The original superstores were designed for full service. They were based on the premise that consumers had very little product information, that products changed only incrementally, and that knowledgeable salesmen could learn enough to sell any category of goods. All that was true in the early '80s. It became dead wrong in the '90s.

In the original superstores, all customers were met and greeted by a salesperson, whether they were buying a dollar battery or a $3,000 home stereo system. As products proliferated and became more complex, we divided the floor into major appliances, TV, and audio. This allowed the salesmen to deepen their product knowledge in a particular category. Except for small items like blank tapes and batteries, the stock on the showroom floor was for demonstration and not for sale. Once customers purchased an item, they went to the adjacent warehouse where a stock person fetched the product and placed it in their vehicle.

In the mid-'80s, while I was still there, Circuit City stores evolved to a split system in which a limited number of younger, less experienced sales personnel were paid by the hour plus a small commission and/or spiffs to explain and sell what we called ACE (advanced consumer electronics) merchandise. Most of these products were stored on the sales floor and would be rung up by the salesperson in the department. Often the customer picked up the product and brought it to a salesperson to ring up.

By the '90s, the volume and variety of the ACE products had expanded dramatically and many "traditional" products, including smaller TVs and portable audio equipment, had declined so much in size and price that a much larger percentage of total sales were now ACE-type products. Shifting the sale of small TVs, for example, to hourly paid people created two problems: There was insufficient space on the sales floor to house backup stock, and the big-ticket TV and audio salesmen resented the fact that a lot of product was now available for sale by hourly paid, less experienced salespeople.

For most of the '90s, Circuit City largely ignored this inherent conflict between the original superstore design and greater reliance on customer self-service. In 2000, facing existential challenges from Best Buy and the mass merchants, the management team needed to decide how to design a store in which a significant portion of the merchandise could be picked up by customers and brought to a central checkout. Should Circuit City opt for shopping carts and a larger selling floor to store the boxed merchandise formerly held in the warehouse? Should it also adopt a staffing model with only hourly salespeople? If it kept commissioned salesmen for bigger-ticket, higher-tech merchandise, could it devise a system in which hourly paid and commissioned salesmen did not compete over which customers they were going to wait on and yet did not ignore any customer who wanted help? Resolving these issues was the number one challenge facing the new management team.

Ready, Fire, Aim

The 2001 Plan's stated goal was that the "Store of the Future" would be "bright, open and inviting" and "created around how customers want to shop," including "shopping carts for merchandise and small children." The "more familiar product categories will be self-service, leaving our more knowledgeable commissioned sales counselors in areas where they are needed most."[251] The plan anticipated an intensive program "to remodel or relocate most of our [570] stores base to achieve our 'Store of the Future Prototype.'"[252] Redesigning the stores for more self-service necessarily required a reexamination of the selling strategy and the roles of commissioned and noncommissioned sales personnel.

Back in the late '90s senior vice president Jack Fitzsimmons, whose responsibilities included real estate, store design, and construction, had led an effort to remodel the Chesterfield (part of the Richmond metropolitan area) store by cutting into the warehouse in order to expand the selling space and thus make room to "bulk out" self-service items. He kept the departmental checkouts in place but added grocery-style registers at the front of the store. The goal was to improve customer service by giving customers the option of talking to a salesperson or picking up a portable product and either paying for it in the department or taking it to one of the registers in the front of the store.

The idea was a good one, but never properly implemented. The new layout required systems changes, such as automatic alerts to the warehouse crew to replenish the bulked-out merchandise on the floor. Supporting these experimental changes was never a priority for the skeptical store operations team and was never accomplished. Following the remodel, there was no lift in sales, and the Best Buy across the street continued to do 50 percent more business than the remodeled Circuit City store.

At the same time he was remodeling the Chesterfield store, Fitzsimmons was also working on a prototype for a brand-new store. He believed that, in store design as in modern architecture, "form follows function." Together with George Pasini, who had an architecture and construction background, and Ann Marie Stephens, who had a marketing background, he created a "play book" for how to design, staff, and run a mixed service "Store of the Future."

Together they created a new store prototype, code-named "Horizon," in a warehouse near the home office. In addition to an enlarged selling floor, the Horizon format included a central checkout and shopping baskets, not carts, for small goods.[253] Fitzsimmons also hired visual or display managers, each assigned to a merchandise category, to help decide how to display the products to best advantage. Once the prototype was established, the plan was to roll it out as new stores were built and, to the extent it was feasible, as older stores were remodeled.

Understanding that a large-scale remodeling effort was needed, McCollough pushed ahead with the Horizon design. In 2001, just as he was assuming the CEO mantle, the fiscal year 2000 Annual Report announced Circuit City would:

> ...remodel 30 to 35 stores in central and south Florida and in Richmond, Va., [providing] easier access to self-service products and expanding our assortments in key areas. [254]

> The Superstores in these markets will be dedicated to consumer electronics and personal computers, creating a high-energy environment for new technologies and permitting expanded assortments of video game hardware and software, entertainment and computer software, peripherals and accessories.[255]

In order to make room for games, computer peripherals, and other small electronics it had not previously carried in depth, Circuit City decided to eliminate appliances in the remodeled stores and use the freed-up space for these new product categories. To maintain the appliance business, the Annual Report announced:

> [W]e will open a limited number of stand-alone major appliance stores, which we believe will increase consumer awareness of our appliance selection and provide an improved selling environment for these products. [256]

Florida Fiasco

The Horizon design was first incorporated into a store that was currently under construction in Jacksonville, Florida. When Fitzsimmons, frustrated by Circuit City's inability to embrace an updated store design and staffing model, departed in early 2000, the company drafted Carl Liebert, a new store operations executive with a strong managerial background at GE, to oversee the ongoing Florida remodeling exercise. Without waiting for Jacksonville to open in August and see what the new store would look like or how it would function, Liebert went ahead with tearing apart twenty-five existing Florida stores that spring and summer. Unfortunately, when the Jacksonville store opened in August, the results were underwhelming, and certainly not sufficient to believe that this was the answer to Circuit City's competitive problems. Evaluation was complicated, however, by the fact that the site was "not the best real estate."[257]

Any multi-store remodeling process is complicated, and this one was especially so. Each store was slightly different because of the size and shape of the original lot or local building code requirements. They were also of different generations, with attendant differences in layout and design. The major changes made were to eliminate the existing red towers and shift the entrance to the center of the store. Inside, the sight lines were lowered so that customers could see all the way to the back wall, and the layout was rearranged to eliminate the "race track" and make the space more like a conventional discount store.

According to executives involved, there was no clear plan to manage the remodeling process.[258] No order was established for which the stores would be remodeled when, and the work within each store was not sequenced in a logical manner. Fixtures and materials were stacked up for months waiting to be installed while other materials were much delayed in arriving. There were frequent change orders during the process, and the prototype layout was changed multiple times, making some of the new fixtures irrelevant or difficult to modify. As much as $12 million worth of fixtures were eventually discarded.[259]

In addition, trying to keep the stores open during remodeling exacerbated the inherent complications. Management was afraid of losing business and perhaps permanently losing customers. Because the issues of electrical and antenna distribution were not thought through in advance, cement floors had to be jackhammered to create channels to run the wires. With all the noise and dust, it was often unclear to customers whether the stores were actually open for business. Indeed, given the disruption and much-reduced sales, they might as well have been closed. To use one observer's analogy, it was like trying to change the tires on a racecar while it was going around the track. In a moment of unusual candor, the 2001 Annual Report observed:

The cost of last year's full remodels and the business disruption to the existing store environment were not acceptable...[and] it is difficult to immediately measure the results of our investment."[260] We will limit our [next year] remodels to 20 to 25 and refine the design so that it is less costly and less disruptive.

Petersburg Prototype

While the Florida remodeling exercise was underway, Ann-Marie Stephens persuaded McCollough to authorize a third new store design based on new bottoms-up research she had done. Under great secrecy, she assembled a team to design and build yet another version of the "Store of the Future" in Colonial Heights, Virginia. It would replace the existing Petersburg store less than a mile away. Stephens's consumer research and interviews had produced several critical findings:

• Women and teenagers did not feel respected by Circuit City's sales personnel. Many reported feeling ignored, talked down to, or, in the case of teenagers, followed around as though they were suspected of shoplifting. On the other hand, teenage kids could comfortably "hang" at Best Buy.

• Teenage comfort was doubly important because adults often rely on their children's and grandchildren's advice about what to buy and where to buy it.

• Customers did not trust the Circuit City sales personnel, believing they had their own commission-driven agenda rather than the customers' best interests in mind.

• Worldwide, there were no successful models for consumer electronics and appliance stores with a commissioned sales force.

• The average Circuit City customer visited the store once or twice per year, while the average Best Buy customer visited eleven to twelve times per year. These repeat visits were due in large part to Best Buy's emphasis on consumables, such as DVDs, CDs, games, and printer ink, while Circuit City studiously avoided these products because of their low margins and slow turnover.

• Customer browse time at Circuit City was eighteen minutes compared to Best Buy's forty-five minutes. Circuit City's commissioned sales counselors would stop a customer as soon as he or she had a product in hand and ask to ring up the sale, at which point the customer would stop browsing.

Stephens' new store design, code-named "Tide," was designed to address these issues. Believing that some women found the superstore claustrophobic, the front of the store was opened up to allow customers to see in from the outside. Once inside, a customer could survey the entire store all the way to the back wall and identify departments by their signage. Most of the 34,000-square-foot store was devoted to showroom, with only a 5000- to 6000-square-foot stockroom. In addition, there was a flexible industrial-style ceiling with "power poles" to conduct the electricity and antenna connections required for running the display items. This eliminated the need to trench the floor, now or in the future. Also, many of the fixtures were on wheels to permit easy rearrangement as new products were introduced.

Believing that Circuit City's sales problem was deeper than simply store layout and design, Stephens also developed an alternative staffing model. The products that most customers were comfortable picking up and taking to the cashier were supported with hourly paid employees. In the "high touch" areas (flat-screen TVs, computers, and car stereos) where knowledgeable sales assistance was still deemed essential, salesmen continued to be paid commissions (at reduced rates) on what they sold.

To create a storewide team with a sense of responsibility for taking care of the customer, every employee received a monthly bonus based on store sales and customer service scores. This gave both hourly and commissioned sales personnel the incentive to see that all customers were helped, regardless of where in the store they were shopping.

The Petersburg store took off. Its sales were 27 percent higher than those of the earlier, albeit smaller and less well-located, store nearby, and it had much better customer feedback, especially from women. Stephens's plan, quite sensibly, was to do a second store, adjusting the model based on what she had learned in Petersburg, and then a third one, before rolling the model out chain-wide. This plan was not to be. McCollough visited the Petersburg store in December of 2000 and liked what he saw. In fact, he liked it so much that, instead of waiting to refine the model, he decided immediately to apply the results to the Chicago stores, where major remodeling was already planned for 2001.

Applying the Petersburg Lessons

Shortly after that, McCollough promoted John Froman from SVP for Merchandising to executive vice president and COO, the number two job in the company. All the stores now reported to Froman, and the Chicago remodeling project fell under his aegis.

Froman had his own ideas about store staffing and design. He did not discuss Stephens's research with her. He had no interest in her new staffing model and did not include Ed Brett, the human resources executive who had spearheaded it, on his Chicago remodeling team. Consequently, executives involved in the process felt a sense of competition, rather than cooperation, between the Petersburg and Chicago remodeling teams.

Although he rejected Tide's human resource initiatives, Froman implemented in Chicago many of the physical changes that Stephens had instructed. He incorporated the power poles. He used a lot of the Petersburg signage and graphics, but, to save money, he eliminated all carpeting and custom displays. Instead he chose standard steel fixtures designed for discount stores. One thing he did not do, even though adding floor space was essential to implementing self-service, was to create a larger sales floor, because he decided that removing the wall between the too-small sales floor and the too-large warehouse would be too expensive.[261]

The Chicago stripped-down remodel was cheaper than the Tide

store in Petersburg or the earlier Horizon model, but it was still very expensive, averaging more than $2 million per store. Most importantly, neither the Florida nor the Chicago remodels significantly increased sales. Since the only changes in Florida and Chicago were to the physical plant and not, as in Petersburg, to the staffing model and commission system, the lack of increased sales suggests that Circuit City's problems were deeper than just store design.

Appliances

Indecision over whether to continue selling appliances severely complicated the remodeling program. Once Circuit City decided early in 2000 to remove appliances from the remodeled Florida stores and create freestanding appliances only stores in those markets, numerous people spent countless hours designing an all-appliance store. In less than a year, the plan was dropped. Some former Circuit City executives believe that the company had already made the decision to exit appliances altogether and that this elaborate study was a charade to fool the appliance manufacturers into believing that the Circuit City was still committed to carrying their products.[262] Others think it was just another example of management's inability to make clean, clear-cut decisions.

McCollough addressed the strategic decision to stop selling appliances in the 2001 Annual Report with a tactical explanation:

> Our original intent was to test a free-standing appliance store. However, as appliance sales softened and competition intensified, we decided to exit that category and re-merchandise the appliance space in all remaining Superstores. That exit cost us approximately 29 cents per share [$60 million total]...[263]

With Circuit City out of the appliance business, Lowe's, Home Depot, and Best Buy fought for the number two spot behind Sears. These big-box retailers' warehouse-style format and low-cost structure allowed them to offer rock-bottom prices, a key to survival in this fiercely competitive industry. Between 1999 and 2004 their combined share of the appliance business grew from 19 to 35 percent, while Sears' share held steady at 39 percent.[264]

The decision to exit appliances remains controversial among Circuit City veterans to this day. One former executive who studied the issue thinks the decision was based on "bad accounting and poor understanding of the economics."[265] On a fully allocated cost basis major appliances were not making much money, but if viewed as a marginal contribution to an electronics store, he believes, they carried their own weight and made a positive contribution.

Another executive thinks that, from a marketing and an operations perspective, the elimination of appliances:

> ...took points off the board. It was a $1 to $1.5 billion business, between 10 and 15 percent of Circuit City's total sales. It confused the customer. It was difficult to take appliances off the table and not alienate core customers or make customers think that Circuit City was going out of business.[266]

Years later, customers were still looking for appliances at Circuit City and were surprised not to find them.[267]

On the other hand, there is no denying that the cost of carrying appliances was high. They were stored in separate warehouses and required special handling for both store and customer delivery. In addition, the industry was getting more competitive, as both Lowe's and Home Depot were challenging Circuit City's number two position in appliance retailing.

Perhaps most important, the superstore selling space was too small. As the 2001 Annual Report stated:

> This move [to eliminate appliances] provided some additional space quickly to expand selections of copiers and cameras; computer software and peripherals; video games and software; DVD movies and cell phones. [268]

While reasonable people can differ over whether the decision to exit appliances was right or wrong, there can be little doubt that the results were disappointing and the process flawed. The new electronics categories were never able to replace the lost appliance volume. To make matters worse, the new merchandise had very low margins. Finally, it turned out that exiting appliances freed up more space than the new products required.[269]

As for the process, Ann-Marie Stephens was in Florida scouting locations for the new appliance-only stores when she got an unexpected phone call to terminate her search and return to Richmond because the decision had been made to abandon appliances altogether. She recalls that the question of exiting appliances had never been raised with the executive committee. John Froman recalls that "we had ex[ecutive]-com[mittee] discussion, but it was not a robust discussion with deep analysis."

Abandoning 10 to 15 percent of one's business is not a decision to be made on the fly or in secret. Because of McCollough's process (or lack thereof), there was no thoughtful consideration among the management team of balancing the cost and benefits in order to arrive at a consensus.

While not fatal, this process was symbolic of Circuit City's more general failure to confront its strategic challenges in an open, honest, and collaborative way. The fallout was a lack of trust on the part of the employees, in this case the appliance buyers, appliance sales force, and appliance warehouse personnel, who had been led to believe that their products were going to remain a part of Circuit City's future.

Band Aids and Chewing Gum

In lieu of a systematic store-redesign program, Circuit City instituted a series of scattershot mini-remodeling exercises. Believing that a full-scale remodeling program to create the "Store of the Future" was too expensive, McCollough developed a "lite" version to be implemented across the chain over five years.[270] The lite version did not increase the selling space to accommodate self-service, nor did it raise the ceilings or otherwise open up the stores to accommodate shopping carts or significant "bulk outs" of pickup merchandise. [271]

The 2001 remodels included the removal of appliances and some new fixtures to make the appliance space usable for other, previously underrepresented products such as video games. In 2003, Circuit City began creating central checkouts as an alternative to departmental checkouts, as well as installing some lighting upgrades and fixture changes in 200 stores. Other than in the Florida and Chicago markets, however, none of the older stores received a major facelift and none had additional space added to the selling floor.

Store Relocations

Remodeling was not a universal cure for what ailed the company. Management recognized that many of Circuit City's nearly six hundred stores needed to be moved rather than remodeled. Some locations had been secondary real estate when acquired.[272] Others had become subprime as trade areas shifted. A few years after the remodeling efforts began in 2003, a comprehensive consultant study documented that one-third of the stores (about two hundred in total) were in need of relocation. [273]

Financially, store relocation involves three principal components: land, construction, and disposing of the old location. Each new store required 3.5 acres of land, at a cost, in the early 2000s, of anywhere from $1.5 to $2.5 million for an average site. For 200 stores, that would have come to $400 million. Construction costs were similar to remodeling costs, $1.7 to $2.4 million per store— or another $400 million.

Finally, the older stores, when placed on the market, were not worth what Circuit City had invested in them. They were held on long-term leases, and, unfortunately, the unique design and layout of a superstore made it almost impossible to sublease. For one thing, less than half the store was air-conditioned. To create a sublease-ready "plain vanilla box" would have cost roughly $1 million per store.[274] To obtain a competitive rent Circuit City would also have needed to provide a subtenant with "a fit-out" allowance, write off its undepreciated fixtures and leasehold improvements, and carry the rent until the store was subleased. That could add another $1 million.

Thus, relocating two hundred stores could cost $400 million for land, another $400 million for construction, $200 million for retrofitting the abandoned stores, and another $200 million for carrying costs and tenant allowances, making a total of $1.2 billion.

For the remaining four hundred stores that did not need relocating, the remodeling cost, including cutting the stock room and expanding the floor, would have been roughly $2.25 million per store or $900 million.[275] Taken together, the relocation of two hundred stores and the remodeling of another four hundred would have cost Circuit City $2.1 billion.

This was a challenging number. It would have required that Circuit City halt all of its planned expansion, possibly abandon some underperforming markets, sell the generic credit card business and possibly the private label card as well, sell (rather than distribute to shareholders) its stake in CarMax, and take other uncomfortable steps, including admitting to Wall Street that its store base was impaired and required major surgery.

To the best of my knowledge, neither McCollough nor the board ever addressed the issue in this comprehensive way or asked the top management team how they could align their store base with the avowed strategy of creating the "Store of the Future around how customers want to shop."[276] The unwillingness to accept the costs required completely to remodel well-located stores or relocate poorly positioned ones, was in my judgment a major strategic error. That, plus the stubborn refusal to reconsider the store staffing model, as Ann Marie Stephens did in Colonial Heights, turned out to be the kiss of death. Whatever chance Circuit City had to challenge Best Buy was, I believe, lost with these decisions. Unlike Ford and IBM, which took bold and decisive action, Circuit

City's failure to implement the stated aspirations of its 2001 Plan explains why Ford and IBM were able to right their ships and stay afloat while Circuit City capsized and sank.

Faulty Metrics

On a more technical level, Circuit City failed to take the necessary steps to reinvent itself because it employed a faulty metric to determine return on investment. It measured the anticipated results of each store remodeling or relocation as a separate and distinct investment. It then estimated the expected increased sales and extrapolated that increase to estimate future profits and the return on investment. Circuit City's minimum internal rate of return on capital for remodeling investments varied between 12 to 15 percent. If the return-on-investment looked good, they could justify the wisdom of their capital expenditure to Wall Street. If not, they passed.

This is the right way to measure ROI for *new investments*. Here, however, the company had major costs it could not easily sell or recoup. If, as I believe, the company needed to be fixed market-by-market so that it could effectively advertise its new look and operating strategy, it should have based its ROI calculations on what it would cost to fix *each market*, not each store individually, and the analysis should have included both relocation and remodeling expenses. Based on the expected future profits from the market, the company would then either make the investment or exit the market altogether. The path they chose left most markets a mixed and confusing bag: some new stores, some remodeled stores without an expanded selling floor, and some old stores left unchanged.

By about 2005, the new CFO, Mike Foss, determined that the Circuit City owned roughly six hundred stores that were unmovable, unalterable, and out of date. As the previous acting CFO, Phil Dunn, observed, "Foss decided we couldn't fix the existing stores and it was more economical to build more because Circuit City could not get rid of old leases economically."[277]

Beyond financial metrics, however, there were also existential issues the company never confronted. With a continuously eroding market share and all of its 571 superstores in need of serious reconfiguration, using a standard ROI approach to decide whether or not to make the needed investment misses the strategic implications of doing nothing. Some of the stores were already generating losses, and any objective analysis would have predicted further declines in almost all the stores unless drastic changes were made. From that perspective, almost any investment that returned a market to profitability would have been justified, regardless of ROI.

In the end, between 2000 and 2004 Circuit City fully remodeled only 46 stores out of a total of 571 (8 percent), and relocated but 38 more (7 percent). All the rest were "remodeled" with Band-Aids and chewing gum that stopped far short of the initial objective to have all the stores "bright, open and inviting" as well as "created around how customers want to shop." In the same period, it opened eighty-two brand-new Circuit City stores in new trade areas, almost as many as the eighty-four that were relocated or remodeled. As a result, the bulk of the existing stores continued to drag the company down.

A Better Way to Face the Brutal Facts?

To the best of my knowledge, Circuit City never seriously faced the brutal reality of its existential plight. It never asked, for example: "If we need dramatically to change the existing store base, as our strategic plan says, are there assets we can sell to raise the cash required? Should we go private, at least for a while, and make these changes out of the glare of being a public company? Is there some other alternative?"

Hindsight is always twenty-twenty. One never knows what he would have done in the circumstances. So it is with some trepidation that I outline an alternative strategy. Nonetheless, I believe that if the model is broken, it is far better to spend whatever time and money are required to fix it than to putter around the edges and allow the problems to fester. That is what we did in selling and closing the many ill-advised acquisitions Wards made in the '70s. That is what Circuit City did in deciding to exit Lafayette in 1986 and to open superstores in Los Angeles. Earnings and the stock price took a hit in the short run, but they were the right decisions for the long run.

The stumbling block to a clear and aggressive operational plan to "fix" the company in 2000 was not money. As of February 28, 2001, six months after McCollough took office, the Circuit City Group (excluding CarMax) had $437 million in cash and $2.2 billion in stockholder equity.[278] If it had issued public debt, it would have qualified for a BB (non-investment grade) bond rating. [279]

Under these circumstances there were many ways to raise cash, including selling stock, selling bonds, disposing of the generic credit card portfolio, or selling the company's remaining interest in CarMax. Another alternative would have been to go private. Ideally, an extensive store-remodeling exercise of this type should be undertaken by a private company that can close stores, lay off employees, and take the hit to earnings over multiple years without the adverse impact of press releases and analysts commenting on disappointing earnings. That is what many retail companies, including Burger King in 2002, Toys "R" Us in 2005, and Dollar General in 2008, have done.[280, 281]

Reluctant to face the brutal facts, the board and management refused to fess up to investors that the model was broken and needed repair. This refusal was grounded in the reasonable fear that the stock market would not accept the radical surgery required. The success of Circuit City in the '90s had, on paper, made most of the management and middle-management team rich beyond their wildest dreams and many of the board members noticeably wealthier. So instead of finding and pursuing a firm and clear alternative that might improve Circuit City's market position in the long run, but adversely affect the stock price in the short run, they ping-ponged between refreshing the store base on-the-cheap and trying to keep earnings in a respectable range for Wall Street. In the end, the unwillingness to face the brutal facts sank the entire company.

Sales Force Productivity

Hollowed-Out Training

Based on its consumer research, Circuit City understood that consumers believed that its salespeople tried to sell what *they wanted the customer to buy,* not what *the customer wanted to purchase.* It also knew that its commissioned sales force entailed a considerably higher expense than its competition. Instead of addressing these strategic weaknesses, the 2001 Plan focused on creating a "learning culture" to maintain "Circuit City's tremendous competitive advantage in selling advanced products."[282]

Circuit City's salesmen earned, on average, $30,000 per year (the equivalent of, roughly, $15 per hour) and quite a few earned well over $50,000 ($25 per hour).[283] Best Buy was paying $10 per hour ($22,000 per year) and mass merchandisers even less.[284] In addition, company employed roughly 25 sales trainers located in major markets around the country whose primary function was to hold sales training classes every couple of weeks, to teach new employees how to sell.[285] The 2000 Annual Report announced that to improve productivity:

> We will begin to introduce state-of-the-art interactive Web-based training for store, service center and distribution Associates....All sales training will take place online, saving the time and expense of off-site travel.[286]

The selling culture that Sam created had already been compromised in the late '80s by the decision to employ part-time salespeople. On the one hand, it was smart to staff the stores so that there were more sales counselors available in the evenings and on weekends, when the traffic was heaviest. In addition, part-timers were not entitled to medical and other benefits, which further reduced their cost. On the other hand, it was difficult, if not impossible, to hold effective weekly sales training meetings before a store opened if a significant portion of the staff was not scheduled to work that morning.

The final nail in the coffin of a well-trained sales force was McCollough' s decision to fire the training staff and put all the training online. Just as you cannot learn to drive a car online or become a doctor without hands-on experience treating patients, you cannot, in my opinion, effectively teach someone how to sell strictly from a computer. Practice and peer review are essential learning techniques.

Like the decision to go to part-timers, the decision to do all training online was largely financially driven. As detailed in the Three Year Plan, the annual savings from switching from human trainers to training online was $16 million over three years, not a lot of money in the scheme of things for a $10 billion company. [287] In addition to saving money, the plan declared, "Such an important asset that provides differentiation [from competitors] deserves to be communicated and celebrated."[288] It turned out to be a liability, not an asset, and the proper celebration would have been a wake. CarMax, which also did a lot of sales training, never stopped using human trainers, demonstrating that the child is sometimes wiser than the parent.

Backing into the Future

As Circuit City's profits sharply declined from their 2000 peak, and Best Buy and the discounters kept taking market share, the company finally decided to make a partial move. The 2002 Annual Report, after proclaiming that "we are committed to an incentive compensation system that rewards sales counselors for assisting the customer," disclosed that:

> After extensive testing, we simplified our commission
> structure in fiscal 2002, adopting fixed commission
> rates across broad product categories.[289]

By eliminating different commissions Circuit City eliminated
a portion of what it had long considered an essential tool for
achieving higher margins. In addition it reduced the number of
sales counselors and cross-trained those remaining to sell more
than one category of goods. The principal motivation was to cut
expense.

The other shoe quickly dropped. Under pressure from the board
to further cut selling expense, the management team proposed
going to an hourly paid model, code-named "Big Red." Following a disappointing Christmas season, the company announced
that earnings for the 2003 fiscal year were likely to be half of Wall
Street's expectations. In a clear effort to offset that bad news with
good, Circuit City disclosed that the previous day it had eliminated commissions altogether and fired 3,900 of its highest-paid
commissioned sales personnel, to be replaced with 2,100 salesmen paid by the hour. That and some other personnel cuts were
estimated to save $130 million per year. [290] In the Annual Report
issued a few months later, the company justified its decision as
follows:

> We believe the change to a single hourly pay structure will:
> • Unify our sales Associates into one team, focused
> solely on customer service.
> • Increase browse time in our stores.
> • Simplify store operations.
> • Reduce operating costs.[291]

Contrary to management fears, margins and ESP sales did not
fall off the cliff. For many years, they had clung to the belief that
without a commission-incentivized push, customers would both
choose the low margin item and refuse to buy ESPs. In fact, within
nine months both ESP rates and margins were higher than before.
John Froman, one of the strongest advocates of commissioned

salespeople, admitted, "Pretty soon we found that the model Best Buy employed of hourly associates motivated to do the right thing and comparing store to store and department to department was a good way to run the business."

In fact, the ability to sell higher-margin products and ESPs without paying commissions should not have been a surprise. Besides observing that Best Buy and others were successful with an hourly paid staff, Circuit City executives had only to look to CarMax. For years, CarMax had paid its salespeople a fixed amount for each car sold, regardless of whether it was a Mercedes or a Hyundai. The goal was to sell the customer something he or she wanted to drive, not what made the greatest profit for CarMax. In the 2001 Annual Report, McCollough boasted that CarMax's flat commission structure "enables each sales consultant to focus on the needs of the customer rather than profit of the deal." So haltingly, reluctantly, Circuit City accepted the reality that a commissioned sales force was no longer a profitable way to sell electronics. With some humility and curiosity, management could have come to that conclusion years earlier, but it had not even been willing to *test the possibility* that hourly paid salespeople could still sell a reasonable mix of better product and ESPs at a lower cost to the company. Management feared that word of a test would leak out and that the company would be faced with an insurrection or mass departures.[292] This was another untested ideological assumption.

Fifty years earlier, Sam had faced a possible insurrection in the sales force when he elevated an African American service technician to the position of salesman. Following his one-face policy of honesty and fair dealing, he called the salesmen together and explained that times had changed in the South and they needed to accept an integrated sales force. When most of the white salesmen caucused and sent word that they would quit, he called them back together and told them he was not backing down. No one left.

A similar tough-love policy would have explained that the competition had changed and no retail TV and appliance company could be competitive with a high-commission structure. That honesty, together with a fair and caring severance program for those who chose to leave, would have gone a long way to making a smoother transition from commissions to hourly wages and minimized the anger it generated among employees and their families as well as the media and general public. Instead, the management team backed into an hourly pay system in the worst possible way.

Merchandising

Once John Froman was promoted to executive vice president and COO, it was necessary to recruit a new top merchant. For the first time in its fifty-year history, the company selected someone from the outside to head its merchandising team. He turned out to be a disaster.

Counterculture

Kim Maguire came to Circuit City from a twenty-year career at Target Stores. McCollough thought that Maguire's experience with Target's well-regarded merchandising system would help Circuit City get its costs in line and create a state-of-the-art supply chain system. Instead he got an individual who either did not know or did not respect the Circuit City culture, and whose personal behavior alienated women in the office. [293] Rather than helping to solve the company's problems, Maguire decimated the merchandising staff, aggravated suppliers, and created the worst inventory glut in Circuit City history.

From the start, Maguire was focused on reducing expenses. Based on his Target experience, he believed the Circuit City buyers were overpaid, so on a Monday morning, without any warning, he fired or demoted several longtime senior buyers, people whom Circuit City had trained over many years and who had strong, long-term relations with the suppliers. [294] Those he did not fire quickly left to find a home where they were not demeaned. In the two and a half years he was there, he created a brain drain of twelve buyers out of a staff of sixteen.

To make matters worse, Maguire severely weakened one of Circuit City's most important assets: its vendor relations. He was not accustomed to dealing with major electronics vendors like Sony, Panasonic, Apple, or HP. As his successor put it, "He was not a student of the business. He went to playbook...what he knew from Target."[295] Once Best Buy passed Circuit City in sales, the company's once-paramount position with its vendors had been weakened. Nonetheless, McGuire went out of his way to alienate suppliers by playing adversarial games. For example, he charged vendors for being one day late with a delivery.

As Sam and Hecht understood from the beginning, in a world of limited suppliers, most of which were far larger and more powerful companies, patience, courtesy, and honey achieve much more than arrogance and vinegar. Circuit City could and did bargain hard, but it respected the fact that there were a limited number of suppliers for most categories of goods and there were limits to what it could expect from any supplier. Under Maguire, the many years of patient relationship building with major vendors went down the drain.

InterTAN

McCollough also wanted to improve margins through private-label goods, but his approach was to add private-label accessories and peripheral items, most of which Circuit City did not already stock. These included small accessories, parts, and "gizmos," similar to what RadioShack carries. The gross margins on such items averaged over 40 percent, almost twice Circuit City's average.[296]

These goods were sourced in Asia, and to expand its assortment, Circuit City would have to set up a buying office in Asia or expand its relations with various importers and jobbers. Instead of doing either, McCollough turned to InterTAN, a publicly owned, 970-store consumer electronics chain based in Canada. It already had an experienced buying staff in Hong Kong, Taiwan, and mainland China. InterTAN had been spun out of RadioShack in 1987 to be an independent public company (hence InterTAN). After shedding hundreds of stores in a dozen or more countries, InterTAN ended up with six hundred company-owned and four hundred affiliated dealers, all in Canada. By 2004 the business, led by Brian Levy, a former RadioShack executive, was doing $400 million in sales, with strong earnings.[297]

In fiscal 2005, Circuit City paid $300 million in cash to acquire the company.[298] The stated reasons were:

> We believe this transaction will bring to Circuit City a management team with extensive sourcing experience for private-label merchandise and creative in-store merchandising capabilities and enable us to accelerate the offering of private-label merchandise to our customers. It also allows us to enter Canada with a company that already has a proven retail format. We also believe the combination of the two companies will create inventory purchasing synergies for both.[299]

The acquisition, however, never lived up to these promises.

While on its face the deal made some strategic sense,[300] the implementation was a disaster. From the beginning, Circuit City buyers (largely Maguire recruits) resisted. A group of them flew to Toronto, where InterTAN merchants presented the choice items in their lineup of four thousand stock-keeping units. But the Circuit City buyers never followed through. Finally, Levy and McCollough came up with a list of three hundred SKUs they thought would do well in the Circuit City stores and arranged for them to be shipped in appropriate quantities. When they arrived at the stores they mostly sat in stockrooms. The Circuit City store managers did not know what to do with them or how to display them.[301] So the store operations staff, like the buyers, was also resistant to change.

In addition to the $300 million in cash, the acquisition demanded a significant investment of time and effort by Circuit City headquarters executives to integrate InterTAN's ordering and re-plenishment system into Circuit City's merchandising systems and to bring InterTAN into compliance with the accounting standards mandated by the Sarbanes-Oxley Act of 2002. Finally, the acquisition galvanized RadioShack to challenge InterTAN's right to use the RadioShack name in Canada. Circuit City lost and was forced to rebrand more than five hundred Canadian RadioShack stores as "The Source by Circuit City," at a cost of $30 million.[302, 303]

In the end, incorporating small-ticket InterTAN gadgets into the stateside Circuit City stores did not provide enough of a lift to offset margin declines in the company's core categories. Adding insult to injury, the Canadian business did not fare well under Circuit City leadership. Its operating earnings fell from a respectable 7.1 percent pretax operating profit in 2005 to losses in 2006, '07, and '08.[304] In short, the effort to solve Circuit City's problems through higher-margin, private-label merchandising only added to the company's woes.

New Blood

After Kim Maguire resigned in April 2004,[305] McCollough's first move was to bring in Doug Moore from the field to run merchandising on an interim basis. Moore was a ten-year Circuit City veteran with experience in both merchandising and store operations. After six months, Maguire told Moore he would be named executive vice president for Merchandising. Then, before the appointment was announced, and while they were en-route to Korea on a business trip, McCollough withdrew the promised promotion, telling Moore that the company had just hired Phil Schoonover to fill the top merchandising job.[306]

Some time earlier, the board had indicated that they wanted to fill the merchandising vacancy with someone who had the potential to succeed McCollough as CEO. They hired Spencer Stuart, a large professional headhunting firm, to conduct a nationwide search and to review internal candidates.[307] Spencer Stuart recommended against the internal candidates but presented Schoonover, Best Buy's EVP of Customer Segments, as its strong recommendation. Schoonover had been with Best Buy since 1995, working in Merchandising, Digital Technology Solutions, and New Business Development.[308] Prior to that, he had held management and sales positions at Appliance City (a mega superstore chain in New Jersey) and Sony Corp. of America.[309]

He was well regarded by vendors and by Best Buy, which was touting his projects at retail industry conferences. McCollough, and especially the board, liked his energy, his focus on innovation, and his Best Buy knowledge and experience. In October 2004, Schoonover signed on as EVP, chief merchandising officer, and heir apparent. His first assignment was to improve Circuit City's merchandise ordering and management systems.

Supply-Chain Management

A quintessential skill for any successful retailer is supply-chain management. Recognizing that Best Buy's inventory turns were far greater than theirs, Circuit City's 2001 Plan called for creating a "World Class Supply Chain." This was not a new idea for Circuit City. Sam had invested in IBM punch card equipment in the early '50s, long before it was fashionable. In the early '80s I purchased Rick Sharp's innovative POS system.

Point of Sale

Over the years the demands on the system had grown as sales expanded into the billions. In 1991, six or seven years after it was purchased, Circuit City did a major rewrite of the original POS, inventory, and back-office system. The upgrade, called DPS, allowed the company to perform complex transactions that its competitors could not. For example, Circuit City sales counselors at one store could sell an item (say, to a parent) and have it delivered (perhaps to a college student) out of the inventory of another store. Over the years, several non-sales functions, like the tracking of employee hours and customer warranties, were added.

As business exploded in the '90s, the increasing demands on the POS systems caused it to degrade relative to both internal requirements and as compared to competitors. By 2000, DPS had difficulty keeping up with the Christmas rush, thereby causing long lines and lost sales. Perhaps more critical, the system was not intuitive. Because of its outmoded architecture, a week of training was needed before cashiers and salesmen could efficiently input transactions. The DPS software code was also quite inflexible, re-quiring significant programmer effort to maintain the system and to accommodate small changes.

In 2002 McCollough directed Dennis Bowman, senior vice president and chief information officer, to upgrade POS. Magel-lan, as the project was called, was designed to reduce training time, increase transaction capacity, and eliminate reliance on spe-

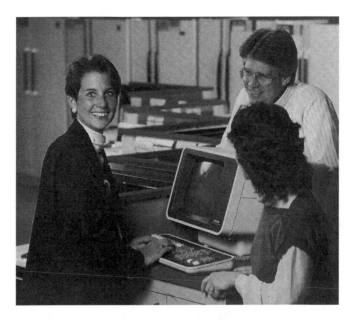

New Point of Sale Terminal

cialty hardware. Bowman decided to replace the build-to-order store controllers with off-the-shelf PCs, the same ones Circuit City sold to customers.

By December 2003, Magellan was installed and working in a hundred of the highest-volume stores at a cost of $25 to $30 million. It was necessary, however, to keep the old system in place for another year to handle the non-sales functions that had been added over the years, including payroll, inventory, and accounting, until those programs could be rewritten and added to the new Magellan sales system. Meanwhile, the store operations team kept changing its expectations for what the new system should do and, at the same time, was uncomfortable with the parallel systems and two terminals at each station.

At a board meeting in late 2003, Bowman explained that for an additional $100 million, mostly for hardware, Circuit City could install Magellan in all six hundred superstores by the following Christmas and, in another year, complete the rewrite of the non-sales functions and add them to the system. The CFO at the time, Mike Foss, pushed an alternative: outsourcing the point-of-sale project to IBM, a move that would spread the $100 million cost over the multiyear life of the contract and thus conserve cash. The board, thinking short-term, opted for the outsourcing, citing limited debt capacity and Wall Street's dissatisfaction with Circuit City's earnings numbers. [310]

Meanwhile, Kim Maguire, in addition to his other shortcomings, had seriously overbought for the 2003 holiday season. Circuit City found itself in January 2004 sitting on $200 million in excess inventory.[311] At that point, McCollough asked Bowman to relinquish his MIS position and take on a special project to correct the defects in the replenishment system. McCollough then tapped Mike Jones, CIO of the credit card bank, to became CIO of Circuit City Stores.

Following Foss's initiative and the board's direction, in the spring of 2004 he engaged IBM, for a fixed price, to create rPOS (replacement POS) as a substitute for both the old DPS system and Magellan. Progress on rPOS was slow and IBM had difficulty staying on budget.

By the end of fiscal 2008 the project's cost had ballooned from the original $69 million contract to $250 million, two and a half times what it would have cost to complete Magellan. Even worse, almost four years after the project was initiated, rPOS was installed in only 26 percent of the stores. Worst of all, the operating results were disappointing: Sales in the locations with rPOS were 10 percent below the company's average.[312] One reason is that the IBM POS terminal, as an off-the-shelf retail product, could not handle many of the unique and consumer-friendly functions that had been built into DPS and Magellan. Once again, the lack of clear planning and effective executive leadership caused an important strategic initiative to fail. Instead of conserving cash, the IBM alternative cost more money and produced worse results.

Inventory Management System

From the beginning of his Circuit City tenure, Schoonover was critical of the company's inventory turns. [313] At his first annual meeting as executive vice president in June 2005, he boldly boasted that going forward Circuit City would not carry any inventory on its books. Turnover would be so high that goods would be sold and the money in the bank before payment to the vendors was due.[314] In fact, Best Buy had never achieved this objective and Circuit City never came close.[315]

Schoonover believed that Circuit City's homegrown merchandise inventory system was to blame for lower-than-desired inventory turns. He wanted to replace it with the Oracle-based system Best Buy used. John Froman defended the differences in turnover, contending that with significant dollars locked into display merchandise in both company's stores, Best Buy's faster turns were primarily attributable to its far higher sales volumes per store rather than its superior inventory system. Schoonover was not persuaded.

Meanwhile, Bowman had corrected the forecasting problems he had been detailed to work on. At his first meeting with Schoonover in October 2005, he outlined the progress achieved. As his reward for giving up the CIO job and fixing the forecasting problem, Schoonover fired Bowman during their second meeting—very likely because he understood that Bowman would be opposed to scrapping the existing inventory management system.

Shortly thereafter, Schoonover put together a team to study what he termed the Merchandising System Transformation (MST) effort. It concluded, just as he had hoped, that the "existing systems do not support the needs of Circuit City."[316]

Up-to-date IT systems, especially for such central functions as retail inventory management, are integral to success in retailing. But changing major systems in a large company is a daunting, disrupting, and perilous task, to be undertaken only if there are no reasonable alternatives. As far as I can determine, the existing merchandising system was not broken. Inventory was being received, distributed, and accounted for without material issues. The improper forecasting that created a glut in 2004 had been fixed with upgraded personnel and improved procedures. There was no compelling need to redo the inventory management system.[317]

Nonetheless Schoonover hired ReTek (later, Oracle Retail) to "transform [Circuit City's] merchandising, supply chain, planning and marketing processes." Implementation was expected in fiscal 2007.[318] The price tag for the new system was $250 million. As late as 2008, four years after Schoonover announced its introduction, the new Merchandise System Transformation was still not fully implemented.

As a result of impetuous and capricious decisions, Circuit City squandered half a billion dollars upgrading its supply chain technology. The $250 million that was spent on the merchandising system upgrade, like the $275 million wasted on a new rPOS system, took a huge bite out of Circuit City's available cash flow—cash that was sorely needed for store remodels, relocations, and other higher-priority projects.

Legacy Issues

In addition to the strategic issues that McCollough confronted in 2000, there were legacy questions to be faced:

- *Spinning off CarMax*. As Circuit City struggled and CarMax grew, managing them under one corporate umbrella became more difficult.

- *Selling the Credit Card Business*. Although not a problem in 2000, the credit card business soon became a lot less profitable and an increasing burden on Circuit City's financial metrics.

CarMax

In fiscal 2000, with forty locations and $2 billion in sales, CarMax turned its first profit: $1 million. Although CarMax did not add any retail locations over the next two years, its focus on improving operations and increasing traffic boosted sales to $3.2 billion and net earnings to $91 million. In July 2001 Circuit City sold an additional 10 percent of CarMax's shares, raising $140 million to fund its own growth.[319] Notwithstanding this success, however, by the following year Circuit City decided it was time to distribute its remaining CarMax shares and set CarMax free as a fully independent company.

The reasons for this decision were several. First, many Wall Street bankers, whether out of self-interest or not, expressed the belief that combining a used car business and an electronics business in one stock reduced the appeal to potential shareholders. Those who liked the car business, they argued, did not want it diluted with TV and electronics, and vice versa. Second, by the late '90s, Circuit City's core business had begun to slip, both absolutely and relative to competitors. Circuit City's ability to finance CarMax's growth was becoming increasingly problematic.[320] Finally, the management of CarMax was frustrated at being tied to the apron strings of the parent company. Having lost confidence in the ability of the parent company to regain industry leadership, the CarMax team was not happy having their compensation fitted into the larger and less successful corporate mold.

Early in 2002, Circuit City management began taking steps to separate the companies. The board of directors cited as its reasons that they were in different industries, that Circuit City's remodeling program was estimated to cost "hundreds of millions of dollars," and that competition for capital could constrain CarMax's expansion program.[321] In September 2002, Circuit City shareholders received nearly one-third of a share of CarMax stock for each Circuit City Group share they owned.[322]

The KMX shares, distributed tax-free to Circuit City shareholders, were worth at the time $1 billion, not a bad return for a six-year, $175 million loan that had been fully repaid with interest. For those shareholders who kept their CarMax shares, the returns have been extraordinary.[323] These days CarMax is a highly successful, independent operation with $8 billion in sales.

Looked at from a long-term perspective, it is disappointing that CarMax did not remain part of the Circuit City portfolio. Its excellent results for the first five years after it was spun out might have helped Circuit City avoid bankruptcy in 2009.[324] Alternatively, if Circuit City had sold its CarMax stock instead of distributing it to shareholders, it could have raised approximately $1 billion to finance its badly needed remodeling efforts.

In reality, CarMax's eventual separation had been building since the tracking stock was created in 1997. The initial premise for CarMax was to create a portfolio of retail companies, so that as one matured another would be coming along to support the growth of the whole. But fashions change on Wall Street, just as they do on Fifth Avenue. By 2000, conglomerates, even those composed exclusively of retail companies, were out of fashion.

The child Circuit City created and nurtured is the parent company's most enduring tangible legacy.

Bank Credit Cards

By the early 2000s the credit card business, the mainstay of Circuit City's earnings in the '90s, had also become problematic. At the same time that Circuit City's operating profits significantly declined, its credit card receivables ballooned to an unwieldy $2.8 billion.[325] For years, Circuit City had found a profitable niche in lower-tier credit customers. By 2000, higher interest rates, an explosion of credit cards in consumers' hands, and rising delinquencies were eroding profitability.

Circuit City, which had sold most of these receivables, was required by its securitization agreements to add additional cash to the securitized pool if delinquencies exceeded designated levels.[326] In fact, the quality of the receivables did deteriorate and the rating agencies increased the amount of security Circuit City was required to hold, thus tying up more millions in cash. As receivables ballooned, this 10 percent retained interest became a bigger and bigger fraction of Circuit City's working capital. As its earnings declined and delinquencies increased, Circuit City became a growing concern to the rating agencies and the banking regulators. Compounding the problem, in 2003 the U.S. Comptroller of the Currency decided, as a matter of policy, that retailers should not own and operate credit card banks. It gave Circuit City and others, including Sears, a difficult time. [327]

Responding to these pressures, in 2003 Circuit City sold its Visa/MasterCard business to FleetBoston Financial and announced the planned sale of the private-label finance operation to Chase Card Services (previously Bank One Corporation). For the private-label sale, Circuit City set up an arrangement whereby Chase would continue to supply consumer credit to Circuit City customers for the ensuing seven years. According to the Annual Report, "We expect that the two sales together will generate new cash proceeds totaling more than $600 million, simplify the investment analysis for our shareholders and remove the earnings volatility of these operations."[328]

There is no doubt that selling the generic Visa and MasterCard receivables was the right move. The portfolio had grown to $1.5 billion by the end of fiscal 2003. Long-term, there was no strategic value in owning and managing a portfolio of receivables for customers not doing business with Circuit City. In addition to weighing down its balance sheet, the portfolio generated a $172 million after-tax loss in the first half of fiscal 2004.[329] Because of the deteriorating quality of the receivables, Circuit City was forced to take an additional $90 million after-tax loss on the sale of the generic portfolio just a few months later.

The wisdom of selling the private-label portfolio is less clear. On the one hand, the sale generated $476 million, $50 million more than its appraised fair market value, and made available to the company the $58 million that First American National Bank (Circuit City's credit card bank) was reserving in cash to guarantee the receivables.[330, 331]

On the other hand, selling the private-label receivables eliminated the strategic advantage of being able to weigh the profitability of the sale against the creditworthiness of the customer rather than relying on a fickle third party to make that judgment. That was the strategic reason to go into the credit card business in the first place. That had not changed.

The McCollough Years

In addressing the five strategic issues outlined in McCollough's 2001 Strategic Plan nothing of substance was achieved.

- Marketing initiatives, despite some innovative and attractive commercials and themes, failed to reverse the deteriorating sales trends.
- The erratic design and relocation effort never effectively came to grips with improving the outmoded and deteriorating store base.
- In merchandising, the search for higher margins led Circuit City into a poorly conceived acquisition that wasted hundreds of millions of dollars and an untold number of management hours.

In addition, new merchandising leadership significantly compromised two of Circuit City's most important assets: a strong merchandising team and long-term vendor support.

• Sales force productivity was destroyed by the continuing refusal to abandon or modify the step-up selling strategy and by a panic-driven decision to abandon sales commissions altogether and terminate many of the company's most experienced salespeople.

• Finally, instead of achieving a world-class supply chain, decisions to abandon, rather than fix, the aging point-of-sale system and to replace the functional merchandise management system led to expenditures of more than half a billion dollars and did not improve functionality.

Need for an Operational Plan

So why did all these initiatives fail?

The main issues identified in the 2001 Strategic Plan—marketing, store relocation and redesign, sales force productivity, and management information systems—were all interrelated and needed to be tackled in a coordinated way. Circuit City needed to make most of these changes market-by-market and not store-by-store. In order to advertise credibly in a market, all or most of the stores in that market had to be redesigned and/or relocated and their selling strategies revamped *before* the new advertising began. Otherwise the store experience would not deliver what the advertising promised.

In short, Circuit City needed a comprehensive *operational* plan to address, specifically and logically, how it would implement its vague, but directionally correct, strategic aspirations. If the company was to update the stores, relocate real estate, and modify store staffing, it would need to: (1) decide how much to expand the sales floor and reduce the warehouse; (2) identify market-by-market those stores that needed to be relocated and those that needed remodeling; (3) set a plan to make the required changes quickly and efficiently; (4) abandon or significantly modify the commission-based step-up selling system; and (5) identify how to pay for the "makeover," and not flinch when the cost threatened to impact the price of its stock.

Management Style

CEOs are necessarily two-faced, not in the sense of being duplicitous but in the mythological sense of being Janus-like, able to look simultaneously in different directions. The CEO of a public company must communicate a sense of the company externally to suppliers, shareholders, and the stock market. And, at the same time, he must look internally and refine and clarify the business strategy with and to employees.

External Style

In facing the market, McCollough was too anxious to please.

Perhaps the best evidence is that, when confronted with the need for a major remodeling and relocation effort costing upwards of a billion dollars, he compromised his judgment of how the new stores should function (shopping carts and bulked-out displays) and went with a low-budget alternative because he thought the costs of doing it the right way would be more than the Street could tolerate. Another piece of evidence is the way Circuit City backed into the future when they moved from a commissioned sales force to hourly workers. Instead of gradually replacing high-priced commissioned personnel, the company put on a show for Wall Street to prove that it was reducing costs and, in the process, alienated its entire workforce along with a significant segment of the public.

A review of the press releases from 2000 to 2004 shows that Circuit City, reflecting the company's preoccupation with pleasing investors, reversed the cardinal rule for such disclosures: It overpromised and underdelivered.

Internal Style

When facing inside, McCollough was also anxious to please, and especially anxious to avoid conflict. He was willing to make decisions but often did not make them collaboratively. This was a change in the culture. Under previous leadership, the company had been run through an executive committee that met once a month to discuss operational decisions before they were implemented. These meetings were often marathon sessions, lasting all day and sometimes into the evening. Participants felt free to speak their minds, even if it meant disagreeing with their boss or their peers. This practice had two main advantages. More input and free debate led to better decisions. And the sense of inclusion ultimately led to greater support, even from those on the "losing" side.

From all reports, McCollough did not welcome debate or conflict. He often tried to work out strategic initiatives with the person most directly involved, bypassing his executive committee. He did this when the company decided to discontinue carrying appliances and when he promoted someone to be head of merchandising one day and demoted him the next. Similarly, he allowed two separate, noncommunicating teams to work on the "Store of the Future" without ever resolving their differences.

This backdoor management style produces inferior decisions. It also leads to frequently having to reverse or modify decisions once other executives weigh in and all of the implications are understood. This, in turn, creates stress and uncertainty among employees. In the process, loyalty and trust both suffer.

During his tenure McCollough experienced an extraordinary amount of turnover among senior staff. Within four years he lost two executive vice presidents, five senior vice presidents, numerous vice presidents, and three long-term senior merchants. This list does not include retirees or lower-level officers. With these departures, the heart of the company had either jumped ship or was thrown overboard. In either case they took with them big swaths of institutional memory.

New Leadership

On February 16, 2005, tragedy struck the Circuit City community. Two company-owned Cessna jets, each carrying six passengers and two pilots, were flying to the West Coast. They needed to stop in Pueblo, Colorado, to refuel. One landed safely in drizzly, freezing weather. The second one crashed, killing all eight aboard. The entire Circuit City family was devastated, especially since the company used its three planes extensively and any one of several hundred people might, but for the grace of God, have been aboard. This added to the sense of malaise and resignation. Was this an omen that Circuit City was somehow doomed to fail?

A year after the crash McCollough decided to step down as Chairman and CEO. He had been thinking about this possibility for some time, but the crash may have accelerated his timing. Jeff Wells, Circuit City's SVP of human resources at the time, believes that McCollough took seriously a chart that Wells had showed him from his days at Sears. Sears managers, the chart indicated, lived on average only 1.5 years past retirement, and for each year worked beyond age 55, their life expectancy was reduced by two years. McCollough was then 57.

Whatever the reason, McCollough decided it was time to move on. The board had reservations about Schoonover's readiness to succeed him but decided not to conduct a search. Schoonover's previous year and a half with the company, they thought, was better than having no Circuit City experience at all, and his Best Buy experience held promise for catching up. McCollough was confident that he was leaving the company in good hands. In his final Annual Report as CEO he wrote,

> Certainly one of our greatest accomplishments has been the transformation of our senior management team. The strength and readiness of this team led in part to my decision to retire as chief executive officer in February and as Chairman at the upcoming 2006 annual shareholders' meeting.[332]

Circuit City Revenues and Earnings 2001-2005

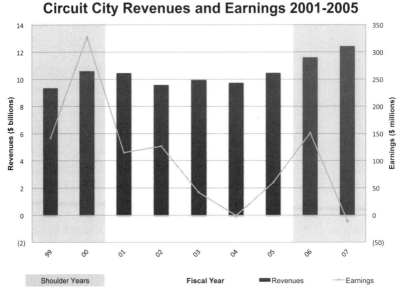

Looking back, it is hard to judge McCollough's tenure as a success. By all accounts, including my own, Alan McCollough is one of the nicest men you will ever meet. He is smart and well spoken, even courtly. Everyone at Circuit City liked him. Leo Durocher once observed, "Nice guys finish last." I do not think that is true. However, a good leader, especially in tough times, needs to make tough calls. As is apparent from the stories I have recounted, and from the testimony of many of his colleagues, McCollough had a hard time making tough decisions and a harder time sticking to them. Given Circuit City's problems, that was a significant handicap.

Based simply on the financial record, McCollough's tenure was disappointing at best. Despite an explosive growth in consumer electronics between 2000 and 2005,[333] Circuit City's sales remained essentially flat at $10 million per year. The sales gained by a net increase of forty-one superstores and expanded e-commerce were offset by same-store sales declines in existing shops.

In addition, earnings dropped precipitously from a high of $327 million in FY 2000, just before McCollough took over, to a loss of

$800,000 in FY 2004, and rebounded to only a modest profit of $60 million in FY 2005. In the same time period Best Buy sales doubled from $12.5 to $25 billion and the mass merchants continued to gain market share.

Much more significantly, however, none of the strategic challenges facing the company in 2000 were successfully resolved. Whatever chance Circuit City had to retool and again challenge for industry leadership was squandered by McCollough's inability to set a bold and coherent plan and execute it.

McCollough chose not to stay on as chairman of the board for Schoonover's early years, and, with that decision, he broke with Circuit City's long-standing tradition of the ex-CEO remaining on the board and mentoring his successor. In February 2006 Schoonover was left alone at the helm with only seventeen months of Circuit City experience under his belt.

Habits of Mind

Be Humble, Run Scared: *Continuously doubt your understanding of things. Business success contains the seeds of its own destruction. Worry about what the competition knows that you do not. Andy Grove, the legendary cofounder of Intel, got it largely right in his book* **Only the Paranoid Survive**.

Despite the obvious deterioration of Circuit City's position vis-a-vis Best Buy and the mass merchants, nowhere in the Three Year Plan or in the board's actions do we see a sense of urgency or an understanding of the existential threat to Circuit City. The board shortsightedly halted the implementation of the point-of-sale upgrade, improvidently approved an unnecessary replacement of the inventory management system, presided over an erratic and undisciplined store improvement program, and wasted $300 million and a lot of management effort on the ill-advised acquisition of InterTAN.

Maintain a Current Road Map: *If you don't know where you are going, any road will take you there. Regular strategic planning based on how the company relates to its external environment, including the economy, competition, and the customer, is essential to success.*

By undervaluing, and then discontinuing, long-range strategic planning, McCollough was, in effect, driving down a dark road without headlights. He faced many serious challenges that needed to be attacked decisively, and in a coordinated manner, but without a strategic plan he was doomed to fail.

Evidence Trumps Ideology: *In business, as in politics, decisions are too often based on unproven assumptions about what works and what doesn't. We all need operating assumptions about human nature, the economy, and the like, but when things do not work out as planned, we need to determine whether our assumptions were based on evidence or ideology. Evidence about the real world trumps ideological assumptions every time.*

McCollough bought into Circuit City's long-held corporate belief that only commissions could motivate salesmen to sell better products and extended warranties. . Best Buy proved that sales people paid by the hour, if properly led, can deliver an acceptable mix of profitable sales at a far lower cost. Once it was forced by unsatisfactory financial results to go to hourly paid sales people, Circuit City discovered that they could, in fact, sell higher-margin products and extended service policies.

Confront the Brutal Facts: *The worst person you can fool is yourself. Ignoring or denying reality does not help it go away. Once you understand the issues, be bold enough to take decisive action.*

When McCollough took over in 2000 there were a lot of brutal facts staring the company in the face. He clearly *understood* the issues, but, because he was not running scared, he did not take swift and decisive action. He tried a lot of things, but none of them consistently or with determination. In short, he failed to...

Boldly Follow Through: *Big ideas require bold leadership and attract loyal* *followers. The effort comes to naught if the execution is tentative or not well disciplined.*

Following his first (and only) comprehensive Three Year Plan, McCollough failed to develop a cohesive operational strategy. The interrelated issues of marketing, store remodeling and relocation, and sales force productivity, all identified in the plan, were attacked piecemeal. Improvements in merchandising and supply-chain management were botched. In each case the company failed to develop a thoughtful set of actions to attack the strategic issues or to stick to a consistent program.

On the other hand, McCollough did boldly and decisively exit DIVX, the credit card business, and CarMax.

Mind the Culture: *Create a caring and ethical culture where employees can make mistakes without fear of adverse consequences. Beware of employees who are more concerned about their own success than the success of the business. Understand, exemplify, and reinforce the company's positive history and culture.*

Maguire destroyed the culture of the merchandising staff and severely weakened the company's standing with vendors. McCollough must have known that morale was being destroyed, yet he did not act. His noncollaborative decision-making style also weakened morale, and the excessive turnover among senior officers further deprived the company of the caring culture that had prevailed in the days when it was thriving.

Another example of countercultural activity includes the decision to abandon appliances in a manner that, at best, was misunderstood by most Circuit City employees, and, at worst, forfeited Circuit City's number two position in a significant segment of the business. Equally counter to the company's long-standing culture was the manner in which thousands of sales personnel were fired without warning, without being offered the opportunity to stay on as hourly employees, and without any clear explanation of why eliminating commissions and their jobs was necessary.

Focus on the Future: *Manage for the long term and not the short. Don't let short-term earnings swings divert a long-term strategy. Ignore the skeptics and short-term market swings. If things go well, the value of your company, whether public or private, will respond over time.*

Too often management and the board made decisions designed to please the market in the short run, rather than build for the long run. These included failing to pursue the store remodeling and relocation programs with discipline and a market focus, the decision not to fully implement the Magellan point-of-sale upgrade, and the preemptive firing of salesmen in a manner that infuriated customers and fellow employees.

Lessons Learned

Know When to Hold and When to Fold: Circuit City made the right move in selling its generic credit card portfolio. It had made a lot of money over the years, but by 2000 it was losing money and tying up the balance sheet for an operation that had no strategic value to the company. The decision to also sell the private-label credit card portfolio was a tougher call. It had strategic value in assisting sales when the customer was only marginally qualified for credit, but it was also another distraction and a financial burden on a weakened company.

Chapter Eleven

GONE

It is an immutable law in business that words are words, explanations are explanations, promises are promises but only performance is reality.

– Harold Geneen

In March 2006, sixteen months after Philip Schoonover arrived at Circuit City to replace Ken Maguire as the chief merchant, he was named president. A month later he was named CEO. Never before in the history of Circuit City had anyone ascended to the top so quickly.

Choosing and grooming a successor is the single most important job of any board and its CEO. One of the reasons Circuit City had been able to develop a culture of teamwork and cooperation is that, from the beginning, the various boards and CEOs had taken their time to evaluate and train future CEOs. This allowed them to ensure that the successors both understood the challenges facing the company and embraced the culture Sam and Hecht had established. Schoonover's appointment was an exception.

The Real World 2006–2009

The external outlook for Circuit City in March 2006 was actually brighter than it had been for a while. The U.S. economy was on an upswing. In 2005 real GDP growth hit 2.7 percent.[334] Consumer electronics industry sales, led by triple-digit growth in flat-panel televisions and portable MP3 players, were $125 billion. This was a very healthy 11 percent increase over the prior year, with 2006 expected to be even better[335]. Circuit City, with an 8 percent market share, sat in third place, behind Best Buy (17 percent) and Walmart (10 percent).[336] Its just-completed fiscal year 2006 had produced $11.6 billion in sales and $151 million in earnings, the best since 2000. Its $24 stock price, the highest since 2002, valued the company at more than $4 billion.[337]

The company had also been dramatically simplified since 2000, when Alan McCollough began his tenure as CEO. DIVX, CarMax, the credit card bank, and the appliance business were all gone, leaving only the core consumer electronics stores. This simplification was partly offset by the acquisition of InterTAN in 2005. As we saw in the '70s, reducing complexity is an important ingredient in profitable growth.

In addition, a number of important strategic changes, albeit badly executed, had been undertaken. In 2003, after 54 years of directed selling, Circuit City eliminated all sales commissions. Although the process destroyed morale and some customer loyalty, the fact is that in a commodity-pricing environment, high-priced commission sales personnel were no longer affordable. The store revitalization program, although it failed to address the strategic objective it set, had made at least cosmetic changes in many stores, and by the end of fiscal 2006, one-third of Circuit City's domestic superstores had been newly constructed, relocated, or partially remodeled in the previous five years.[338]

Nonetheless, there were still many problems. One-third of the stores[339] were still locked into suboptimal real estate with long-term leases the company could not easily shed. Analysts worried that the overall increase in revenue Circuit City had shown in recent quarters had been the result of merchandise price cuts that could not be sustained.[340] Most crucial, Circuit City was still generating less than half of Best Buy's volume per store.[341] And at the end of fiscal 2005, Best Buy had, for the first time, more stores—608 as compared to Circuit City's 604.

Innovation

Schoonover brought a new perspective to the company. He had participated in the Best Buy turnaround in the mid-'90s, when Ar-

Phillip Schoonover, CEO 2006-2008

thur Andersen's consulting arm, Accenture, reengineered its methods of doing business and RHR International helped change its culture to accept Andersen's more rigorous and accountable methods.

While he declined to be interviewed for this book, I have no doubt that Schoonover believed Circuit City also needed to be made over. Given Best Buy's success, he understandably used that turnaround as his model. During his tenure he hired from Best Buy four buyers plus the four key officers in any retail operation: general merchandise manager, retail operations manager, supply chain manager, and CFO.

To his credit, instead of simply copying Best Buy, he also began a process of exploring new ways to do business. He said in his first annual report:

> We are creating an innovation engine. Innovation teams will generate many ideas, then pursue, develop and test concepts aimed at the creation of real value and the transformation of our business for the future. Expect to see us try many new things, some of which will likely fail, but all of which will result in learning. [342]

Shortly after becoming CEO, Schoonover had the entire top management team of a hundred people retreat to the University of Virginia for a weeklong "Innovation Boot Camp," run by the Boston Consulting Group.[343] In addition, he hired a University of Michigan professor to expose store employees from around the country to innovative thinkers in order to generate new ideas from the store level up. The two hundred participants were required to spend eight to ten hours a week over many weeks attending meetings in Richmond, reacting to new ideas and to touchy-feely books like *Tuesdays with Morrie*.[344]

The downside of this program, however, was that, with all the normal responsibilities already on their plate, many of the participants resented the additional time required to participate in thought experiments and what-if scenarios. One observer believed that store execution suffered because so many of the best people were attending seminars. Most thought it was a colossal waste of time and money.

Hiring an abundance of consultants on multimillion-dollar contracts also went against the Circuit City culture. One senior executive estimated that, in two years, Schoonover spent over $50 million just on strategy and store-design advisers.[345] Previous CEOs had retained consultants sparingly, generally for their expertise in specific areas like tax planning, pension benefits, or distribution technology, not to tell Circuit City how to run its business or to recommend strategic initiatives. That was the responsibility of top management, not to be delegated to consultants, however smart they might be.

Schoonover Initiatives

With the new CEO came a new strategic direction. As Schoonover wrote in the 2007 Annual Report:

> We see enormous opportunities with the four pillars of our strategy to win in home entertainment, grow our services business, leverage the shift to multi-channel retailing and significantly improve our real estate position.[346]

Although three of the four pillars were largely recycled from the Best Buy playbook of earlier years,[347] they were worthwhile goals for Circuit City.

"Win in Home Entertainment"

At an analyst conference in May of 2005, Circuit City's management had described its focus on television and audio as "the heritage of our brand."[348] Under Schoonover's merchandising leadership that historic emphasis on television had been paying off. From the time he became chief merchant in October 2004 until he became president in March 2005, the company's share of the U.S. flat-panel television market increased from 15 percent to 22.8 percent in units and from 12.6 percent to 18.9 percent in dollars.[349] Led by triple-digit comparable store sales growth in flat panel TVs, Circuit City posted its best results in years: $11.6 billion in sales and $151 million in earnings for fiscal 2006. Shortly after the numbers were released, the company's stock price peaked at over $31 per share, a level it had not achieved since 2000.[350]

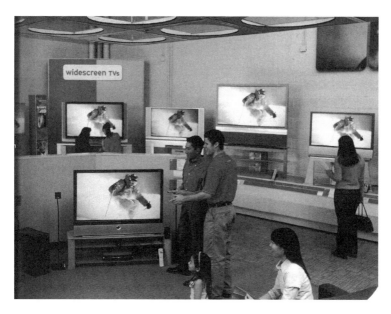

Wide Screen Display – circa 2005

That success, however, was short-lived. During the 2006 holiday season the market took an unexpected turn. A year earlier, one of Circuit City's best-selling televisions had been Panasonic's 42-inch HD flat panel, which retailed for $2,800.[351] The company could not keep enough in stock. By October 2006, however, supply had caught up to demand and Panasonic was overstocked. Instead of turning to Best Buy or Circuit City to solve its inventory problems, it sold 50,000 units to Walmart at a price that was low enough for Walmart to promote them on Black Friday (the day after Thanksgiving) for $1,294. Other manufacturers scrambled to match or beat Panasonic's offer, thus setting off an industry-wide price war.[352] All other retailers, including Circuit City, had to write down the value of their entire flat-screen inventory. As a result, in fiscal 2007 Circuit City posted a net loss from continuing operations of $10 million. Panasonic's move may well have taken everyone by surprise, but if a company is going to "win in home entertainment," it has to be faster on its feet and merchandise entertainment products smarter than its competitors.

In-Home Service

The second pillar of Schoonover's strategy, in-home service for the set-up and repair of home theaters and other complex digital equipment, including computers, was long overdue. Best Buy had much earlier recognized that as high-tech products became increasingly commoditized and their installation and maintenance more complex, an important path to profits lay in providing in-home services. This thinking led Best Buy to acquire the Geek Squad in 2003.[353] Within three years, the Geek Squad was contributing an estimated $1 billion in annual revenue and $280 million in profits to Best Buy's bottom line.[354]

In fall 2006, three years after Best Buy, Circuit City launched its response: Firedog. As the 2007 Annual Report explained:

> Firedog services include in-store and in-home PC services, available through Circuit City's more than 600

Superstores across the country; home-theater installations, available within 25 miles of Circuit City locations; and remote technical assistance for PCs through
www.firedog.com 24 hours a day, 7 days a week.[355]

Firedog was a big step in the right direction. Like Answer City
before it, it met a strong consumer need. In fiscal 2007 Firedog
generated $200 million in revenue, which grew to $270 million in
2008.[356] More important, the initiative created a platform for Circuit
City to rise above competing on price alone and to distinguish itself
from the mass merchants. In the company's own words, "Through
Firedog, Circuit City provides a profitable, differentiated offering
in the high-growth consumer services market that we estimate will
reach $20 billion in fiscal 2010."[357] Unfortunately, Circuit City was
already burning, and Firedog arrived too late to put out the blaze.

Multi-channel Integration

Since 1999, when it became the first national brick-and-mortar
specialty retailer to sell consumer electronics over the Internet,
Circuit City's online store had been the industry leader.[358] In
2006, management made several key observations:

- Seventy percent of Circuit City shoppers visited the website
  before buying online or in-store.
- Circuit City's website influenced $3 to $4 billion of in-store sales.
- Sixty percent of online sales in fiscal 2006 were picked up in-store.
- Multichannel shoppers (defined as online customers who also
  shop in-store or on the telephone) shopped more often, were
  more satisfied with Circuit City, and spent five to six times more
  than customers who bought only on the website.[359]

An independent 2004 survey showed that Circuit City ranked third
in overall customer satisfaction among electronics e-tailers and first
for in-store pickup.[360] In light of these findings, management knew
the company needed to maintain its lead in multichannel shopping.

To enhance its e-commerce sales, in 2005 Schoonover launched
the 24/24 Pickup Guarantee. It promised that qualifying purchases

made through Circuit City's website or call centers would be ready for in-store pickup at a customer-designated location within twenty-four minutes or the customer would receive a $24 Circuit City gift card.[361] Not a bad idea. Unfortunately, the twenty-four-minute promise was undercut by the fact that Circuit City stores did not have separate checkout lines for online customers, and this sometimes irritated web shoppers who had to wait longer than they hoped to check out.[362] In-store pickup of online purchases was further complicated by two pricing policies that had been in place since 2001. One assured online customers that Circuit City would match the price of any *stocking e-commerce retailer,* that is, one that had the product in stock. The second assured in-store shoppers that they would receive the lower of either Circuit City's in-store price or its web price.

Now, in an effort to ratchet up web sales, Schoonover decided to match any competitor's web price for online customers, regardless of whether the competitor stocked the product. Needless to say, it's easy to offer popular products at uneconomically low prices if you don't have any in stock and have no intention of delivering them! By matching phantom competition online, Circuit City's web prices consistently ran lower than its in-store prices. Schoonover further insisted that, if challenged by a customer, Circuit City's posted in-store price would be reduced to match its own web price. As a result, in-store staff were constantly taking markdowns to meet web-pricing at the point of sale, thereby severely eroding gross margins.

In 2007, when Chief Merchandising Officer Doug Moore brought the problem to Schoonover's attention, not only did the CEO fail to correct the issue, he fired Moore for insubordination. When Jim Marcum became acting CEO after Schoonover's own firing a year and a half later, one of the first moves he made, at the urging of his management team, was to discontinue matching phantom prices on the web. Marcum believes that Schoonover's insistence on matching web-pricing in the stores was a significant factor in Circuit City's demise. In effect, multichannel integration turned out to be a broken crutch rather than a pillar.

Real Estate: the City Stores

The final column in Schoonover's strategy was to modify Circuit City's real estate program. In the 2007 Annual Report, he wrote:

> We are transforming our real estate position primarily by opening incremental stores in new trade areas and relocating stores to better locations in existing trade areas...[363]

In FY 2008 Circuit City opened forty-three new superstores and relocated eighteen more at a cost of $106 million.[364]

In addition, 2008 saw the debut of a new store format designed to reinvigorate the Circuit City brand. Schoonover concluded that despite the fact the company had tried before and failed, it could put smaller stores in smaller markets and make money.[365] By year-end, Circuit City had opened twenty-two stores called "the city."[366] Each measured 20,000 square feet, 60 percent the size of Circuit City's principal prototype. The innovation featured "partners" (sales associates) and "guests" (customers) working together on a tablet PC containing interactive merchandise displays to develop personalized solutions for each "guest."[367]

Circuit City had high expectations for "the city," declaring that the concept "is not only exciting, it's inspiring."[368] Customer feedback was positive.[369] Unfortunately, the financial results were not. Unsure of the company's ability to recoup the $1.2 million in construction costs per store, CFO Bruce Besanko, without consulting Schoonover, cut the number of stores in the pipeline, from 112 to 54. Nonetheless, in FY 2009, its final year of life, Circuit City spent $254 million on new stores and remodeling. Pouring millions into an unproven concept further eroded the company's financial reserves and left it unprepared to weather a financial storm.

Given more time, management might have figured out how to translate positive consumer reviews for "the city" into financial success or improved customer satisfaction chain-wide. But building 54 stores based on untested assumptions was another nail in Circuit City's coffin.

Maintaining the Culture

From the beginning, Schoonover's hiring had sent a dissonant message to the Circuit City rank and file. For years Best Buy had been the enemy. Now, suddenly, "one of them was our leader."[370]

Sales Commissions: Shooting Yourself in the Head

I described earlier how, in 2003, Circuit City precipitously reversed more than fifty years of commission selling and fired 3,900 of its highest-paid sales personnel, replacing them with hourly paid salespeople. As if the turmoil created by these dismissals were not enough, Circuit City doubled down in 2007 and fired another 3,400 commissioned employees. A press release, again written for Wall Street applause, stated:

> The company has completed a wage management initiative that will result in the separation of approximately 3,400 store Associates. The separations, which are occurring today, focused on Associates who were paid well above the market-based salary range for their role. New Associates will be hired for these positions and compensated at the current market range for the job. [371]

The press noted that the "company saved $130 million in 2003 by eliminating commissions for salespeople, instituting hourly rates and terminating 1,800 jobs."[372] In essence, everyone who had been earning more than $18 per hour, roughly $37,000 per year for a forty-hour week, was let go. They were not offered jobs at the new ceiling ($18 per hour) because management believed their attitudes would be hostile and would contaminate the remaining pool of employees. The company gave the dismissed workers severance pay and told them that after ten weeks they were free to apply to get their old job back at a lower wage.[373]

The firings came as a complete surprise. According to one reporter, the Asheville, North Carolina, store manager broke the news to the dismissed employees during an 8:15 a.m. meeting and immediately escorted them out of the store.[374] As a result of these dismissals, the most-talented salespeople, those in whom the company had invested untold training dollars over the years, walked out the door with their lists of long-time customers and intense resentment at the way they had been treated. As one might imagine, morale and loyalty among those who remained at all levels of the organization was never the same.

> "The mood has been bad for about a week," said Tracy Novak, a business analyst at the chain's corporate offices. "Everyone was afraid, nonproductive, standing around. You were looking around when a door slams or a phone rings. Everybody was on pins and needles." [375]

Not surprisingly, Circuit City was hit with the worst round of adverse publicity imaginable. Journalists and various politicians, among them Senators Hillary Clinton and Chris Dodd, expressed outrage at the callous firings. Once again, Circuit City had managed a strategic transition in a ham-handed way.

Management Style

The bedrock of the company's culture was the "one face" philosophy that Sam and Hecht had established from the very beginning. By the time Schoonover arrived, most of the institutional memory concerning that culture was gone. But even if the memory had survived, Schoonover marched to a different drummer. Schoonover saw the Circuit City culture as lacking a sense of urgency.[376] He was in a hurry to turn things around. Unfortunately, one former executive thinks, "His inconsistent management style and failure to gain people's trust left him with very little internal support."[377] And, as another executive stated: "Alan McCollough was an empathetic person. When he left, the organization was heartless."[378] One former Best Buy colleague who followed Schoonover to Circuit City said: "As the chief merchant, he was a popular leader. When Phil became CEO, he became isolated and may have lost a sense of perspective. He is a very strong-willed individual. He should have put strong-willed people around him. But he did not."[379]

Whatever credibility he might have had with the rank and file was destroyed once and for all in the spring of 2007 when he called all of the Richmond employees together and rented a tent to hold the crowd. The event cost more than $1 million to stage—and this was shortly after the company had laid off 3,400 salesmen plus 500 home-office employees. At the meeting he attempted to identify with the employees, but instead of answering their questions he said he should be questioning them and then bragged about his expensive new boat. He was totally insensitive to the layoffs and to the fears of his remaining staff.[380] The upshot was an anonymous hate e-mail, full of defamatory allegations about Schoonover, which was placed on the Circuit City server and circulated among employees. Sporadic e-mails with similar content continued for years.

Over the last few years of its existence, Circuit City was not a pleasant place to work. One associate said the leadership "was feudal and paranoid. Initially, Schoonover appeared to be a visionary leader. We all wanted him to succeed. He proved to be a ruthless, superficial and vindictive person. He was an embarrassment to everyone. We never had a chance after he settled into power."[381]

Given his management style, it is no surprise that there was extraordinary turnover at the highest levels. Over the course of his three years as CEO, Schoonover brought in thirteen new people to the fourteen-person team of senior executive officers.[382] In one observer's opinion, the quality of personnel at the executive committee level had deteriorated. Many of the new hires thought of their new jobs as short-term.

In addition, the executive officers did not function as a team. Decisions were made by whoever had the power. They were eleven silos, many of whom focused only on their own issues and rarely, if ever, worked well together or spoke truth to power. The General Merchandise Manager, Doug Moore, lost his job by arguing with Schoonover over merchandise-pricing policy. Besanko,

Schoonover's handpicked CFO, cut the pipeline of new stores by half without Schoonover's knowledge because he feared the financial impact would sink the company. Mike Jones, former CIO, summed it up:

> I left in 2007 because I began seeing the decline in our business, and rather than building one strong, cohesive team, founded on trust and support, we were building our team around fear and intimidation. Those elements are not aligned with my definition of success. [383]

In short, during Circuit City's last five years the company's culture of honesty and fair dealing with employees and suppliers, the bedrock of its success, was systematically destroyed. So far as I can tell, the board stood by and took no action.

It would be hard to overestimate the damage that Phil Schoonover inflicted on Circuit City. Some of his strategic initiatives, particularly Firedog and the emphasis on flat-screen TVs had merit. The rest were either too late or poorly executed. On the other hand, he pursued reckless spending on IT, new stores, and, as we will see, reckless stock buybacks. Most important, he destroyed the Circuit City culture, which had already been weakened by McCollough's lack of decisive leadership and inconsistent decision-making.

Role of the Board: 2000–2009

Many have asked, how could all this happen? If management was tone deaf, where was the board? Unfortunately, the board also failed in many of its essential duties.

In the first two years of McCollough's term as CEO, six of the twelve long-standing directors resigned.[384] The directors McCollough chose to replace them had impressive résumés and several had strong business backgrounds, but only two had prior retail experience. Also, two of McCollough's recruits left after two years, adding to the turnover. In the last seven years of its existence,

Circuit City brought a total of twelve new outside directors on to its thirteen- or fourteen-member board. At the end, only three of the thirteen outside directors had been there before McCollough became CEO in 2000. As a result, both institutional memory and continuity suffered.

Looking back over the last decade of Circuit City's existence, there are four major areas in which the board failed in its duties:

- Its governance procedures were lax.
- It failed to manage CEO succession successfully.
- It failed with several merger and acquisition opportunities.
- It failed to manage the cash.

Governance Failures

Unfortunately, only a few of the directors with whom I served and none of the directors who joined after I departed were willing to talk to me about governance issues.[385] As a result, I am not aware of *how* the board functioned after 2000. Nonetheless, it is possible to form some judgments based on the public record of *what* it did and did not do during that time.

The board of the last twenty or more years of Circuit City's existence, while clearly "independent," was, by today's more stringent governance standards, formally deficient. Until 2004, when it selected its first lead director, it rarely met in executive session and it did not regularly evaluate the CEO, except through its compensation committee, which the CEO in effect appointed. It had no formal plan of succession and, until the end was in sight, did not stand up to, much less fire, the CEO despite poor performance.

Formalities aside, in the mid- to late '90s the board also failed in its substantive duties to shareholders by failing to intervene while Circuit City lost its market position. It did not appreciate Circuit City's strategic weakness as Best Buy overtook the company. It did not require management to present a clear and viable plan to set the ship aright. It also failed by accepting McCollough's pie-in-the-sky Three Year Plan in 2000 and allowing him to discontinue the three-year planning process thereafter.

In a nutshell, the board perpetuated the laissez-faire environment that had prevailed through most of the Sharp years. Management was in charge and the board, so far as I can tell, questioned little and challenged almost nothing. Only when the company was staring bankruptcy in the face did the board members wake up and begin to take charge. By then it was too late.

Succession Failures

The absolutely indispensable obligation of any corporate board is to select a capable CEO and to remove an unsuccessful one. The board is also responsible for the internal health of the company culture and for ensuring that there is a proper fit between the company's goals, the culture of the organization, and its CEO. In his book, *The CEO's Boss*, William Klepper discusses the need for a "social contract" between a board and the CEO and describes the contract's main elements as a mutual commitment to: [386]

- The stakeholders, including customers, suppliers, communities, and employees.
- Risk assessment and managing the company's risk profile.
- Transparency and honesty in dealing with each other.
- Outside professional coaching for a new CEO to manage more effectively and for the board to govern better.

It appears that, in selecting McCollough or Schoonover, these mutual commitments were not undertaken by the board and CEO, either explicitly, as Klepper recommends, or implicitly.

In considering Sharp's replacement, the Circuit City board—and I was there at the time—simply ratified Sharp's earlier commitment to recommend McCollough as his successor. Without any in-depth discussion of qualifications or fit, the board went along. Since the board had acquiesced in Sharp's effort to reverse McCollough's decision to leave in 1997, it would have been awkward to raise objections when Sharp retired. Despite the moral dilemma, however, the board had a fiduciary obligation to revisit its earlier acquiescence and consider McCollough's fitness to succeed Sharp in 2000. The board knew McCollough, but it never asked itself, either in 2000 or earlier, whether he was the right person to lead Circuit City. I share the blame for that.

Similarly, when McCollough suddenly resigned, the board accepted his recommendation that Schoonover succeed him. It did not engage a headhunter to do a search to find the best person for the job.[387] Instead the board went along with McCollough's recommendation, despite the reservations of at least one director. In both cases the board made a mistake in their choice, but, more significantly, they failed to follow a process that might have prevented their errors.

Mergers and Acquisitions Failures

Another major failing was the board's willingness to accept, without skepticism or independent analysis, management's recommendations with regard to mergers and acquisitions. In its later years the company took several bad swings at wild pitches.

InterTAN

The acquisition of InterTAN is a case in point. The board failed to ask tough questions of the management team and allowed itself to be seduced by optimistic forecasts.[388] It turns out that the cross-sell and synergy projections were never validated with senior merchants,[389] nor did the company consider the possibility of a lawsuit from RadioShack. Just one week after Circuit City announced the acquisition agreement, RadioShack sued for the wrongful use of its name in Canada. The lawsuit came as a complete surprise, and Circuit City was forced to spend $30 million redoing the signs on the RadioShack stores. When, in 2007, the company was required by its accountants to take an "impairment charge" of $92 million, the board woke up and finally recognized its mistake. It authorized management to "explore strategic alternatives for InterTAN, Inc,"[390] but the company was unable to find a buyer. After spending $300 million and countless hours of management time integrating the purchase, Circuit City died with InterTAN still part of the company.

Acquisition Overtures

In the early 2000s Circuit City's substantial coffers of cash and its volatile stock price made it an attractive buyout candidate. Between 2003 and 2005, the company received two acquisition offers.

The first came on June 16, 2003, from Carlos Slim Helu, a Mexican billionaire and notorious bottom-fisher. Slim, who already owned 9 percent of Circuit City, offered shareholders $8 per share, an 18.5 percent premium over the then-current stock price of $6.75.[391] Slim cited buying synergies with CompUSA, which he already owned, as the reason for his offer. Analysts, however, were skeptical. Two days later, at the Annual Meeting, Circuit City shareholders and the board of directors rejected the offer, and rightly so: More than half of the $1.5 billion Slim would have paid was sitting in Circuit City's own cash accounts.[392]

The next acquisition offer was both more serious and more realistic. On February 11, 2005, following several years of off-and-on discussions, Highfields Capital Management came forward with an offer to purchase the company for $3.2 billion in cash, or $17 per share, a 20 percent premium over the then-current price of $14.14.[393] Highfields, which already owned a 6.8 percent stake in Circuit City, was a well-regarded $6.5 billion hedge fund run by a former manager of the Harvard endowment and backed by a major investment from Harvard.[394]

In a letter to McCollough, Highfields said that it was disappointed with the company's operating performance and "suboptimal capital structure," which it attributed partially to:

> ...the demands and scrutiny that come with being a public company (i.e. emphasis on monthly sales, quar-

terly earnings and other short-term targets) and partially to the Company's historical inability to react to the increasing competitive nature of the business.

[W]e believe that Circuit City may be better suited to execute its business plan as a privately-held company. Such a transformation would eliminate the public-company transparency into the Company's operating strategy that is uniquely damaging in a highly competitive industry where Circuit City is going head-to-head with a tough and entrenched competitor.[395]

Analysts' responses were mixed. Some thought the offer was a good one and that Highfields would be more aggressive in cutting costs than Circuit City's current management team. Some argued that the premium was not high enough.[396] Others pointed out that Highfields had little experience with takeovers in general and retailing in particular, although it had made several small private-equity investments over the years.

As required by corporate law, Circuit City's directors took the bid seriously and engaged some of Wall Street's best-known take-over defense bankers and lawyers.[397] As is required in these situations, the board directed management to compare the $17 per share offer with the likely price of the stock if the company stayed independent. Naturally, the management team built a set of optimistic projections. They showed that, given the plans to improve the business, Circuit City's stock price would exceed $17 in a relatively short time.

On March 7, 2005, a month after receiving the Highfields offer, McCollough announced that the directors had rejected it and decided not to consider any other offers or conduct an auction to obtain a higher price. Instead, the directors had determined that Circuit City could "best maximize shareholder value by continuing aggressively to implement the strategic, operational and financial [initiatives] under way and contemplated for the future."[398]

All boards and management teams instinctively want to maintain their independence. Most are reluctant to face the brutal facts or run up a white flag. But under the circumstances, it is hard to understand how the board could have rejected this offer.

- For a decade Circuit City had been losing market share to Best Buy and the mass merchants.
- Since 2000 total sales had stagnated and declined on a per-store basis as more stores were built.
- Earnings had shown severe continuing declines since 2000, with the company losing money in 2004.
- Most of the strategic operational and financial initiatives outlined in the 2000 Three Year Plan had failed.

Highfields' point, that a private company is in a better position to restructure out of the glare of publicity and the demands of shareholders with short-term horizons, was valid. As if to prove the point that the restructuring was not working, between receipt of Highfields' offer and its rejection, Circuit City announced mediocre earnings for fiscal 2005 ($59 million) and the third straight quarter of declining same-store sales.

No company lasts forever. Ultimately the endgame for any business enterprise is to merge or be liquidated. Every board, like any poker player, needs to think about when to hold and when to fold its cards. It seems clear, certainly in retrospect, that the Circuit City board made a huge mistake in rejecting the Highfields offer out of hand and not making a counteroffer.

Cash Management Failures

Perhaps the greatest failure of the board was its inability to manage the cash of the company in a prudent manner. Record earnings in 2000, plus McCollough's decision to sell the bankcard and private-label credit portfolios and to spin off CarMax, and moderately decent earnings in 2001 and 2002,[399] had left the company with hefty cash balances for most of its last nine years. From 2000 to 2007 its year-end cash balances fluctuated between $650 million and $1.2 billion. However, when cash balances exceeded $1 billion, McCollough felt under a lot of pressure from Wall Street investors[400] who thought it should be distributed as dividends or used to support the share price by buying back company stock. Always anxious to please the Street, McCollough, sitting on $900 million in cash, asked the board to approve a stock buyback program. As the 2003 Annual Report explained,

> Our confidence in the strategies and initiatives underway led the board of directors in January 2003 to approve a $200 million stock buyback program. We believe, given the current stock market conditions, a stock repurchase program is a prudent use of our cash resources and an attractive means to enhance shareholder value.[401]

The chart below shows how cash was managed over the last nine years of Circuit City's existence.

Given that Circuit City had been in a deteriorating competitive situation since the mid-'90s and had shown no improvement in same-store sales since 2000, it is hard to imagine on what "strategies and initiatives" the board's confidence was based. In fact, in each of the next two years the company lost money. For the five years following the first buyback (FYs 2003–08) the company earned a total of $240 million on sales of $54 billion, a 0.44 percent returns on sales. Nonetheless, the board authorized four stock buybacks between 2003 and 2007. In the process, Circuit City had spent almost $1 billion buying its own stock.[402]

The alleged "attractive means to enhance shareholder value" was more imaginary than real. The $966 million expenditure purchased 48 million shares, or 18 percent of the shares outstanding when the buyback program began early in 2003.[403] As a result, the impact on stock pricing could hardly have been more than 20 percent. In fact, Circuit City's stock price did rebound from $6 per share in January 2003, reaching a post-2000 peak of $30 in May 2006. That improvement, however, was largely attributable to improved earnings, which almost quadrupled from a meager $41.6

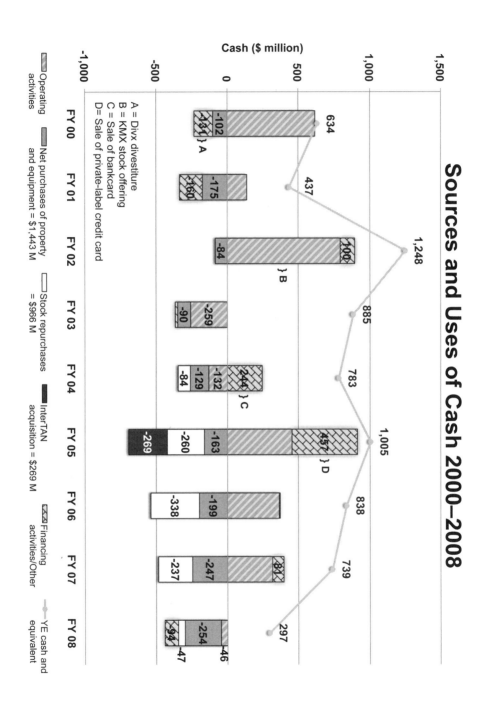

Sources and Uses of Cash 2000–2008

Cash ($ million)

A = Divx divestiture
B = KMX stock offering
C = Sale of bankcard
D = Sale of private-label credit card

Operating activities

Net purchases of property and equipment = $1,443 M

Stock repurchases = $966 M

InterTAN acquisition = $269 M

Financing activities/Other

YE cash and equivalent

FY 00: 634, -102, -131, } A
FY 01: 437, -175, -160
FY 02: 1,248, 100, -84, } B
FY 03: 885, -259, -90
FY 04: 783, -84, -129, -132, 244, } C
FY 05: 1,005, -269, -260, -163, 437, } D
FY 06: 838, -338, -199
FY 07: 739, -237, -247, 81
FY 08: 297, 46, -254, -47, 94, 47

million in FY 2003 to a still slim but more respectable $151 million in FY 2006. When Circuit City announced in April of 2007 that it expected a loss of $70 to $80 million for the first quarter, the stock, which had already dropped significantly from its $30 high, hit $17.45, and by year-end it was at $4.20. Meanwhile the company paid an average of $20.12 per share. In the end, buybacks can only enhance shareholder value for a company that is consistently generating more cash than it can effectively invest. Buybacks can no more hide or offset poor earnings performance than you can turn a sow's ear into a silk purse.

Cash Crisis

For the fiscal year ending February 28, 2007, despite strong demand for consumer electronics, the company lost $10 million. Nonetheless, Schoonover and the operating management team budgeted a very healthy $250 million profit for FY 2008. Mike Foss, the strong-minded CFO since 2003, had resigned in April 2007 and a new CFO did not arrive until July. In the interim, the acting finance team of Phil Dunn and Chip Malloy went to Schoonover to urge him to lower the profit forecast for the current year. Schoonover declined.

Meanwhile, Dunn worked to lower expectations. On April 30, 2007, the company formally withdrew earnings guidance for the first half of the year, leaving the impression that any shortfall would be made up in the second half. Then on June 20, the company withdrew all financial guidance for the year. When Bruce Besanko, the new CFO whom Schoonover had recruited from Best Buy, finally arrived ten days later, he also found the profit forecast for the year unrealistic. Within a few days he took it from a $250 million profit to a $125 million loss. A few months later he revised that to a $150 million loss. In October he further reduced the forecast to a $250 million loss, a $500 million swing from Schoonover's original projection. With losses running $1 million per day, Besanko began worrying about liquidity and possible bankruptcy. Circuit City's cash balance at August 31, 2007, stood at $91 million, a paltry sum for a $12 billion company. With the financial crisis gathering, there could not have been a worse time to have so little cash on hand.

In November, Besanko flew to New York to meet with the Bank of America, the company's lead bank, about an expanded revolving credit agreement, and to meet one-on-one with several board members. [404] At the December 2007 board meeting, the board reviewed Besanko' s new financial forecast. Besanko told them the estimated $250 million loss projected for the current fiscal year (2008) was "light" and that the company was at risk of a liquidity crunch without additional credit. There was stunned silence: The board wanted to know what had happened to the cash. The answer was that in the four fiscal years 2004 to 2007, $966 million had been spent on buybacks, $365 million on IT, and $587 million on store expansion and remodeling.[405]

After the board understood the company's financial position, it went into executive session to discuss whether to fire Schoonover. Immediately before the meeting Blockbuster had called and asked to look at the books in advance of a potential offer to buy the company. The leadership discussion thus turned on whether the company would be better off negotiating to sell itself with or without a CEO. There were two camps: those who wanted to fire him immediately, and those who wanted keep him in place to conduct negotiations with Blockbuster. The latter prevailed. Whether that was the right decision is open to debate. Meanwhile, the company continued in free fall.

Last Tango

The board was understandably reluctant to allow Blockbuster to examine the books. For starters, there was no offer on the table, just a request to look at the books in advance of a possible offer. In addition, the board had legitimate doubts about Blockbuster's ability to finance the deal since it would have to pay more

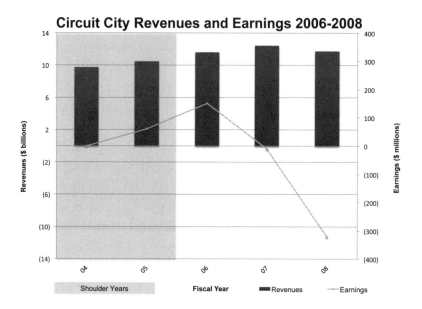

Circuit City Revenues and Earnings 2006-2008

than its own market value for the purchase.[406] The board also had legitimate doubts about the long-term viability of Blockbuster's store-based video rental business. Netflix was becoming a powerful competitor and the long-predicted possibility of downloading movies on demand was increasingly imminent. While discussions continued, Circuit City refused to open it books.

Finally, in February 2008, Blockbuster made a nonpublic offer: $6 to $8 per share, subject to due diligence. That amounted to a premium of between 54 percent and 105 percent over the then-current stock price of $3.90 and valued the firm at $1 billion to $1.35 billion. The market value of the company's outstanding shares just prior to the Blockbuster offer was $659 million.[407]

While the board considered the Blockbuster offer, Mark Wattles, a longtime industry veteran and founder of Hollywood Video, launched a proxy fight for control of the board. He had accumulated a 6.5 percent stake in Circuit City. On April 2, 2008, he announced that he wanted Schoonover fired and the entire board replaced with a slate of new directors that he proposed. And he insisted that Circuit City open its books and allow Blockbuster to conduct due diligence.

In response to the proxy battle, Circuit City's lead director, Mikael

Salovaara, began discussions with Goldman Sachs, experienced attorneys and proxy solicitors. Based on these discussions, the board decided not to allow Blockbuster to see Circuit City's books but to settle the proxy fight with Wattles. Meanwhile, Blockbuster, ramping up the pressure, went public in early April with its bid of $6 to $8 per share and announced that Blockbuster's largest shareholder, billionaire Carl Icahn, would put up the capital if Blockbuster could not.

In a settlement dated May 8, 2008, Circuit City accepted three of Wattles' five proposed directors and put them on the Circuit City board. At the same time, the board could no longer justify stonewalling Blockbuster and agreed to open its books. After one quick look, Blockbuster decided it did not like what it saw, or, as some suspect, Carl Icahn decided he would no longer backstop Blockbuster's offer. In any case, on July 2 Blockbuster withdrew its offer, explaining it had determined "that it is not in the best interest of Blockbuster's shareholders to proceed with an acquisition of Circuit City."[408]

Without Blockbuster in the picture, Circuit City's board evaluated its options and realized they were grim. A few days before, Circuit City had reported a net loss of $165 million for the first quarter of fiscal 2008. Its share price had fallen to $2.55, down from $15.33 one year earlier.[409] The company was losing one million dollars every day. After considering and rejecting a plan to reorganize out of court, the company opened the door to all potential buyers.[410] Now that the Blockbuster negotiations were at an end, the board let Schoonover go. [411]

Last Gasp

Following Schoonover's departure, the board, on August 14, 2008, elected Jim Marcum to be CEO.[412] Marcum was one of the three directors who had joined the board in May 2008 as part of the settlement with Wattles Capital. A CPA by training, he had worked at Melville Corp., a large retail conglomerate with roots in the shoe business. He got to know Wattles through Hollywood Entertainment, where Marcum had turned around a failing video rental business, and they had also worked together in the restructuring of Ultimate Electronics, a midsize electronics retailer with stores in the Midwest and Rocky Mountain states that Wattles had bought while it was in bankruptcy. While he had never run a multibillion-dollar business, he had a lot of experience that would be relevant to attacking the issues at Circuit City.

The week before joining Circuit City he got a haircut in New Hampshire. The barber was talking to a girl in the next chair who was recounting her recent visit to a Circuit City store. Her baby was due shortly and she was anxious to get a camera to record the first days. She complained that at Circuit City she could not get anyone to help her. She ended up buying at Target.

When he came on board, Marcum found that the story he heard in New Hampshire was all too common. The "service standards in the showrooms," he said, "were abysmal." Once, when he went to a store unannounced, he waited forty-two minutes to be waited on. On other occasions it took up to twenty minutes for any sales person to make eye contact. Stock levels were also poor. If he tried to buy something, he frequently found that the items were not available. Marcum came to believe that what killed Circuit City was word of mouth about poor service and high out-of-stock condition.

Marcum's first move was to try to gain the confidence of the executive team. He found that they were beaten down, discouraged, and lacking in self-confidence. So he sat thirty or more top players around a conference table for "a deep dive into what happened and how to repair it." He promised that if they were straight with him, he "would not shoot the messenger." They needed, he felt, "to arrive at a common understanding of the problems and end the wars between various silos."

After examining Circuit City's problems, Marcum believed that the real estate was not the main culprit. He compared all ages and prototypes of stores and found that no one version performed better or worse than the others. While it was too late to do anything about it, he questioned exiting the appliance business, especially since he found that the space vacated by appliances was generally a "dirty hole" that did not produce much revenue. He also believed that giving up commissions had been a big mistake. "It gutted the culture at the wrong time," he said. In short, he concluded that Circuit City had lost sight of how it was relevant to its customers. Finding a niche, fixing the broken culture, and reengaging those customers would take time.

Meanwhile, to staunch the bleeding, he stopped the practice of meeting phantom web pricing. Marcum believed that Schoonover's insistence on matching lower prices, whether the item was in stock or not, both on the web and in the stores, eroded customer confidence, discouraged salesmen, and needlessly reduced gross margins; after all, the online business was only $1.4 billion compared to in-store volumes of $10 billion. Before he could get traction on any of the big issues, however, the storm hit.

A Perfect Storm

One cannot imagine a worse time than August 2008 to become the CEO of a weakened company. The eye of the worst financial hurricane the world had seen since the Great Depression was about to land. Trouble had been brewing in the financial markets for several years, as the Fed steadily reduced interest rates and enhanced liquidity. Beginning in late 2007, announcements of financial distress had been arriving with increasing regularity and severity. In August 2007 the Bank of America announced it was buying the preferred stock of Countrywide Financial, a large, failing thrift and mortgage lending institution, and in January 2008, it bought the whole company. In March, J.P. Morgan acquired Bear Stearns, a leading Wall Street investment-banking firm on the verge of bankruptcy, for an unimaginable $2 per share, quickly revised to $10.

In July, IndyMac, a sizable mortgage savings and loan, was seized by the Office of Thrift Supervision. That same month the

Treasury announced a "temporary increase" in the lines of credit available to Fannie Mae and Freddie Mac, and in September the FHA placed them in receivership. The coup de grâce came in September with the bankruptcy of Lehman Brothers. A few days later, several money market funds "broke the buck" when their net asset values dropped below a dollar a share. Financial institutions and investors worldwide were paralyzed with fear. Circuit City's cash levels were at the lowest point in a decade. Meanwhile, Christmas was coming and there were simply not enough goods in the stores or in the warehouses for even a poor Christmas selling season. Many long-term banks and important vendors were refusing credit. Others were reducing credit availability or demanding cash on shipment. If the music stopped, no vendor wanted to be left without a seat.

Marcum's immediate priority was to buy goods for Christmas. On November 10 the company announced that it had "filed a voluntary petition for reorganization relief under Chapter 11 of the United States Bankruptcy Code." To cut operating losses and preserve cash Marcum announced plans to exit the Atlanta and Phoenix markets and close, in total, 155 stores, 21 percent of the store base.[413] By closing the least-productive stores and relocating their inventory, he raised cash, cut expenditures, and reduced future store-level losses by two-thirds.

Reorganization under Chapter 11 allowed the banks to infuse new cash and vendors to extend new credit on a priority basis while the company reorganized. With the filing, the company announced that it had negotiated a $1.1 billion debtor-in-possession (DIP) credit facility to replace its revolving line of credit and to supplement its working capital, enabling it to purchase goods again. Under Chapter 11 Circuit City could also renounce the leases on the 155 soon-to-be-closed stores as well as the leases on previously closed and not yet subleased stores,[414] and it could also unburden itself from other contracts.

Seeing the problem as a temporary liquidity crisis, the board and management believed that a restructuring plan would "allow Circuit City to emerge as a stronger business with an improved national distribution channel for its vendors and a more compelling offering for its customers."[415] The hope was to get through Christmas, the most profitable time of the year; restructure the company; and move forward as a slimmer, trimmer, and profitable entity.

In the financial storm of 2008, however, hope was not enough. The company had posted just one profitable quarter since mid-2006.[416] It owed its creditors more than $1.5 billion, including $650 million to its suppliers and $900 million to its banks.[417] It was bleeding cash, having run through more than $200 million between March and August of 2008 and who-knew-how-much since then. Its net worth had shrunk to little or nothing. In less than three years it had shed more than $5 billion in stock market value.

Despite the new credit facility and reduced expenditures, with more and more vendors demanding cash in advance or on receipt of goods it quickly became apparent that Circuit City could not be reorganized. The high-handed destruction of supplier confidence that occurred earlier in the decade had left its mark. The die was cast. There were just too few believers that the company could reorganize successfully.

During the final weeks of its existence there were furious negotiations to sell the company as a going concern. Marcum, together with CFO Bruce Besanko, was trying desperately to find a buyer. On January 7 and 8, 2009, they met with two potential buyers and several key vendors in Las Vegas, the site of the annual Consumer Electronics Show. Although not actually at the gambling tables, Circuit City, its creditors, and the potential buyers were all playing for high stakes. The two possible purchasers were Ricardo Salinas, a Mexican billionaire who, among many other things, owned Latin America's largest chain of consumer electronics stores, and Golden Gate Capital, a California-based private equity firm. Both were interested, but only at a rock-bottom price.

Because of their differing priorities under the bankruptcy laws, the various creditors had significantly different interests. Some creditors wanted the company liquidated; others wanted it to continue on a smaller scale. One option was to reduce the chain to 350 of the best store locations. Another scenario would shrink the company to 180 stores, all operating on the East Coast. The key question was whether vendors, in any of these scenarios, would agree to ship new goods under normal credit terms. Some did. So with $400 million unofficially pledged in vendor support, Circuit City emerged from the Las Vegas meetings somewhat optimistic. But the feeling did not last long. Back in Richmond, on January 9, U.S. Bankruptcy Judge Kevin Huennekens, sensing an impasse, dropped a time bomb: Circuit City had one week to make a deal with both creditors and potential new investors.

On January 12 the company and its creditors virtually took over the offices of Skadden, Arps, Slate, Meagher & Flom LLP in Manhattan. On one floor, Circuit City's top executives met with rep-

Going Out of Business Sale Johnstown, PA

resentatives from Ricardo Salinas' Grupo Salinas. Golden Gate's executives were in touch by phone. On another floor, Circuit City executives negotiated with members of the creditors' committee. On two other floors, liquidation specialists pored over inventory sheets and lists of furniture and fixtures, preparing to make their bids and readying to pounce if a deal could not be made.[418]

In bankruptcy, the creditors are in charge. The purpose of this three-sided negotiating exercise was to determine if the creditors would be better off liquidating the company or having it sold to a viable buyer who would keep at least some of the stores open. Complicating the issue was the recent change in the bankruptcy laws that gave recovery priority to vendors who had shipped goods in the twenty days preceding bankruptcy filing. Those vendors who were owed more for goods shipped after the cutoff than for goods shipped prior the twenty-day cutoff, were better off with liquidation. Conversely, those who were owed more for their earlier sales preferred the company be sold to a viable buyer: They would likely not be paid in full if Circuit City were liquidated.

While Bank of America, the lead lender of a bank consortium, was generally supportive of the reorganization, the bank put a $600 million limit on how much additional money it would lend. Furthermore, the pall of the Lehman bankruptcy hardened every creditor's concerns and Bank of America was having problems of its own. It was discovering more troubles than it expected from the purchase of Countrywide Financial and was under attack for the controversial acquisition of Merrill Lynch.

The auction of the company's assets, which the judge originally scheduled for January 13, was postponed as Circuit City executives struggled to reach a deal. On January 15, the day before Circuit City's scheduled appearance in bankruptcy court, Salinas backed out of negotiations. Some earlier problems with the SEC in a totally unrelated transaction made it impossible for Grupo Salinas to borrow the money in time to make the purchase. Golden Gate Capital was still interested in buying the company but was unable to convince the creditors to give it even a few extra days to complete its due diligence. The creditors' committee was convinced that Circuit City was toast.[419] At 10 p.m. that night Great American Group, a liquidation firm, made a lowball offer of $900 million for the company's assets—primarily inventory, furniture, and equipment. It was the highest bid Circuit City received.

The next morning, the courtroom was crowded with reporters, numerous lawyers for Circuit City, its suppliers, and the creditors' committee. Tensions were running high. The parties and their counsels were tired and frustrated at not having reached any kind of agreement.

Judge Huennekens, in what he said was one of the hardest decisions he had made during his two years on the bench, understood that he had no real option. Nonetheless, as a Richmond native he also understood that more than 1,500 local employees would lose their jobs and that a pillar of the Richmond business community was about to fall. He struggled to find a way out and asked Circuit City's counsel, Gregg Galardi, if, given three more days, the company could strike a deal with a buyer.

Galardi hung his head. Not possible, he said. It would take at least a month, and even then he was not confident that a deal could be struck. The vendor support was not there, adequate purchaser financing was not available, and interested buyers were not sufficiently motivated.

Reluctantly, Judge Huennekens raised his gavel and brought it down with a bang. He ordered Circuit City Stores Inc. to close all 567 remaining store locations by March 31 and to liquidate all its assets, leaving 34,000 employees out of work.[420] Going-out-of-business sales at Circuit City stores all over the country were to begin immediately. At 2:45 in the afternoon on January 16, 2009, in the same city where it began sixty years before, Circuit City was GONE.

Habits of Mind

Confront the Brutal Facts: *The worst person you can fool is yourself. Ignoring or denying reality does not help it go away. Once you understand the issues, be bold enough to take decisive action.*

In the early 2000s the brutal fact was that Circuit City needed every dime it had to fix its broken business model. Instead of boldly attacking the issues of store design, obsolete locations, and sales compensation the management and the board paid out $900 million to repurchase its own stock. That did not add to long-run shareholder value. To the contrary, it doomed the company to collapse for lack of cash or credit in 2008.

Mind the Culture: *Create a caring and ethical culture where employees can make mistakes without fear of adverse consequences. Beware of employees who are more concerned about their own success than the success of the business. Understand, exemplify, and reinforce the company's positive history and culture.*

While excessive turnover and lack of attention to "fair dealing" weakened the Circuit City culture in the early years of the decade, Schoonover systematically destroyed the culture that Sam and Hecht had developed and that Sharp and I had perpetuated. Careless hiring and precipitous firings of executives and the wholesale dismissal of salesmen and support staff wrecked employee morale and loyalty.

The cavalier treatment of suppliers and the incredibly rapid turnover of buyers and merchants eroded the patiently crafted support that Circuit City had built among the limited set of vendors in the TV and appliance business.

Pass the Torch with Care: *Succession is critical. Most companies cannot withstand successive top management failures. CEOs need to select and groom their successor with care. Boards need to be bold enough to replace the CEO when necessary and to take the time to be sure the right successor is in place.*

McCollough and the board failed to pass the torch with care. Schoonover, while a good merchant, was not prepared to run a $10 billion company, and McCollough's abrupt departure deprived the board of his ability to advise them on how Schoonover was handling his new responsibilities.

Lessons Learned

Know When to Hold and When to Fold: Since the mid-1990s, Circuit City management and the board had not had a viable plan to stem the decline in the company's market share or the decline in its stock price. When, in 2005, the company received a takeover offer at $17 per share, 20 percent more than the current market price, the board allowed itself to be persuaded by the management team that they could magically reverse the slide and get the company back on track and the stock to higher levels.

HABITS OF MIND REVISITED

The art of progress is to preserve order amid change, and to preserve change amid order. Life refuses to be embalmed alive.
— Alfred North Whitehead

In the end, success in business—and this includes the business of not-for-profit organizations—comes down to two things: strategy and execution.

Strategy is the art and science of harmonizing organizational goals, resources, and talent with the relevant external environment. This requires the hard work of developing realistic organizational goals as well as objectively assessing organizational capacities, and the equally difficult task of understanding the environment and sorting out what aspects of that environment are relevant to success. Strategic planning is an analytical process that takes both time and mental effort. The task is too important for the CEO to delegate and too burdensome to be done annually.

Execution is about management, and management is about achieving results through the efforts of other people. This requires being a leader, motivating others, setting standards, and demanding accountability. Being a good leader has more to do with values, feelings, assumptions about human nature, empathy, and a host of other "soft" skills. Here analytical thinking is a lot less relevant, and may, on occasion, be counterproductive.

Habits of Mind, as I have used that term, encompass both strategic, analytical skills and "softer" execution skills.

The Habits of Mind that I have identified fall into several categories. A few are personality traits: **Curiosity** and **Humility**, for example, are typically inborn. It is hard, but not impossible, for someone who is not naturally curious or humble to become so. **Boldness** and the willingness to **Chase the Impossible Dream** are also personality traits that are more often native to the individual than learned.

Other Habits of Mind are learned at an early age in the family or in school. They include being willing to **Confront the Brutal Facts** and being able to understand and believe that **Evidence Trumps Ideology.** Both are based on intellectual honesty, a quality one acquires early in life. **Creating a Road Map, Passing the Torch with Care,** and **Keeping it Simple and Accountable** are learned skills for making one's way in the world that can, after a while, become habits.

Finally, there are traits that fall between native and learned. For example, **Encouraging Debate** is something one can learn, but it can be hard to implement unless one is comfortable with conflict and ambiguity. **Focusing on the Future** requires one to tolerate short-term adversity and criticism in the service of long-term success. It requires a level of self-confidence that is generally learned early in life. **Dreaming an Impossible Dream** requires both **Boldness** and a comfort with ambiguity. **Minding the Culture** requires both sensitivity to what the organization values and the patience to make changes slowly.

The bottom line is that Habits of Mind, like leadership, are sometimes "inborn" but can also be mastered and further developed through understanding and hard work. Understanding one's weaknesses in any of these areas is the beginning of wisdom and the key to self-improvement.

The Legacy

Circuit City lives on in the hearts and minds of former employees and their families. For sixty years, Circuit City enabled them to lead a better life. Many a Circuit City employee started in the stockroom and ended up a vice president.

In late 2010, hundreds of former employees and their families gathered in Richmond to view a ninety-minute film, created by a former management trainer, to document the rise and fall of Circuit City. They spoke of being part of a "family" that had gone from Good to Great and then, sadly, to Gone.

June, 2012

NOTES

All of the Circuit City specific source materials on which this book is based are deposited with the Virginia Historical Society: 428 North Boulevard, Richmond, VA 23220-3307, Tel. (804) 358-4901.

PROLOGUE

1. Llovio, L, & Martz, M. (November 11, 2008). Circuit City files for bankruptcy. Richmond Times-Dispatch Retrieved from http://www2.timesdispatch.com/business/2008/nov/11/circ11_20081110_213227-ar-103460/
2. Clothier, M., & McCarty, D. (2008, November 10). Circuit City, electronics retailer, seeks bankruptcy. In Bloomberg. Retrieved from http://www.bloomberg.com/apps/news?pid=newsarchive&sid=aOl7tdCatQU4& refer=home
3. At the date of the original filing petition for bankruptcy on November 8, 2008, Circuit City had 712 superstores and approximately 39,600 employees. Declaration of Bruce H. Besanko, executive vice president and chief financial officer of Circuit City Stores, Inc., in support of Chapter 11 petitions and first day pleadings, dated November 10, 2008, filed in The United States Bankruptcy Court for The Eastern District of Virginia - Richmond Division, pp. 6 and D9. Retrieved from http://www.scribd.com/fullscreen/7858787
4. Llovio, L., & Ress, D. (2009, January 17). Unable to find buyer, Circuit City will fold. Richmond Times-Dispatch. Retrieved from http://www2.timesdispatch.com/business/2009/jan/17/circ17_20090116-223008-ar-100075
5. For more on the theory and history of cycles in retailing see: Introduction to Retailing, Patrick M. Dunne Robert F. Lusch, James R. Carver. Cengage Learning Asia Pte Ltd. 2011, pp. 113–117.
6. Collins, J., and Poras, J. (1994). Built To Last (p. 48). New York, NY: HarperCollins.

CHAPTER ONE

7. At the end of 1948, the year that WTVR went on the air, there were only twenty-seven TV broadcast stations in the U.S. Retrieved from http://www.earlytelevision.org/us_tv_sets.html
8. At the end of 1948 fewer than 1.2 million American households (2.6 percent) had TV sets. Retrieved from http://www.earlytelevision.org/us_tv_sets.html
9. http://www.earlytelevision.org/us_tv_sets.html
10. Johnson, H. (1995, July 26). What it meant to America. The Washington Post.
11. U.S. Bureau of the Census. (1975). Historical statistics of the United States, Colonial Times to 1970, Bicentennial Edition, Part 1. Retrieved from http://www2.census.gov/prod2/statcomp/documents/CT1970p1-01.pdf. In the same timeframes, the birth rate spiked from 19.4 percent in 1940 to 20.4 percent in 1945 to 24.1 percent in 1950. (US Statistics). Retrieved from http://www.infoplease.com/ipa/a0005067.html

12. Council on Environmental Quality. Table 1.4 U.S. Populations in Urban, Suburban, and Rural Areas, 1950–1998. In National Environmental Policy Act. Retrieved from http://ceq.hss.doe.gov/nepa/reports/statistics/tab1x4.html

13. Burck, G., & Parker, S. (1954, August). The consumer markets: 1954–1959. Fortune.

14. In 1942, there were only five thousand sets in operation nationwide. Production of new TVs, radios, and other broadcasting equipment for civilian purposes was suspended. Following our entry into World War II, most of the handful of TV stations then in operation suspended broadcasting. Of the few that remained, the programs included sporting events, illustrated war news as well as training for air raid wardens. After the war regular network television broadcasts began on the Dumont Television Network in 1946, on NBC in 1947, and on CBS and ABC in 1948. By 1949, the networks stretched from New York to the Mississippi River, and by 1951, to the West Coast. Retrieved from http://en.wikipedia.org/wiki/History_of_television#United_States

15. Bondi, V. (1995). American Decades: 1940–1949. Detroit, MI: Gale Research, Inc.

16. U.S. Bureau of the Census. (1999). Communications and Information Technology. In Statistical Abstract of the United States. Retrieved from http://www.census.gov/prod/99pubs/99statab/sec18.pdf

17. In 1960, there are 52 million TV sets in American homes. [Source: Jordan, W. (1996). The Americans. Boston: McDougal Littell.] That year, 34,000 households had color television [Source: Television Bureau of Advertising. (2004). TV Basics 2004: A Report on the Growth and Scope of Television. Retrieved from LexisNexis Statistical Database.] Even accounting for the possibility that some of these households had multiple color television sets, it is safe to say that at least 50 of the 52 million TV sets in the US in 1960 were black and white.

18. Seligman, D., & Parker, S. (1954, March). Upheaval in home goods. Fortune.

19. Bowden, S., & Offer, A. (1994). Household appliances and the use of time: The United States and Britain since the 1920s. The Economic History Review, 47(4), 725–748. Retrieved from http://www.j-bradford-delong.net/Teaching_Folder/Econ_210c_spring_2002/Readings/Offer.pdf

CHAPTER TWO

20. Sam was deeply involved in the Richmond Jewish community and initially his corporate and personal philanthropy expressed itself primarily in that arena. By the early 1970s Circuit City was regularly donating 5 percent of pretax profits allocated to a broad array of primarily local charities and civic ventures. For example, Sam led an effort to create the Richmond Community Foundation and was involved in hospital planning for the metropolitan area.

21. Unpublished interview found in Sam's papers.

22. Ibid.

23. Ibid.

24. McGregor, D (1960). The Human Side of Enterprise. New York, NY: McGraw-Hill.

25. Theory X and Theory Y. In Reference for Business, Encyclopedia of Business, 2nd edition. Retrieved from http://www.referenceforbusiness.com/management/Str-Ti/

Theory-X-and-Theory-Y.html

26. This was the terminology before "Human Resources" became the accepted term.

27. While I do not believe he invented the phrase, Jim Collins made this a major point of his book Good to Great. Collins, J., and Porras, J. (2001). Good to Great. New York, NY: HarperCollins.

28. Unpublished interview found in Sam's papers. Obviously some positions, such as in accounting, programming and even truck driving, for example, require a certain level of prior training and experience.

29. Unpublished interview found in Sam's papers.

CHAPTER THREE

30. Bowen, W. (1967, March). The U.S. economy enters a new era. Fortune, 111.

31. Sienkiewicz, S. (2001, August). Credit cards and payment efficiency. In Federal Reserve Bank of Philadelphia. Retrieved from http://www.philadelphiafed.org/payment-cards-center/publications/discussion-papers/2001/PaymentEfficiency_092001.pdf

32. U.S. Department of Labor. Annual average unemployment rate, civilian labor force 16 years and over. In Bureau of Labor Statistics. Retrieved from http://www.bls.gov/cps/prev_yrs.htm

33. Federal Reserve Bank of St. Louis. Consumer Price Index for All Urban Consumers: All Items. Percent Change from Year Ago, Monthly. In Federal Reserve Economic Data. Retrieved from http://research.stlouisfed.org/fred2/graph/?chart_type=line&s[1][id]=CPIAUCSL&s[1][transformation]=pc1

34. Survey Research Center: University of Michigan. University of Michigan: Consumer Sentiment. In Federal Reserve Economic Data. Retrieved from http://research.stlouisfed.org/fred2/series/UMCSENT

35. Siskind, D. (1982, May/June). Housing starts: Background and derivation of estimates, 1945–1982. Construction Review. Retrieved from http://www.michaelcarliner.com/files/Data/CB82Hous_Start_Revised_History1945-82.pdf

36. Breckenfeld, G. (1972, October). Downtown has fled to the suburbs. Fortune.

37. Ann and Hope was a sailing ship lost off the coast of Rhode Island in 1806. Today the successor company operates a small chain of home fashion outlets, garden outlets and dollar outlets in Rhode Island, Massachusetts and Connecticut. Retrieved from http://en.wikipedia.org/wiki/Ann_%26_Hope

38. Silberman, C. E. (1955, August). Retailing: It's a whole new ballgame. Fortune.

39. Kmart Corporation. In Funding Universe. Retrieved from http://www.fundinguniverse.com/company-histories/Kmart-Corporation-Company-History.html

40. Target Corporation. In Funding Universe. Retrieved from http://www.fundinguniverse.com/company-histories/Target-Corporation-Company-History.html

41. Walmart Stores, Inc. In Funding Universe. Retrieved from http://www.fundinguniverse.com/company-histories/WalMart-Stores-Inc-Company-History.html

42. Whitaker, J. (2006). Service and Style: How the American Department Store Fashioned the Middle Class. New York, NY: St. Martin's Press.

43. In 1972, Sears' sales accounted for 1 percent of GNP. [Source: Katz, D. R. (1987). The

Big Store. New York, NY: Penguin Books.] Around that time, according to the 1970 and 1975 Statistic Abstracts of the United States, retail trade accounted for 10 percent of GNP. [Source: U.S. Bureau of the Census. (1985). In Statistical Abstract of the United States.] Retrieved from http://www2.census.gov/prod2/statcomp/documents/1985-06.pdf

44. Layman, R. (1994). American Decades: 1950–1959. Detroit, MI: Gale Research Inc.

45. http://en.wikipedia.org/wiki/Ultra_high_frequency

46. Mayer, L. A. (1968, June). The troubling shift in the trade winds. Fortune, 76.

47. In 1975, the timeframe was amended to twenty-four months. Halfhill, T. R. (2006, September). The mythology of Moore's Law: Why such a widely misunderstood 'law' is so captivating to so many. Solid-State Circuits Newsletter, IEEE. Volume: 20, Issue: 3, 21–25. Retrieved from http://ieeexplore.ieee.org/xpl/freeabs_all.jsp?arnumber=4785856

48. Layman, R. (1995). American Decades: 1960–1969. Detroit, MI: Gale Research Inc.

49. Stein Bros. & Boyce. (1961, December). Wards Co. Incorporated Prospectus.

50. They had given their chief financial officer, Marty Ross, most of the 16 percent balance.

51. Rivas, Bill. Interview with Carl Brauer, for unpublished book on the history of Circuit City, p.13.

52. Richmond Times-Dispatch. (1965, December 6), p. 22.

53. Collins, J. (2009). How the Mighty Fall. New York, NY: HarperCollins.

54. Wards Company Inc. (1969). Annual Report, 5.

55. The handheld calculator was invented at Texas Instruments in 1966, the year I joined Circuit City. They were not generally available to purchase until the early 1970s. Retrieved from http://www.ideafinder.com/history/inventions/handcalculator.htm

56. For the year ended March 1970, the company reported sales of $48 million and profits of $529,500 (1.1 percent), well below the prior two years. Wards Company Inc. (1970). Annual Report, 1.

CHAPTER FOUR

57. Roosa, R.V. (1971, September). A strategy for winding down inflation. Fortune, 70.

58. National Bureau of Economic Research. Business Cycle Expansions and Contractions. Retrieved from http://www.nber.org/cycles/cyclesmain.html

59. Beman, L. (1974, November). Inflation: Winners are hard to find. Fortune, 143.

60. U.S. Department of Labor. Annual average unemployment rate, civilian labor force 16 years and over. In Bureau of Labor Statistics. Retrieved from http://www.bls.gov/cps/prev_yrs.htm

61. Meyer, H. E. (1976, May). Why corporations are on the move. Fortune, 252.

62. Saxenian, A. (1994, July). Lessons from Silicon Valley. Technology Review.

63. Hobbs, F., & Stoops, N. Demographic trends in the 20th century, November 2002. In Census 2000 Special Reports. Retrieved from http://www.census.gov/prod/2002pubs/censr-4.pdf

64. Kessler-Harris, A. (2003). Out to Work: A History of Wage-Earning Women in the United States (pp. 300–304). New York, NY: Oxford University Press.

65. 1962 to 1972: The birth of discounting. (2002, August). DSN Retailing Today, 41 (15).

66. Ibid.

67. Ibid.

68. Annual TV Sales in the USA—Color v. Black & White Sets—1973 to 1977. In Television History—The First 75 Years. Retrieved from http://tvhistory.tv/TV_Sales_70-77.JPG.

69. Television Bureau of Advertising. (2004). TV Basics: Multi-Set & Color TV Households. In Media Trends Track. Retrieved from LexisNexis Statistical Database.

70. Bondi, V. (1995). American Decades: 1970–1979. Detroit, MI: Gale Research Inc.

71. Robertson, W. (1974, December). Merchants fight it out in a less affluent society. Fortune, 128.

72. Brauer, C. (1997). History of Circuit City, 4–21. Unpublished manuscript.

73. Circuit City Stores Inc., 1973 Three Year Plan, p.30.

74. Ibid, p.26.

75. Ibid, p.26–27.

76. Ibid, p.29.

77. Ibid, p.29.

78. Ibid, p.29.

79. Ibid, p.29.

80. Ibid, p.29.

81. Ibid, p.29.

82. Ibid, p.30.

83. Ibid, p.30.

84. Ibid, p.29.

85. Ibid, p.30.

86. Hildebrand, C. (1997, March 15). CIO Magazine. Retrieved from http://books.google.com/books?id=hAYAAAAAMBAJ&pg=PA26&dq=Peter+Drucker+AND+naval+AND+gazing&hl=en&sa=X&ei=ED8wT9K4LO7XiALi2d2vAw&ved=0CEEQ6AEwAg#v=onepage&q=Peter%20Drucker%20AND%20naval%20AND%20gazing&f=false

87. http://research.stlouisfed.org/fred2/data/PRIME.txt

CHAPTER FIVE

88. Although their relationship was strained for at least five years, they gradually resumed their friendship and were often seen bicycling together in the mornings.

89. Richmond Times-Dispatch. (1968, September 13).

90. Bruckart, Walter. Interview with Carl Brauer, for unpublished book on the history of Circuit City (p.3).

91. Drucker, P. (1967). The Effective Executive (p. 90). Burlington, VT: Elsevier Ltd.

92. Wards Company, Inc. (1984). Annual Report.

93. If you run a company based on open budgets and open results for each profit and expense center, it is easy for people to figure out what others are earning.

CHAPTER SIX

94. Greenberg, Joshua F. Enforcement, Criminal Sanctions and Private Actions; 53 Antitrust L.J. 1045 (1985).

95. I do not recall their other suggestions, nor did I give it a tremendous amount of thought and concern. I have long believed that the "magic" in names is overemphasized, particularly by consulting firms that want to charge huge fees to research and suggest a new name. In my experience, the name a company uses takes on a connotation based on how the company advertises and performs. For years "Sears" meant quality hard goods while "Penney" connoted affordable clothing. In the same way, "made in Japan" had the connotation of shoddy goods until they began to emphasize quality. I chose a name that suggested electronics and appliances in an open-ended way. It takes time and money to get a name that has no objective meaning, like Wards or Sears, to develop a secondary meaning based on what it stands for in the marketplace. So a generic name that described what we did was a cheaper, faster way to go.

96. Kennedy and Cohen is now known nationally. (June 22, 1971). The Miami News, advertising section. Retrieved from http://news.google.com/newspapers?id=K8QlAA AAIBAJ&sjid=FPQFAAAAIBAJ&pg=728,778408&dq=kennedy-and-cohen&hl=en

97. Landow, Melvin. Your People Are Your Business: A Manager's Manual for Making Millions in Merchandising. Exposition PR of Florida, 1973.

98. Collins, J., and Poras, J. (1994). Built To Last (p. 48). New York, NY: HarperCollins, 1994.

CHAPTER SEVEN

99. Bondi, V. American Decades: 1980–1989. Detroit, MI; Gale Research Inc. 1996, 146.

100. Ibid.

101. U.S. Department of Labor. Annual average unemployment rate, civilian labor force 16 years and over. In Bureau of Labor Statistics. Retrieved from http://www.bls.gov/cps/prev_yrs.htm

102. Bondi, V. (1996). American Decades: 1980–1989. Detroit, MI; Gale Research Inc., 150

103. U.S. Department of Commerce: Bureau of Economic Analysis. Real Gross Domestic Product. In Federal Reserve Economic Data. Retrieved from http://research.stlouisfed.org/fred2/data/GDPCA.txt

104. U.S. Census Bureau. Table P-1: Total CPS Population and Per Capita Income (All Races). In Historical Income Tables—People. Retrieved from http://www.census.gov/hhes/www/income/data/historical/people/index.html

105. U.S. Census Bureau. (2002, 2006, 2008). Current Population Reports. From Statistical Abstract of the United States. Retrieved from http://www.census.gov/prod/2005pubs/censr-24.pdf, http://www.federalreserve.gov/releases/Z1/current/z1r-2.pdf, http://www.infoplease.com/ipa/A0880690.html

106. U.S. Department of Commerce: Bureau of Economic Analysis. Real Personal Consumption Expenditures. In Federal Reserve Economic Data. Retrieved from http://research.stlouisfed.org/fred2/data/PCECCA.txt

107. McConnell, T. (2001). American Decades: 1990–1999. Farmington Hills: Gale Group.

108. U.S. Department of Labor. Annual average unemployment rate, civilian labor force 16 years and over. In Bureau of Labor Statistics. Retrieved from http://www.bls.gov/cps/prev_yrs.htm

109. Barua, A., Pinnell, J., Shutter, J., Whinston, A.B. (1999, June). The Center for Research in Electronic Commerce at The University of Texas at Austin. Measuring the Internet Economy. Retrieved from http://ai.kaist.ac.kr/~jkim/cs492a/internet_economy-UT.pdf

110. U.S. Bureau of the Census. (2002). Productivity and Related Measures: 1980 to 2001. In Statistical Abstract of the United States (Labor Force, Employment, and Earnings). Retrieved from http://www.census.gov/prod/2003pubs/02statab/labor.pdf

111. McConnell, T. (2001). American Decades: 1990–1999. Farmington Hills: Gale Group.

112. U.S. Census Bureau. Table P-1: Total CPS Population and Per Capita Income (All Races). In Historical Income Tables—People. Retrieved from http://www.census.gov/hhes/www/income/data/historical/people/index.html

113. U.S. Bureau of the Census. Table HH-1: Households by Type: 1940 to Present. In Families and Living Arrangements. Retrieved from http://www.census.gov/population/www/socdemo/hh-fam.html#ht

114. Colvin, G. (1984, October 15). What the baby-boomers will buy next. Fortune. 110.

115. Leonhardt, D. (1996, June 3). Like totally big spenders. BusinessWeek. 8.

116. Bhambhani, D. (2000, September, 18). Web site helps youth manage allowances. The Washington Times. p. D3.

117. Leonhardt, D. (1996, June 3). Like totally big spenders. BusinessWeek. 8.

118. http://en.wikipedia.org/wiki/Shopping_mall

119. Crowley, W., with Dorpat, P. (photography editor). (1998). National Trust Guide: Seattle. New York, NY: John Wiley & Sons, Inc., 1998. 209. Retrieved from http://www.historylink.org/index.cfm?DisplayPage=output.cfm&File_Id=3186

120. Data provided by International Council of Shopping Centers.

121. Bondi, V. (1996). American Decades: 1980–1989. Detroit, MI: Gale Research Inc. 385.

122. Mayer, C.E. (1986, April 14). Rapid growth of Circuit City sending waves across industry. The Washington Post, B1.

123. The Fact Book. (1999, July) Discount Merchandiser, 39.

124. The True Look. (1993, June). Discount Merchandiser, 33.

125. Sieling, M., et al. (2001, December 1). Labor productivity in the retail trade industry, 1987–1999. Monthly Labor Review, 24.

126. See Chart on p. 159, Consumer Electronics Factory Sales, 1978–1986.

127. Marcom Jr., J. (1986, June, 4). Consumer Electronics: Latest gear takes aim at the trade-up buyer. The Wall Street Journal. p. 1.

128. Until 1976, the actual phone instruments were bundled with the price of monthly telephone service. The decision of the FTC to allow customers to buy their own phones, rather than rent them from their telephone company opened a big market for retailers. [Source: Stuart, R. (1997, March 2). F.C.C. lets phone customers provide equipment without a 'protective' fee. The New York Times, p. 61.

129. Sanger, D. E. (1986, January 10). Electronics Fads Cooling Off. The New York Times, p. D1.

130. Marcom Jr., J. (1986, June,4). Consumer electronics: Latest gear takes aim at the trade-up Buyer. The Wall Street Journal, p. 1

131. U.S. Bureau of the Census. (1999). Utilization of selected media: 1970 to 1997.

In Statistical Abstract of the United States (Communications and Information Technology). Retrieved from http://www.census.gov/prod/99pubs/99statab/sec18.pdf

132. Cusumano, M.A.., et al. (1992, Spring). Strategic maneuvering and mass-market dynamics: The triumph of VHS over Beta. The Business History Review, 66.

133. U.S. Bureau of the Census. (1999). Utilization of Selected Media: 1970 to 1997. In Statistical Abstract of the United States (Communications and Information Technology). Retrieved from http://www.census.gov/prod/99pubs/99statab/sec18.pdf

134. Schrage, M. (1986, July 17). Home electronics boom slowed in '84. The Washington Post, p. D2.

135. Sanger, D. E. (1986, January 10). Electronics fads cooling off. The New York Times, p. D1.

136. Schrage, M. (1983, August 7). Consumer electronics industry has everything but the profits. The Washington Post, p. G1.

137. Television Bureau of Advertising. (2004). TV Basics: Personal Computer & Digital TV Sales. In Media Trends Track. Retrieved from LexisNexis Statistical Database.

138. Ibid.

139. The Consumer Rush is On for Anything Electronic. (1984, February 27). Business Week, 148.

140. Schrage, M. (1985, January 7). Home Electronics Boom Slowed in '84. The Washington Post, p. D2.

141. Ibid

142. Schiller, Z. (1986, August 4). Turning Up the Heat in the Kitchen. BusinessWeek, 76.

143. Circuit City Stores, Inc., Three Year Plan, FY 1989–1991, 4–8.

144. Energy Information Administration. (2006, July). Annual Energy Review. Retrieved from LexisNexis Statistical Database.

145. For the most part, our competitors sent their car stereo customer to an installation shop that also sold car stereo. So this was both a profit opportunity and a competitive advantage.

146. Three hundred miles is as far as a truck could go and hope to get back the same day.

147. Sam Antar Speaks his Mind. Retrieved from http://www.whitecollarfraud.com/947660.html

148. HFD-The Weekly Home Furnishings Newspaper. (1986, July 28), 1.

149. Wards Company, Inc., 1986 Annual Report,33.

150. Admiral Hyman Rickover was the highly demanding head of the U.S. Navy's nuclear submarine program.

151. The nature and function of Coffee Conferences is discussed in Chapter 2.

152. It was not until 2000 that women became members of the top management team and served on the executive committee.

153. Calculation based on selling space only. Circuit City Stores, Inc., Annual Report, 1989, 18.

154. It is impossible without the detailed data to calculate actual same store sales, but

adding up the annual same store increases gives a good idea.

155. Circuit City Stores, Inc., Annual Report, 1988, 3.

CHAPTER EIGHT

156. Circuit City Stores, Inc., Annual Report, 1988, 4.

157. Circuit City Stores, Inc., Annual Report, 1993, 31.

158. Circuit City found that default rates on refrigerators and washers, for example were lower than on entertainment equipment, presumably because consumers were more reliant on their refrigerator and reluctant to have it repossessed. Hence, it was safer to extend credit for such items. It also makes sense to take a bit more risk with high margin items, such as audio speakers, than low margin items such as receivers.

159. Circuit City Stores, Inc., Annual Report, 1995, 30.

160. Circuit City Stores, Inc., Annual Report, 2000, 61.

161. In FY 1996 and 1997 total contributions from the bank were $101m and $130.8m. Three Year Plan, FY 1999-2001, VII-11. Circuit City Group's earnings before income taxes and Inter-Group Interest in the CarMax Group in 1996 and 1997 were $295.9m and $236.0m, respectively. Circuit City Stores, Inc., 1997 Annual Report, 42; Circuit City Stores, Inc., Annual Report, 1998, 44.

162. Bankcard business earned $42.9m and $25.6m after tax in 2002 and 2003, respectively. The effective income tax rate applicable to results from continuing operations was 36.7 percent in 2002 and 3.3 percent in 2003. Circuit City Stores, Inc., Annual Report, 2004, 19.

163. When Circuit City announced it was selling its private-label credit card business to Bank One, it estimated that the arrangement would produce pretax income of approximately $30 million per year, "which is similar to the finance income we would have generated if we had maintained ownership of the private-label receivables." Circuit City Stores, Inc., Annual Report, 2004, 18.

164. Circuit City Stores, Inc., Annual Report, 1990, 7.

165. Kirkpatrick, D., & Furth, J. (1994, February 21). How PCs will take over your home. Fortune.

166. Trost, M. (1986, January 9). Consumer Electronics: VCR Sales Explosion Shakes Up Industry. Advertising Age. Vol. 57, 14.

167. Bob Appleby (personal communication, October 27, 2010).

168. As more stores were added, the customer could also view cars at another CarMax store. For a small transfer fee, CarMax would bring the car to the customer's store. If the customer bought the car, the transfer fee would be applied to the purchase price.

169. Securities and Exchange Commission. CarMax, Inc.—Separation from Circuit City Stores, Inc.: No Action, Interpretive and/or Exemptive Letter. Retrieved from http://www.sec.gov/divisions/corpfin/cf-noaction/carmax120602.htm

170. Circuit City Stores, Inc., Annual Report, 2002, 60.

171. Circuit City Stores, Inc., Three Year Plan, FY 1999–2001, p. 1–2.

172. The company took post-tax losses on discontinued DIVX operations of $20.6m, $68.5m, and $16.2m in fiscal 1998, 1999, and 2000, respectively. In those years, the

company received tax benefits of $12.6m, $42m, and $9.9m. Additionally, the company took a loss on the disposal of DIVX of $114m after a tax benefit of $69.9m. Circuit City Stores, Inc., Annual Report, 2000, 62.

CHAPTER NINE

173. Associated Press. (1990, June 19). Sears to open 198 brand-name units. The New York Times, p. D5.

174. http://www.fundinguniverse.com/company-histories/Best-Buy-Co-Inc-Company-History.html

175. http://www.fundinguniverse.com/company-histories/Best-Buy-Co-Inc-Company-History.html

176. S.C. Biemesderfer Corporate Report Minnesota, quoted in http://www.fundinguniverse.com/company-histories/Best-Buy-Co-Inc-Company-History.html

177. Bill Zierden. Interview by the author.

178. Best Buy Co, Inc. In Funding Universe. Retrieved from http://www.fundinguniverse.com/company-histories/Best-Buy-Co-Inc-Company-History.html

179. Ibid.

180. Gibson, E., and Billings, A. (2003). Big Change at Best Buy: Working Through Hypergrowth to Sustained Excellence. Palo Alto, CA: Davies-Black Publishing.

181. Circuit City Stores, Inc., Three Year Plan, FY 1993–1995, 1-1

182. Circuit City Stores, Inc., Three Year Plan, FY 1993–1995, 3-6

183. Circuit City Stores, Inc., Three Year Plan, FY 1993–1995, 3-12.

184. BrandsMart operated five large stores in Florida, each at least 55,000 square feet of showroom, plus a large warehouse. Florida's BrandsMart electronics chain thriving, expanding. (Originated from The Miami Herald). Knight Ridder/Tribune Business News. (Nov. 21, 1996). Tops' stores ranged in size between 45,000 and 120,000 square feet. http://www.fundinguniverse.com/company -histories/Tops-appliance-City-Inc-Company-History.html

185. Circuit City Stores, Inc., Three Year Plan, FY 1995–1997, IV-25.

186. Circuit City Stores, Inc., Three Year Plan, FY 1997–1999, IV-2.

187. Circuit City Stores, Inc., Three Year Plan, FY 1997–1999, IV-3.

188. Circuit City Stores, Inc., Three Year Plan, FY 1997–1999, IV-16-7.

189. Circuit City Stores, Inc., Three Year Plan, FY 1997–1999, IV-12.

190. At this point in time, all sales were entered by a salesman on computers located throughout the store. The new system for ACE (Advanced Consumer Electronics, an acronym for small portable electronics) allowed the customer to pick up certain, but not all, low price items and take them directly to a cashier for payment.

191. Steven Richman. Interview by the author.

192. Circuit City Stores, Inc., Three Year Plan, FY 1999–2001, IV-13.

193. Ibid.

194. Ibid.

195. Circuit City Stores, Inc., Three Year Plan, FY 1999–2001, IV-18.

196. Circuit City Stores, Inc., Three Year Plan, FY 1999–2001, IV-14-15.

197. Ironically, most of the management was unaware of Circuit City's own limited operating profitability, absent the bank earnings.

198. Sam Winokur graduated first in his class at Yale Law School and went on to join Sullivan and Cromwell and then headed White Rose Tea, a large grocery distributor in the Northeast. Hyman Meyers took a small family furniture store chain in the South and turned it into one of the largest publicly traded home-furnishings retailers in the United States with sales reaching $1 billion. Rick Dean, a Boston born graduate of Harvard, rose in Richmond banking circles to become the chairman of Signet Bank, a leading Richmond financial institution. Morton Wallerstein presented himself as a "country lawyer," but his "down home" exterior belied the fact that was a graduate of Harvard Law School who founded and ran a leading Richmond law firm.

199. Our attorney, Bob Burrus, the managing partner of one of Richmond's leading law forms, McGuire Woods, was one of Richmond's most sought after lawyers. He attended every Circuit City board meeting and spoke freely on business and legal matters. He just did not vote. Our investment and commercial bankers attended as appropriate.

200. Full disclosure: Cooper was my college roommate and Drysdale advised us on the tax aspects of the Lafayette acquisition.

201. Author's letter to Richard Sharp, dated July 2, 1998 following the 1999-2001 Three Year Planning meeting.

202. Circuit City Stores, Inc., Three Year Plan, FY 1999–2001, IV-14-15.

CHAPTER TEN

203. Best Buy Co, Inc., Annual Report, 2000. Retrieved from http://media.corporate-ir.net/media_files/irol/83/83192/reports/bby_fy00ar.pdf

204. Circuit City Stores, Inc., Annual Report, 2000, p.47.

205. As sales per store grow, rent and advertising as a percentage of sales decline. If the rent for a desirable new location was a million dollars, that turned out to be 5.9 percent of sales for Circuit City and only 2.7 percent for Best Buy. Circuit City's goal was to keep rent at 3 percent of sales. The same inexorable arithmetic applied to advertising costs as well.

206. Circuit City Stores, Inc., Annual Report, 2001, 54, 55. These figures are for the Circuit City Stores Division, excluding CarMax.

207. History of IBM (n.d.). Wikipedia, the Free Encyclopedia. Retrieved April 6, 2011 from http://en.wikipedia.org/wiki/History_of_IBM

208. Reed, J. (2011, March 17). Alan Mulally: In the driving seat at Ford. Financial Times. Retrieved from http://www.ft.com/cms/s/0/eda88d96-4410-11e0-8f20-00144feab49a.html#axzz1j5IXz4lh

209. Dow Jones Industrial Average. In Google Finance. Retrieved from http://www.google.com/finance?q=INDEXDJX%3A.DJI

210. Stone, B. (2000, December 25). Finally, the Net gets real. Newsweek,66.

211. Dow Jones Industrial Average increased from 7,489 on July 24, 2002, to 14,279 October 11, 2011. Retrieved from http://finance.yahoo.com/q/hp?s=%5EDJI&a=06&b=1&c=2002&d=09&e=30&f=2007&g=d&z=66&y=1320

212. Retrieved from http://research.stlouisfed.org/fred2/graph/?chart_type=line&s[1][id]=GDP&s[1][range]=1yr

213. U.S. Department of Commerce: Bureau of Economic Analysis. Personal Savings Rate. In Federal Reserve Economic Data. Retrieved from http://research.stlouisfed.org/fred2/series/PSAVERT?cid=112

214. Federal Reserve Bank of St. Louis. Real Retail and Food Service Sales. In Federal Reserve Economic Data. Retrieved from http://research.stlouisfed.org/fred2/series/RRSFS?cid=6

215. Datamonitor. (2008, June). Online retail in the Unites States: Industry Profile. Retrieved from EBCSOhost Business Source Complete.

216. Masters, G. (2003, July). DVD is the place to be. Retail Merchandiser, 12.

217. U.S. Bureau of the Census. (2009). Information and Communications, 21. In Statistical Abstract of the United States. Retrieved from http://www.census.gov/prod/2008pubs/09statab/infocomm.pdf

218. U.S. Bureau of the Census. (2009). Information and Communications, 21. In Statistical Abstract of the United States. Retrieved from http://www.census.gov/prod/2008pubs/09statab/infocomm.pdf

219. Gartner. Various Press Releases. In Gartner Newsroom. Retrieved from http://www.gartner.com/it/page.jsp?id=939015, http://www.gartner.com/it/page.jsp?id=1076912, http://www.gartner.com/it/page.jsp?id=1207613, http://www.gartner.com/it/page.jsp?id=1279215, http://www.gartner.com/5_about/press_releases/2002_01/pr20020118a.jsp

220. U.S. Bureau of the Census. (2009). Information and Communications. In Statistical Abstract of the United States. Retrieved from http://search.census.gov/search?q=households+with+computers+2000&btnG=Search&entqr=0&ud=1&output=xml_no_dtd&oe=UTF-8&ie=UTF-8&client=default_frontend&proxystylesheet=default_frontend&btnG.x=15&btnG.y=7&sort=date%3AD%3AL%3Ad1&site=census

221. Palenchar, J. (2005, February 21). This Week in Consumer Electronics Magazine. Retrieved from http://www.twice.com/article/252349-MP3_Saves_Portable_Audios_Aspirations.php

222. Profit Parade. (2009, August 24). This Week in Consumer Electronics Magazine. Ebsco, MasterFILE Premier.

223. Chen, K. (1999, November 22). Measure is cleared to let satellite TV show network fare. The Wall Street Journal, p. B8.

224. The Nielsen Company, 2009 Media and Communications Trends, October 15, 2009. 21. Retrieved from http://enus.nielsen.com/content/dam/nielsen/en_us/documents/pdf/Webinars/2009%20Media%20and%20Communications%20Trends.pdf

225. Tarr, G. (2006, April 10). Flat-Panel TV makers brace for spike in sales. This Week in Consumer Electronics Magazine. Retrieved from http://www.twice.com/article/248836-Flat_Panel_Makers_Brace_For_Spike_In_Sales.php

226. Tarr, G. (2007, March 26). Flat-Panel TVs begin to dominate US Market. This Week in Consumer Electronics Magazine. Retrieved from http://www.twice.com/article/246908-Flat_Panel_TVs_Begin_To_Dominate_U_S_Market.php

227. Wolf, A. (2003, November 24). Top 100 top $100 billion in CE sales. This Week in Consumer Electronics Magazine. Retrieved from http://www.twice.com/article/240447-Top_100_Top_100_Billion_In_CE_Sales.php

228. Olenick, D. (2006, September 1). More Installation Services on the Way: Adam Levin. This Week in Consumer Electronics Magazine. Retrieved from Ebsco MasterFILE Premier.

229. Circuit City Stores, Inc., U.S. Economy, Three Year Plan, FY 2001–2003, 1.

230. Circuit City Stores, Inc., Changing Consumers, Three Year Plan, FY 2001–2003, 2.

231. Circuit City Stores, Inc., Changing Consumers, Three Year Plan, FY 2001–2003, 4.

232. Circuit City Stores, Inc., Changing Consumers, Three Year Plan, FY 2001–2003, 4.

233. Circuit City Stores, Inc., The Digital Product Cycle, Three Year Plan, FY 2001–2003, 1.

234. At the end of fiscal 2000, Circuit City had 571 stores and Best Buy had 357. Best Buy does not publicly release the number markets in which it is located, only the number of states. In 2000, Best Buy was located in thirty-nine states and Circuit City in forty-three. However, in many states, Best Buy had only one city, while Circuit City was in multiple markets. [Sources: Circuit City Stores, Inc., Annual Report, 2000 p. 83. Best Buy Co., Inc. (2000). Annual Report. 46.] Retrieved from http://media.corporate-ir.net/media_files/irol/83/83192/reports/bby_fy00ar.pdf

235. Circuit City Stores, Inc., Best Buy, Three Year Plan, FY 2001–2003, 19.

236. Circuit City's gross margins were 25.2 percent vs. 19.8 percent for Best Buy, a 5.4 percent advantage. It's store operating expenses were 18.6 percent vs. 12.9 percent for Best Buy, a 5.7 percent disadvantage. Circuit City Stores, Inc., Competitive Analysis, Three Year Plan, FY 2001–2003, 24.

237. Circuit City Stores, Inc., Best Buy, Three Year Plan, FY 2001–2003, 8.

238. The internal rate of return (IRR) of an investment is the discount rate at which the net present value of costs (negative cash flows) of the investment equals the net present value of the benefits (positive cash flows) of the investment. Internal rates of return are commonly used to evaluate the desirability of investments or projects.

239. Circuit City Stores, Inc., Best Buy in Three Year Plan, FY 2001–2003, 24.

240. Circuit City Stores, Inc., Fully Integrated Marketing, Three Year Plan, FY 2001–2003, 1.

241. Circuit City Stores, Inc., Reinventing Our Store Format, Three Year Plan, FY 2001–2003, 1.

242. Circuit City Stores, Inc., Developing a Learning Culture, Three Year Plan, FY 2001–2003, 1.

243. Circuit City Stores, Inc., Creating a World Class Supply Chain, Three Year Plan, FY 2001–2003, 1.

244. In fact, for the next three years together Circuit City made less than in 2000. Net profits for FY 2001-3 were: $115m, $127m, and $46m, respectively.

245. Circuit City Stores, Inc., Fully Integrated Marketing, Three Year Plan, FY 2001–2003, 1.

246. Circuit City Stores, Inc., Executive Summary, Three Year Plan, FY 2001–2003, 2.

247. Ibid.

248. Circuit City Stores, Inc., Annual Report, 2000. 3.

249. Circuit City Stores, Inc., Fully Integrated Marketing, Three Year Plan, FY 2001–2003, 2.

250. Between 2000 and 2005 Circuit City's sales hovered around $10 million (see chart on p. 275). Meanwhile Factory shipments of consumer electronics rose by 46 percent between 2000 and 2005 and another 32 percent between 2005 and 2009. http://www.census.gov/prod/2009pubs/10statab/manufact.pdf

251. Circuit City Stores, Inc., Reinventing Our Store Format, Three Year Plan, FY 2001–2003, 1.

252. Circuit City Stores, Inc., Reinventing Our Store Format, Three Year Plan, FY 2001–2003, 1.

253. The choice of baskets symbolizes Circuit City's continued schizophrenia about central checkout. Carts would have required wider aisles and thus a bigger showroom. Baskets meant that customers could pick up only small, lightweight items, not most portable TVs, boom boxes, or audio components.

254. Circuit City Stores, Inc., Annual Report, 2000, 3.

255. Circuit City Stores, Inc., Annual Report, 2000, 5.

256. Circuit City Stores, Inc., Annual Report, 2000, 5.

257. Alan McCollough, Interview by the author. According to McCollough, the shopping center did not get much traffic.

258. James Wimmer, interview by the author.

259. Bruce Lucas, interview by the author.

260. Circuit City Stores, Inc., Annual Report, 2001, 3.

261. In new stores, however, Froman expanded the selling floor space at the expense of the warehouse, built higher ceilings and used brighter lighting.

262. Steven Richman. Interview with author.

263. Circuit City Stores, Inc., Annual Report, 2001, 3.

264. TWICE Magazine's annual appliance registry includes only the top 100 major appliance retailers, which generally account for 90 percent of total industry revenue. [Sources: The top 100 major appliance retailers. (2000, November 20). This Week in Consumer Electronics Magazine. Retrieved from Ebsco MasterFILE Premier; Wolf, A. (2005, June 20). Top major appliance dealers see 10% sales gain in 2004. This Week in Consumer Electronics Magazine.

265. Austin Ligon. Interview with the author.

266. Richard Birnbaum. Interview with the author.

267. Jim Marcum. Interview with the author.

268. Circuit City Stores, Inc., Annual Report, 2001, 3.

269. Edward Brett. Interview with the author.

270. Twenty percent of the stores of stores would be upgraded each year. But the degree of "upgrade" varied. In the high-volume, high-profit stores, the renovations were more extensive. McCollough retired before the process was complete. Steven Richman, interview with author.

271. Circuit City spent $25 or $30 million per year on these upgrades, for an average cost of less than $100,000 per store per year.

272. In the early 1980s, when Sharp and I were building superstores, there was little

competition from either mass merchants or specialty stores. As a result, the additional cost of a first rate location was harder to justify. Later, in the late '80s and throughout the '90s, when Circuit City was growing very fast, it sometimes acquired less than ideal locations to fill out a market or meet Wall Street's growth expectations. In hindsight, all of these compromises were mistakes.

273. There were 571 Circuit City superstores as of February 28, 2000. Circuit City Stores, Inc., Annual Report, 2001. It was not until 2004, when Circuit City commissioned a comprehensive study of its store locations, that it definitively established that around one-third of its existing stores needed to be moved. The 2004 Annual Report stated that "since the beginning of fiscal 2001, we have relocated, fully remodeled or newly constructed 131 stores. We believe that approximately one-third of our remaining stores would produce stronger returns if moved to better locations and that we can build approximately 100 stores in newly developed trade areas . . ." Circuit City Stores, Inc., Annual Report, 2004, 4.

274. Bruce Lucas. Interview with the author. The estimate is based on $30 per foot to add air conditioning, remove the warehouse wall and relocate electrical power. In a hundred or so older stores the firewall between the warehouse and showroom was load bearing and would have increased the construction cost by another $100,000.

275. The Florida remodeling exercise was unnecessarily expensive because it was poorly conceived and coordinated and because the stores were kept open during construction. On the other hand, the remodeling effort did not include converting 10,000 square feet of warehouse to showroom. I am assuming that these factors would have roughly balanced each other, but added $250,000 per store as a cushion.

276. Circuit City Stores, Inc., Reinventing Our Store Format, Three Year Plan, FY 2001–2003, 1.

277. Philip Dunn. Interview with author.

278. Circuit City Stores, Inc., Annual Report, 2001, 55.

279. Circuit City Stores, Inc., Circuit City Financing Summary, Three Year Plan, FY 2001–2003. BB+ is the highest non-investment grade bond rating by S&P.

280. Private Equity Council. Burger King: Expertise, Commitment and Capital Rebuild a Business. Retrieved from http://www.privateequitycouncil.org/wordpress/wp-content/uploads/burger-king-case-study-final-oct3107.pdf

281. Toys "R" Us becomes a private company. (2005, July 21). Msnbc.com - Breaking News, Science and Tech News, World News, US News, Local News- Msnbc.com. Retrieved from http://www.msnbc.msn.com/id/8658948/

282. Circuit City Stores, Inc., Developing a Learning Culture, Three Year Plan, FY 2001–2003. 1.

283. Alan McCollough and John Froman. Interviews with author. Hourly calculations based on forty hours per week and fifty weeks per year.

284. Edward Brett. Interview with author.

285. Product knowledge, as distinct from selling technique, was centrally created and distributed in workbook form, and later digitally, so that both new and experienced salespeople could learn and be tested on the constantly changing product specifics.

286. Circuit City Stores, Inc., Annual Report, 2000, 11.

287. Circuit City Stores, Inc., Developing a Learning Culture, Three Year Plan, FY 2001–2003, 3.

288. Circuit City Stores, Inc., Annual Report, 2000, 4.

289. Circuit City Stores, Inc., Annual Report, 2002, 9.

290. McWilliams, G. (2003, February 6). Circuit City profit to fall short. The Wall Street Journal, p. B4.

291. Circuit City Stores, Inc., Annual Report, 2003, 2.

292. Alan McCollough. Interview with the author.

293. In addition to "demeaning women, he had as reputation as a 'skirt chaser' and did not care who knew it." Jo Ann Cronin. Interviews with Steven Richman and the author.

294. David Cecil. Interview with the author.

295. Doug Moore. Interview with the author.

296. Circuit City Stores, Inc., Annual Report, 2005, 21.

297. Circuit City Stores, Inc. (2004, March 31). Written communication relating to an issuer or third party. In SEC EDGAR Filing Reports. Retrieved from http://sec.gov/Archives/edgar/data/104599/000010459904000028/ccs033104sctoc_ex5d.txt

298. Circuit City Stores, Inc., Annual Report, 2005, 35.

299. Circuit City Stores, Inc., Annual Report, 2004, 5.

300. See Board of Directors, InterTAN (p. 350), for a discussion of whether this was a sensible use of $300 million.

301. Brian Levy. Interview with author.

302. Circuit City Stores, Inc., Annual Report, 2005, 35.

303. Circuit City Stores, Inc., Annual Report, 2006, 27.

304. Circuit City Stores, Inc., Annual Report, 2005, 19; Annual Report, 2006, 23 & 2007, 31; Annual Report, 2008, 29.

305. Circuit City Stores, Inc., (2004, May 7). Definitive Proxy Statement. In SEC EDGAR Filing Documents. Retrieved from http://sec.gov/Archives/edgar/data/104599/000119312504082198/ddef14a.htm

306. Douglas Moore. Interview with the author.

307. Jeffrey Wells, Alan McCollough. Interviews with the author.

308. Best Buy Co., Inc., Annual Report, 2004. In SEC EDGAR Filing Documents. Retrieved from http://www.sec.gov/Archives/edgar/data/764478/000104746904014114/a2134459z10-k.htm

309. Demery, P. (2005, December 19). Philip Schoonover picked to succeed Circuit City's CEO. In Internet Retailer. Retrieved from http://www.internetretailer.com/2005/12/19/philip-schoonover-picked-to-succeed-circuit-city-s-ceo

310. Dennis Bowman. Interview with the author.

311. Based on comparing Circuit City 3Q SEC Reports in November 2002 and November 2003.

312. Phillip Dunn. Interview with the author. Bruce Besanko, Circuit City's last CFO, called the transition from POS to Magellan to rPOS one of the worst managed IT projects he had ever seen.

313. At an inventory turnover rate of 5.3 times per year, Circuit City compared poorly to

Best Buy's 7.7. Calculated from 2005 Best Buy and Circuit City Annual Reports using COGS and average inventory.

314. While this is theoretically possible, I am not aware of any retail store chain that has accomplished this goal. High-volume Internet retailers have a better chance since they do not have store shelves to stock. Successful membership stores, such as Costco, that have both high turnover and hold significant membership fees that offset inventory carrying costs, also have an advantage.

315. As Best Buy's sales grew from $12.5 billion in 2000 to $27.4 billion in 2005, its inventories at year-end ranged from $1.2 billion to 2.8 billion, roughly 10 percent of sales. While considerably better than Circuit City's, where inventories averaged 13 to 15 percent of sales, it is a long way from zero.

316. Circuit City Stores, Inc. Board Presentation: Merchandising System Transformation Slides, from USB drive

317. Dennis Bowman. Interview with the author.

318. Circuit City Stores, Inc., Annual Report, 2007, 7.

319. Circuit City Stores, Inc., Annual Report, 2002, 60. This implied an enterprise value for CarMax of $1.4 billion. Following the sale, Circuit City continued to own 64 percent of CarMax.

320. While CarMax did not require cash to finance its expansion program, Circuit City's implicit and explicit guarantees were an important factor in obtaining attractive rates on the sale and leaseback financing of its stores, the financing of its inventories and the sale of consumer paper. The CarMax related debt weighed on Circuit City's overall credit rating.

321. CarMax S-4 registration statement, filed May 14, 2002. In SEC Edgar Filing Documents, p. 22. Retrieved from http://access.edgaronline.com

322. Circuit City Stores, Inc., Annual Report, 2003, 36.

323. As of January 15, 2011 those shares were worth $32.60, roughly four times their value at the spinoff. Put another way, a Circuit City shareholder who bought stock when the company went on the NYSE in 1984, held on loyally thru the demise of the company, but also kept their KMX distribution from 2002, has outperformed the S&P 500 over that twenty-seven-year period simply because of the value of the CarMax distribution.

324. For the fiscal years 2004–07, CarMax's sales soared from $3.5 to $7.5 billion and earnings from $89 to $198 million. In SEC Edgar Filing Documents. Retrieved from http://access.edgaronline.com

325. From its all-time high of $324 million in FY 2000, net income fell to $115 million in FY 2001, and to $128 in FY 2002 and $42 million in FY2003. FY 2003 excludes CarMax. Circuit City Stores, Annual Reports.

326. At February 28, 2003, the total principal amount of credit card receivables managed was $3.7 billion of which $3.2 billion was securitized. Circuit City's retained interest in these receivables was $560 million, roughly 15 percent. Circuit City Stores, Inc., Annual Report. pp. 31, 38–9. At that time, FNANB had cash and cash equivalents of approximately $280 million and capital of approximately $250 million. Circuit City's net worth was $2.3 billion. Quarterly Report for the Period Ending November 30,

2002. In SEC Edgar Filing Documents. Retrieved from http://sec.gov/Archives/edgar/data/104599/000010459903000001/ccs0311_10q.txt

327. In 2003 Sears sold its credit card business to Citicorp. http://en.wikipedia.org/wiki/Sears

328. Circuit City Stores, Inc., Annual Report, 2004, 3.

329. Circuit City Stores, Inc., (2003, October 22). Current Report in SEC Edgar Filing Documents. Retrieved from http://sec.gov/Archives/edgar/data/104599/000010459903000115/0000104599-03-000115.txt

330. Circuit City Stores, Inc., Annual Report, 2005, 16.

331. Circuit City Stores, Inc., Annual Report, 2004, 22.

332. Circuit City Stores, Inc., Annual Report, 2006, 6.

333. From 2000 to 2005, retail sales at electronics and appliance stores grew from $82.4 billion to $101.6 billion, a 23 percent increase. [Source: U.S. Bureau of the Census. (2009). Wholesale and retail trade, 644. Statistical Abstract of the United States. Retrieved from http://www.census.gov/prod/2008pubs/09statab/domtrade.pdf

CHAPTER ELEVEN

334. Real Gross Domestic Product, Annual, Percent Change. Federal Reserve Economic Data. Retrieved from http://research.stlouisfed.org/fred2/graph/?chart_type=line&s[1][id]=GDPCA&s[1][transformation]=pch

335. Another record year for CE sales in 2005; '06 forecast bright. (2006, January 30). In This Week in Consumer Electronics Magazine. Retrieved from http://www.twice.com/article/243835-Another_Record_Year_For_CE_Sales_In_2005_06_Forecast_Bright.php

336. Based on industry total of $138.5b. [Sources: Wolf, A. (2006, May 8). Flat-Panel fever sends top 100 over $108.5b. In This Week in Consumer Electronics Magazine, 18. Retrieved from Master File Premier. The top 100 consumer electronics retailers. (2006, May 8). In This Week in Consumer Electronics Magazine, 22. Retrieved from Master File Premier.]

337. Circuit City Stores, Inc., (2006). 10-K, 36. Based on March 2006 stock price and 175 million shares issued and outstanding. Retrieved from http://finance.yahoo.com/echarts?s=CCTYQ.PK+Interactive#symbol=CCTYQ.PK;range=my

338. Circuit City Stores, Inc., 2006 SEC Filing, 10-K, 6.

339. Circuit City Stores, Inc., Annual Report, 2004, 4.

340. Heller, L. (2006, January 9). Will Circuit City find its way to turnaround city? DSN Retailing Today. Retrieved from ABI/Inform.

341. In fiscal 2006, Circuit City generated sales of about $17.5 million per store, based on $10.97 billion in domestic sales across 626 superstores. That year, Best Buy averaged $38.9 million per store across 742 stores. Sources: Circuit City Stores, Inc., 2006 SEC Filing 10-K, 3. Best Buy Co., Inc. 2006 SEC Filing 10-K, 6. Retrieved from http://library.corporate-ir.net/library/83/831/83192/items/199546/bby_ar06.pdf.

342. Circuit City Stores, Inc., Annual Report, 2004, 4

343. Michael Jones. Interview with the author.

344. The story of a young man who rekindles a friendship with an older man dying of Lou Gehrig's disease.

345. Michael Jones. Interview with the author. Philip Dunn remembers that Circuit City paid Deloitte a minimum of $10 million per year for various consulting services including store design and spent over $50m with Deloitte alone in a three-year period. Philip Dunn. Interview with the author.

346. Circuit City Stores, Inc., Annual Report, 2007, 1.

347. Best Buy's four key strategic initiatives for 2004 were: Customer Centricity, Efficient Enterprise, Win the Home with Service, and Win in Entertainment. Best Buy (2004). Annual Report. 22–23. Best Buy had addressed multichannel retailing two years earlier. Its real estate was not a major problem.

348. Circuit City Stores, Inc. (2006). Analyst Conference, 27 on USB drive.

349. Circuit City Stores, Inc. (2006). Analyst Conference, 23 on USB drive.

350. CCTYQ Historical Stock Price. In MarketWatch. Retrieved from http://www.marketwatch.com/investing/stock/cctyq/historical

351. Dive into HDTV. (2005, November 7). In Bloomberg BusinessWeek. Retrieved from http://www.businessweek.com/magazine/content/05_45/b3958401.htm

352. Gogoi, P. (2007, April 23). How Walmart's TV Prices Crushed Rivals. Bloomberg. Retrieved from http://www.msnbc.msn.com/id/18274443

353. Best Buy Co., Inc. (2006). Annual Report. 6. Retrieved from http://sec.gov/Archives/edgar/data/764478/000110465906033306/a06-10808_110k.htm

354. Tapscott, D., & Williams, A.D. (2007, March 26). The wiki workplace. In Bloomberg BusinessWeek. Best Buy does not release Geek Squad data. These are industry analyst estimates. Retrieved from http://www.businessweek.com/innovate/content/mar2007/id20070326_237620.htm

355. Circuit City Stores, Inc. (2007). Annual Report, Cover.

356. Circuit City Stores, Inc. (2008). Annual Report, 23.

357. Circuit City Stores, Inc. (2007). Annual Report, Cover.

358. Circuit City Stores, Inc. (2001). Annual Report, 5.

359. Circuit City Stores, Inc. (2006). Analyst Conference, 27 on USB drive.

360. Circuit City Stores, Inc. (2006). Analyst Conference, 28 on USB drive.

361. Circuit City Stores, Inc. (2006). Annual Report, 4.

362. Michael Jones. Interview with the author.

363. Circuit City Stores, Inc. (2007). Annual Report, Letter to Shareholders, 2.

364. $20.9 million for relocation expenses plus $1.4 million of capital expenses per new or relocated store. Circuit City Stores, Inc. Annual Report, 2008, 32 and 39.

365. Perhaps there was no one left that could tell Schoonover that this had been tried unsuccessfully in the late '80s and into the '90s.

366. Circuit City Stores, Inc. (2008). Annual Report, 5.

367. Circuit City Stores, Inc. (2008). Annual Report, Inside front cover.

368. Ibid.

369. Ibid.

370. Jerry Lawson. Interview with the author.

371. Circuit City, Inc. (2007, March 28). [Press Release] Retrieved from http://access. edgaronline.com/DisplayFilingInfo.aspx?TabIndex=2&FilingID=5062131&company id=2212&ppu=%252fprofile.aspx%253fcompanyid%253d2212&type=convpdf

372. Mui, Y. Q. (2007, March 29). Circuit City cuts 3400 'overpaid' workers. The Washington Post, p. D1.

373. Ibid.

374. Ibid.

375. Kelley, J. (2007, May 31). Circuit City slashes hundreds of jobs. Richmond Times-Dispatch, p. A1.

376. Bruce Besanko. Interview with the author.

377. Philip Dunn. Interview with the author.

378. Mike Jones, Interview with the author.

379. This source requested anonymity.

380. Source requested anonymity.

381. Robert Appleby. Email to the author.

382. Three in 2006, five in 2007, and five in 2008.

383. Michael Jones. Interview with the author.

384. Rick Sharp, Alan Wurtzel, John Snow, Edward Villanueva, Walter Salmon, and Hugh Robinson.

385. Some of them expressed concern that with the company still in liquidation and the statute of limitations not expired they could become involved in litigation. Nor would the company's bankruptcy counsel allow me to obtain copies of the minutes of meetings over the past ten years. In late 2010 several former directors were in fact sued for their approval of the InterTAN acquisition. How many knew or suspected this was coming, I do not know, but their fears were real.

386. Klepper, W. (2010). The CEO's Boss (pp. 5–13). New York, NY: Columbia University Press.

387. The board had used a search firm when it hired Schoonover and some board members may have felt that was adequate, even though the search was for a chief merchant and not the CEO.

388. Dennis Bowman. Interview with the author.

389. Dennis Bowman. Interview with the author.

390. Circuit City Stores, Annual Report, 2007, 3.

391. Circuit City Stores, Inc. ((2003, June 26). Form SC 13D—General statement of acquisition of beneficial ownership. In SEC EDGAR Filing Documents. Retrieved from http://sec.gov/Archives/edgar/data/104599/000089914003000511/ccs1224365.txt

392. As of February 28, 2003, Circuit City had $885 million in cash and cash equivalents. Circuit City Stores, Inc. Annual Report, 31.

393. Circuit City Stores, Inc. (2005, February 15). Form SC 13D—General statement of acquisition of beneficial ownership. In SEC EDGAR Filing Documents. Retrieved from http://sec.gov/Archives/edgar/data/104599/000119312505030004/dsc13d.htm

394. Sorkin. A., and Atlas, R. (2005, February 17). A spark for Circuit City's shares. The New York Times, Technology Section.

395. Circuit City Stores, Inc. (2005, February 15). Form SC 13D—General statement of

acquisition of beneficial ownership. In SEC EDGAR Filing Documents. Retrieved from http://sec.gov/Archives/edgar/data/104599/000119312505030004/dsc13d.htm

396. Barbaro, M. (2005, February 16). A bid for Circuit City; hedge fund makes $3.3 billion takeover offer, plans to take electronics retailer private. The Washington Post, p. E1.

397. Sorkin, A., and Atlas, R. (2005, February 17). A spark for Circuit City's shares. The New York Times, Technology Section.

398. McWilliams, G. (2005, March 8). Circuit City rejects takeover bid, won't consider any other offers. The Wall Street Journal. p. A8.

399. $115 million in 2001 and $127 million in 2002.

400. Alan McCollough. Interview with the author.

401. Actually $966.3 million. Circuit City Stores, Inc. Annual Report, 2004, 4.

402. Beginning in fiscal 2004, Circuit City made stock repurchases totaling $84.4m, $259.8m, $338.5m, $236.9m, and $46.7m, for a total of $966.3m. Compiled from Circuit City Annual Reports.

403. At the end, Circuit City had 168.1 million shares outstanding. Circuit City, Inc. SEC 10Q (2008, August 31). As of February 28, 2003, there were 209.9 million shares outstanding. During the period 2003 through 2008 Circuit City bought back 48 million shares and issued 7 million shares, primarily for the exercise of stock options.

404. In fact, Bank of America was willing to do a $1.3 billion revolver. It closed in January 2008, after Circuit City had filed for bankruptcy.

405. Capital expenditures discussion in MD&A. Circuit City Stores, Inc. Annual Reports 2004–2007.

406. Circuit City Stores, Inc. (2008). At the end of the most recent quarter, Circuit City's market capitalization was $1.1 billion, compared to Blockbuster's $870 million. Circuit City had 168 million shares outstanding as of 11/30/07 at $6.69 per share. Quarterly Report for the quarter ended November 30, 2007. In SEC EDGAR Filing Reports. Retrieved from http://sec.gov/Archives/edgar/data/104599/000119312508003994/d10q.htm. CCTYQ Historical Stock Quotes. In MarketWatch. Retrieved from http://www.marketwatch.com/investing/stock/cctyq/historical

Blockbuster, Inc. (2007). Blockbuster had 121 million shares of Class A common stock as of 11/6/07 at $4.72 per share and 72 million shares of Class B common stock at $4.18 per share. Quarterly Report for the quarter ended September 30, 2007. In SEC EDGAR Filing Reports. Retrieved from http://sec.gov/Archives/edgar/data/1085734/000119312507242082/d10q.htm

BLOKA Historical Stock Quotes. In MarketWatch. Retrieved from http://www.marketwatch.com/investing/stock/bloka/historical . BLOKB Historical Stock Quotes. In MarketWatch. Retrieved from http://www.marketwatch.com/investing/stock/blokb/historical

407. Bloomberg. Retrieved from http://www.bloomberg.com/apps/news?pid=20601103&sid=aEdwJiAyBqkU

408. Llovio, L. (2008, July 2). Blockbuster withdraws its offer to buy Circuit City. Richmond Times-Dispatch. Retrieved from http://www2.timesdispatch.com/news/2008/jul/02/-rtd_2008_07_02_0174-ar-122209/

409. Ibid.

410. Philip Dunn. Interview with the author.

411. SEC Edgar On Line. Retrieved from http://access.edgaronline.com/DisplayFilingInfo. aspx?TabIndex=2&FilingID=6167294&companyid=2212&ppu=%252fprofile.aspx %253fcompanyid%253d2212&type=convpdf

412. SEC Edgar On Line. Retrieved from http://access.edgaronline.com/DisplayFilingInfo. aspx?TabIndex=2&FilingID=6112532&companyid=2212&ppu=%252fprofile.aspx %253fcompanyid%253d2212&type=convpdf

413. Circuit City Press release accompanying SEC 8K filing Nov. 10, 2008, retrievable at SEC Edgar On Line: http://access.edgaronline.com/DisplayFilingInfo.aspx?TabIndex =2&FilingID=6244471&companyid=2212&ppu=%252fprofile.aspx%253fcompanyi d%253d2212&type=convpdf

414. As of August 31, 2008, Circuit City was paying rent on 98 closed locations of which 37 were subleased.

415. SEC Edgar On Line. Form 8 K filed 11/12/08. Under Chapter 11, the Circuit City board and management team, as the "Debtor-in-Possession" could continue to run the business under court supervision. Vendors and Banks which extended credit would have the first priority on being repaid. Retrieved from: http://www.sec.gov/Archives/ edgar/data/104599/000010459908000085/0000104599-08-000085-index.htm

416. Llovio, L, & Martz, M. (2008, November 11). Circuit City files for bankruptcy. Richmond Times-Dispatch. Retrieved from http://www2.timesdispatch.com/ business/2008/nov/11/circl1_20081110_213227-ar-103460/

417. Clothier, M., & McCarty, D. (2008, November 10). Circuit City, electronics retailer, seeks bankruptcy. In Bloomberg. Retrieved from http://www.bloomberg.com/apps/ne ws?pid=newsarchive&sid=aOl7tdCatQU4& refer=home

418. Llovio, L., & Ress, D. (2009, January 25). The final moments of Circuit City. Richmond Times-Dispatch. Retrieved from http://www2.timesdispatch.com/business/2008/ nov/11/circl1_20081110_213227-ar-103460

419. The Wall Street Journal. (2009, January 17), p. B1.

420. At the date of the original filing petition for bankruptcy on November 8, 2008, Circuit City had 712 superstores and approx 39,600 employees. http://www.scribd.com/fullscreen/7858787

421. http://mobithinking.com/mobile-marketing-tools/latest-mobile-stats

422. Laurie Burkitt and Bob Davis, (June 15, 2012) Wall Street Journal. Chasing China's shoppers p.B1.

423. General merchandise sales, GAFO, are sales of General merchandise, apparel Furniture and Other. It is essentially all retail sales excluding food and automobiles. Retrieved from http://www.census.gov/retail/#arts

424. Ibid.

425. Amazon Inc. SEC 10K for 2010, 25, 27. Retrieved from http://access.edgar-online. com/DisplayFilingInfo.aspx?TabIndex=2&FilingID=7677121&companyid=7235&p pu=%252fProfile.aspx%253fColLeft%253d75acdace-2e0d-43ab-ab8c-bde7ebb0468c %2526ColRight%253d2ec6feae-23aa-4275-beef

426. Retrieved from http://en.wikipedia.org/wiki/Systemax

INDEX